UPLIFTING THE RACE

The Black Minister in the New South 1865-1902

Edward L. Wheeler, Ph.D.

UNIVERSITY
PRESS OF
AMERICA

LANHAM • NEW YORK • LONDON

Copyright © 1986 by

University Press of America,® Inc.

4720 Boston Way
Lanham, MD 20706

3 Henrietta Street
London WC2E 8LU England

Library of Congress Cataloging-in-Publication Data

Wheeler, Edward L., 1946-
  Uplifting the race.

  Bibliography: p.
  1. Afro-American clergy—Southern States—History—
19th century. 2. Afro-American churches—Southern
States—History—19th century. 3. Southern States—
Church history. I. Title.
BR563.N4W48   1986   305'.92'08996073   85-26537
ISBN 0-8191-5161-0 (alk. paper)
ISBN 0-8191-5162-9 (pbk. : alk. paper)

TO

Mary Susan, Dawn, Wendi

and

Loren

with all my love and gratitude

PREFACE

Uplifting the Race is a revision of my doctoral dissertation completed in 1982. It is in part the result of my academic interest in the black church, but I must confess that my interest has not been and is not now totally academic. I am a product of the black church and this book has grown out of that fact. When I was a child my parents took my brother and me to Sunday School and church services on a regular basis. Our Sundays were filled with church-related activities and our weekdays were sprinkled with a generous portion of choir rehearsals and junior usher board meetings. Having made a public confession of faith when I was eight years old, I was baptized when I was nine. My relationship with the black church deepened when at fifteen I responded to a call to the ministry. I was ordained as a Baptist minister during my senior year at Morehouse College. It has been my privilege to have served as an assistant pastor of a Baptist Church in Georgia and as the pastor of the Trinity Emmanuel Presbyterian Church in Rochester, New York. I have worked in Baptist denominational structures since 1974 and have seen the black church at its best and worst. Currently serving as the Dean of the Morehouse School of Religion and soon to assume duties as the Pastor of Zion Baptist Church in Cincinnati, I do not examine the black church with the eyes of an unconcerned observer. I trust, however, that my training has prevented me from losing my objectivity to the point that my conclusions are invalid.

My desire to write this book also emerges from my appreciation for what the black church has meant to the black community, its witness to the broader Christian community and the potential power it has for the future. That potential will not be realized, however, if past contributions are not recognized and past mistakes avoided. I trust my efforts will place both the contributions and errors of the black church in the proper historical context so that they may be evaluated on their own merits. This should help the black church chart a course for the future with more confidence.

At best this book is a down payment on the unpayable debt I owe to many people who helped influence my life for the better. Though time, space, nor memory will permit me to recall them all, a few must be mentioned. Among these are Mrs. Violet H. Miller; the Rev. & Mrs.

vii

Lucius M. Tobin; Dr. Wendell P. Whalum; members of the Union Baptist Church of Hempstead, Long Island, New York; the Rev. James A. Wilborn, Sr., and the members of the Union Baptist Church of Atlanta, Georgia; faculty, staff, and students at Morehouse College from 1964-69; the Colgate-Rochester Divinity School Community 1969-72; and the many family members who loved enough to discipline me. Above all I owe a debt of love to my father and mother, Joseph and Fannie Wheeler, and to my brother, Joseph Russell Wheeler, Jr. Throughout my childhood and through my journey to manhood it was their love, encouragement, trust, and faith that helped me know that with God all things were possible.

This book represents the culmination of many years of work and sacrifice. While I take full credit for its weaknesses, it could not have been completed without the combined efforts of many people. My research was done in many libraries but my efforts would have been severely hampered had it not been for the gracious, competent, and helpful assistance I received at two libraries in particular. Ms. Gloria Mims and her staff at the Special Collections department of the Trevor Arnett Library at Atlanta University and Mr. Wilson Flemister and his staff at the library for the Interdenominational Theological Center went beyond the call of duty in allowing me access to their collections which proved invaluable to my research. It is fitting that they are now working together at the new Woodruff Library for the Atlanta University Center. In addition, my work could not have been completed without the help and patience of the faculty of the Department of Historical Studies in the Division of Religion of Emory University's Graduate School of Arts and Sciences. Their concern was exceeded only by their competence as scholars. No one on the faculty deserves more credit than my advisor, Dr. E. Brooks Holifield. We worked together from the start of my doctoral studies at Emory and it was Dr. Holifield who recommended that I seek to publish my work.

I also owe a debt of gratitude to Ms. Mary Larche, Rev. Frederick D. Meredith and Mr. Alvin Walker. Ms. Larche is the Administrative Assistant at Morehouse School of Religion and Alvin is a student-assistant in my office. They have been responsible for typing and editing the manuscript for the book. Their expertise and conscientious dedication to a tedious task deserves recognition and has earned my sincere gratitude.

Most importantly I wish to thank my wife and daughters for the love, patience, and dedication they exhibited throughout the years of study that have culminated with this book. I know it was not easy for them. All too often I was with them only in "spirit," but their complaints were few for they shared my dream. I salute Mary Susan, Dawn, Wendi, and Loren. I love them very much and I hope this book gives evidence that their sacrifice was not in vain.

Finally, I thank God for the health, strength, and mental stability I needed to complete this work. I only hope that my efforts testify to my love for Him and my gratitude for the blessings that have come as a result of the opportunity I have had to engage in this intellectual endeavor.

INTRODUCTION

The Union victory in the Civil War officially ended over 200 years of legal black enslavement in America. But while emancipation was a welcome reality to some 3.5 million black people who had been slaves in the South, the end of the war proved to be only the beginning of an equally important struggle by the ex-slave population. This was the struggle to be accepted as equal partners in American society. Though this struggle continues, the thirty-seven years between 1865 and 1902 mark a time when the effort to gain a place of dignity in the society was intense and pivotal. W.E.B. Dubois wrote of the period as a time when the freedman tried to merge his African and American identities into a better and truer self that reflected the best of both cultural traditions.

> *In this merging he wishes neither of the older selves to be lost. He would not Africanize America, for America has too much to teach the world and Africa. He would not bleach his Negro soul in a flood of white Americanism, for he knows that Negro blood has a message for the world. He simply wishes to make it possible for a man to be both a Negro and an American, without being cursed and spit upon by his fellows, without having the doors of opportunity closed roughly in his face.[1]*

The ex-slave wanted to achieve equality and full humanity in America. This task would have been difficult under the best of circumstances, but in the years immediately following the end of the war, several factors made the task even harder to achieve.

First, most freedmen had little or no conception of what freedom really meant. Although blacks had been a part of American society for over two centuries, they had viewed freedom through the distorted vision of slaves. Charles Boothe, a black Baptist minister from Alabama who had been a slave, reflected on the problem in 1895 when he published his **Cyclopedia of the Colored Baptists of Alabama.**

> One of the saddest mistakes of the
> slave was, that he thought so much of the
> pleasures of freedom and so little of its weighty
> obligations. To him freedom meant mansions,
> lands, teams, money, position, educated sons
> and refined daughters, with liberty to go
> and act as he pleased. If he might have
> burdened his mind with thoughts of his sore
> destitution of heart, of intellect, of purse;
> if he might have thought of his poverty as
> to skill in the arts, sciences and professions
> of life, as to social status, as to domestic
> relations, as to opportunities to succeed in
> a wrestle for life by the side of the victorious
> white man - if he might have seen that to
> make himself a strong manhood was his first
> and his most important duty - if his mind
> might have been full of these thoughts, it
> had been a thousand fold better for him.[2]

The freedman saw the opportunities of freedom but had little understanding of the responsibilities; he dreamed of freedom's benefits, but rarely realized what it would take to translate the dreams into reality.

The freedman had a second obstacle to overcome in order to gain equality. That was the fact that slavery had not prepared the ex-slave to assume the responsibilities of freedom, even if he knew what they were. At war's end, most blacks were illiterate. In any relationship that required contracts or written agreements this placed them at the mercy of employers and merchants who could read and write. The ex-slave was usually an unskilled laborer, who depended on the land for survival; land he rarely owned. Early hopes that the government would provide the freedman with "forty acres and a mule" were dashed when land reform legislation failed to gain the needed support in Congress and previously confiscated land was returned to the original owners. The family structure which gave the freedman a sense of identity and purpose was intact for some, but for others slavery had effectively destroyed any recognizable family ties. Furthermore, from the perspective of the black clergy, unscrupulous masters had encouraged a licentiousness that dulled the sense of morality in some black men and women, who therefore exhibited a minimal commitment to the broader society's definitions of responsible sexuality. The black clergy also believed that slavery had not taught the values of honesty very well either. Edward M. Brawley, a black Baptist minister, was only one of many who tied the behavior of the freedman directly to the slave experience. In an article written in 1902 he said that "the two great vices charged against the Negro race are theft and adultery. Whatever truth there is in this charge is due to the long training slavery gave. Indeed, slavery was largely a training in moral evil."[3]

A third factor that made the achievement of equality difficult was the failure of the majority of white Americans to accept the possibility that the freedman was or could be equal. Ending slavery was one thing; ending racial prejudice and establishing a free and open society was quite another.[4]

The predicament of the freedman was at best precarious. It was clear, however, that if the race was to survive (and there were those in the dominant society who did not believe it would), it had to accept the obligations that accompanied freedom, throw off the liabilities inherited from slavery, and show white America that black people were indeed capable of surviving, prospering, and achieving great things as a free people. The concept of "uplift" was descriptive of the process by which the freedman was to overcome oppression and achieve the goal of equality.

The word "uplift" was a common term in England and America in the nineteenth century. While its meanings were broad, the word frequently meant moral elevation, the improvement of physical conditions, intellectual enlightenment, and spiritual elevation.[5] The concept of uplift therefore seemed especially relevant to the condition of the ex-slave. In fact, the concept was in use by black leaders in the antebellum North who were very much aware of the need for blacks to improve themselves.[6] The concern to "elevate the race" was one of the motivating factors behind the establishment and continuation of the Negro Convention movement between 1830 and 1864.[7] But though the concern for uplift was not an innovation of the post-Civil War period, it was only then that there was even the slightest chance that the hope for uplift could be translated into reality.

Following the Civil War the leading voices within the black community adopted the word "uplift" as their own; it was the term that best described the goal they had in mind for their people. Edward R. Carter, the well-respected pastor of the Friendship Baptist Church of Atlanta, Georgia, wrote in the introduction of his book, **Biographical Sketches of Our Pulpit,** that "the pulpit, fireside and schoolroom are the levers that must lift up our down-trodden race. . . ."[8] Thomas O. Fuller, a preacher, politician and educator, wrote in the preface of his autobiography that he had devoted the last twenty years of his still young life to "uplifting my race."[9] Daniel W. Culp used the term in the preface of his book, **Twentieth Century Negro Literature,** published in 1902 explaining that one of the objects of his book was,

> " . . . to point out, to the aspiring Negro youth, those men and women of their own race who, by their scholarship, by their integrity of character, and by their earnest efforts in

> *the work of uplifting their own race, have*
> *made themselves illustrious.*[10]

J.W.E. Bowen, a Methodist minister, and I. Garland Penn an editor and newspaper publisher, wrote that one of their intentions in publishing a book based on the proceedings of the Negro Young People's Christian and Educational Congress of 1902 was to assist their "Brothers in Black" in every endeavor that sought their uplift and that of society as a whole.[11] The book contained essays written by recognized black leaders on a variety of themes referring to "uplift" such as: "To What Extent Is the Negro Pulpit Uplifting the Race?", "What Role Is the Educated Negro Woman to Play in the Uplifting of Her Race?" and "What Is the Negro Teacher Doing in the Matter of Uplifting the Race?"[12]

Leaders who did not use the term "uplift" nevertheless alluded to the concept in their writing. In the introduction to E.R. Carter's, **The Black Side**, published in 1894, Henry M. Turner, then a bishop in the African Methodist Episcopal Church, wrote of the past degradation of black people and of their future hope.

> *Let us admit that the Negro was a degraded*
> *being during the days of our enthrallment*
> *and forced dehumanized condition. . . .*
> *Were not the whites, to whom we belonged,*
> *equally degraded, and did they not close the*
> *doors of every avenue that looked toward*
> *our elevation? . . . While we may not entirely*
> *forget the past, we may remember it only*
> *as an incentive to achieve grander results*
> *in the progressive hereafter.*[13]

A.W. Pegues, author, educator and pastor, wrote in **Our Baptist Ministers and Schools** in 1892 that "there is one ever onward and upward movement of man; a movement peculiar to no one race or people."[14] Peques' opinion was that every race was responsible for its own success or failure to be a part of that movement, and he was proud that the Baptist ministry had contributed to the onward, upward movement of the black people in this country. William J. Simmons, a leading Baptist minister, educator, and denominational worker, implied the concept of uplift when he wrote the preface to **Men of Mark.** One of his purposes in writing this book of biographical sketches was to inspire the readers to emulate men who had excelled and brought recognition and honor to themselves and the race.[15]

Uplifting, improving, elevating the race had to be an urgent concern of the black community in the decades following emancipation if black people were to remain free and become equal. Whites were free to assist blacks uplift the race, but the concept of uplift advocated self-help and self-improvement. If the race was to be uplifted, black people would have to assume major responsibility for the task. Because the black church was the only post-Civil War institution black people could claim as their own, it is not surprising that the church spearheaded the drive for uplifting the race. The church was the center of the freedman's community, and as a result of the church's prominence, the black minister was in a unique position to be a leading advocate of uplift.

Recognizing the pivotal role of the black minister in the black community, this book proposes to examine the black ministry as a social institution in the period from 1865 to 1902. This thirty-seven year span begins with the conclusion of the Civil War and ends with a major religious meeting held in Atlanta designed to assess black progress since emancipation. **Uplifting the Race** will focus on an elite group of seventy-eight ministers who lived and served in the South for no less than five years during the period. Limited reference will be made to an additional one hundred-seventy ministers. The subjects of the study were selected because they wrote books, published articles and sermons, were the subjects of biographers and local historians, were pastors of influential churches, and held positions of leadership in their denominations. Through an examination of materials written by and about this group, I hope to discover the place these men held in their communities, how they attempted to achieve the goal of uplifting the race, and the effect uplift had on their positions of leadership.

This book makes two claims that are important for the study of American Church History in general and of the Black Church in America in particular. The basic claim is that the study of the Black Church in America is a valid enterprise which should be taken seriously by American Church historians. Robert T. Handy made this point over fourteen years ago in his article, "Negro Christianity and American Church Historiography" in Volume 5 of Gerald Brauer's **Essays in Divinity.** But despite Handy's plea and such pace-setting efforts as Sidney's Ahlstrom's inclusion of several chapters dealing with the black religious experience in his outstanding text, **A Religious History of the American People,** few historians have done much in the field. As a result, the religious heritage and the religious contributions of 25 million black Americans is still generally ignored. No less a scholar than Winthrop S. Hudson, who nurtured my love for American Church History as my professor in seminary, was guilty of this oversight in his numerous publications, including earlier editions of his standard text **Religion in America.** This book, **Uplifting the Race,** challenges and calls for a reassessment of the opinions of those who have assumed that sources were not available for the study of the Black Church and those who have assumed that such a study would produce little that was new or of importance in the area of American Church History.

The second claim is that the work of those who have endeavored to interpret the Black Church has been incomplete, insofar as it has ignored the theme uplift and its importance as an aid in interpreting the activities of the ministerial leadership and the black church between 1865 and the turn of the century. Though E. Franklin Frazier, a noted black sociologist, and James Cone, the father of black theology, would no doubt disagree with each other on several points regarding the Black Church, their evaluations of the church in the post-Civil War era are quite similar. Frazier wrote the "Negro's church . . . aided the Negro to become accommodated to an inferior status" in a white-dominated society and provided black people with an escape from the harsh realities of the society.[16] James Cone reached the same conclusion five years later in his **Black Theology,** writing that "the black church gradually became an instrument of escape instead of, as formerly, an instrument of protest."[17] Furthermore Cone provides a negative assessment of the part the black minister played in the transition. "The black minister . . . became a devoted 'Uncle Tom,' the transmitter of white wishes, the admonisher of obedience to the caste system . . . . More than any other person in the black community, the black minister perpetuated the white system of black dehumanization."[18]

Gayraud Wilmore, in **Black Religion and Black Radicalism,** was more charitable in his assessment than Cone or Frazier. Yet Wilmore still interprets the black church in terms of a narrow definition of liberation which leads him to conclude that only the northern black church prior to abolition, and a handful of southern black church leaders after emancipation were really involved in what he calls the "freedom movement." Because he views this movement as the touchstone for determining the church's authenticity, it is no surprise that he agrees with the critics who charge that the leaders of the black church were "too imitative of the white clergy in their politics and given to moralizing and peacemaking." Wilmore concedes that this criticism "was perhaps true of the majority of Black preachers, most of whom were in the South, but such men had little influence upon the highly significant [freedom movement] events we have just recounted."[19] He implies that the southern black church was not involved in the liberation of black people and that the southern black minister was insignificant in the "freedom movement" of both the pre-and post-Civil War eras. Though less explicit in his criticism, Wilmore's position is no less damaging to any suggestion that the black church and the black minister were assets rather than liabilities to the freedman.

Cecil Wayne Cone, a young theologian, is one of the few who have called for a reassessment of the black church during the post-Civil War era. In his book, **The Identity Crisis in Black Theology,** Cone argues that "black religion after the Civil War was and is a continuation of the same tradition" that characterized black religion before the War.[20] He also believes that those who view black religion as compensatory and other-worldly have failed to grasp the full meaning of the language and perspective of the black church.[21] Like W.E.B. DuBois in his **The Souls of Black Folk,** Cone sees the black church as a significant positive force in the black community, but unlike DuBois, Cone does not fully discuss the role of the black minister. Though a welcome corrective to the negative evaluations, Cone does not provide a synthesis that recognizes the problems within the black church and yet balances that recognition with an appreciation of the way in which the post-Civil War black minister and black church contributed to the struggle for dignity. **Uplifting the Race** attempts to do just that.

The black church did move toward accommodation during the post-Civil War era. Accommodation to the dominant white society was a part of what "uplift" meant as it was interpreted by leading ministers. Recognizing that, the book attempts to show some ways accommodation was achieved. Yet the move toward accommodation was filled with ironies, for accommodation itself was also the affirmation of possibility. The concept of "uplift," as formulated and perpetuated by the ministerial leadership, was filled with intimations of possibility for the ministers, the black church, and black people. Accommodation, which of course had a submissive tone, also had a subversive quality. On the one hand, uplift meant accommodation and surrender to the concepts, principles, and ideals of the dominant society. On the other, uplift was a denial of what white society meant by accommodation, for it spoke of a possibility to move beyond the limits prescribed by the dominant society.

The scholars, who have seen the post-Civil War black minister and black church as being one-dimensional, have missed the dialetical quality of the period. It is my claim that the concept of uplift provides a framework for understanding the rich interplay of accommodation and possibility, which I believe characterized the period between 1865 and 1902. The failure to recognize the importance of the concept of uplift leads to a truncated evaluation of the black church and ministerial leadership in the New South.

In addition to this introduction, **Uplifting the Race** consists of four substantive chapters and a conclusion. The first chapter attempts to place the ministerial elite within the broader black community. An examination of their place in the community should give us clues concerning how they could hope to accomplish the goal of uplift. The second chapter will focus on the theological framework that informed and shaped much of the ministers' conclusions about uplift. Chapter three provides the opportunity to investigate how the ministerial elite were influenced by the concept of uplift in the political sphere. The fourth chapter assesses the elite ministers' acceptance of education as essential to uplift and explores the consequences for uplift that their views on education implied.

This study does not attempt to paint a definitive portrait of black ministry in the South and probably does not provide an accurate picture of the "typical" black minister of the period. I contend, however, that an examination of this elite group of men can provide insight into how the concept of uplift helped to define them as an extraordinary powerful group within the black community. It also illustrates how this group used the concept of uplift to establish objectives for and gives direction to the development of their community.

NOTES

[1]*Three Negro Classics.* (New York: Arno Press, 1965), **The Souls of Black Folk,** by W.E.B. DuBois, p. 215.

[2]*Charles Octavius Boothe, D.D.,* **The Cyclopedia of the Colored Baptists of Alabama: Their Leaders and Their Work,** *(Birmingham, Alabama Publishing Co., 1895), pp. 31-32.*

[3]*E.M. Brawley, "Is the Young Negro an Improvement, Morally, on His Father?" in* **Twentieth Century Negro Literature,** *ed. D.W. Culp (J.L. Nichols and Co., 1902; reprint ed., Miami: Mnemosyne Publishing Co., Inc. 1969), p. 255.*

[4]*Historians of the Reconstruction era differ in their interpretations of the nature of race relations in the South in the period following the Civil War. Some, continuing the basic argument of C. Vann Woodward in* **The Strange Career of Jim Crow,** *contend that the strained race relations and the Jim Crow restrictions that characterized the 1890's and much of the twentieth century, developed rather suddenly after the breakdown of those forces which had theretofore kept extremism in check. (See C. Vann Woodward,* **The Strange Career of Jim Crow,** *Second Revised Edition (London: Oxford University Press, 1966). I tend, however, to agree with those historians who see the rise of legalized segregation as simply the institutionalization of long held racial views. H. Shelton Smith in his classic work on Southern religion,* **In His Image, But . . . ,** *demonstrates the long standing racial animosities that had set boundaries for race relations long before Jim Crow legistation. The articulation of the elements of "racial orthodoxy" by the Southern Baptist, Henry Holcombe Tucker, in 1883 adequately reflected the limits beyond which few went. He exposued the inequality of the races, the inferiority of the Negro, the harm of racial fusion, and the sinfulness of free social intermingling between black and white. The basic assumptions were not new and were accepted by conservatives and moderates alike. There was room for some differences in the precise way the assumptions were applied, e.g., moderates felt blacks could be improved with a liberal education or at worst would benefit from vocational training. Some conservatives, on the other hand, questioned whether most blacks could be educated beyond the most elemental levels. Moderates and conservatives alike, however, were remarkably loyal to the maintenance of the tenets of "racial orthodoxy." (See H. Shelton Smith,* **In His Image, But . . .** *(Durham: Duke University Press, 1972), pp. 264 ff., and Rufus B. Spain,* **At Ease in Zion** *(Nashville: Vanderbilt University Press, 1967), pp. 113-119.*

[5]A word study, using the following dictionaries: **The Oxford English Dictionary**, 1933; **A Dictionary of the English Language**, 1819; **An American Dictionary of the American Language**, 1850; **A Dictionary of American English on Historical Principles**, 1944; and **The Century Dictionary**, 1911 confirms the stated use of the word uplift and related words in the period under study. Mitford Mathews edited **A Dictionary of Americanisms on Historical Principles** (1951) that contained an illustration from an 1873 book that demonstrated one way the word was used. "It is impossible that he could know what an uplift he gave to the life to which he ministered." (p. 1802) That illustration was used in at least one other dictionary. Furthermore, an examination of dictionaries devoted to American slang and less respected terms, such as the **Dictionary of Americanisms**, 1848, and **A Dictionary of Slang and Unconventional English**, 1961, shows that the term uplift was not considered slang or unconventional.

[6]See Frederick Cooper, "Elevating the Race: The Social Thought of Black Leaders, 1827-1850," **The American Quarterly** 24 (1972): 604-625.

[7]See Howard Holman Bell, ed., **Minutes of the Proceedings of the National Negro Conventions**, 1830-1864 (New York: Arno Press, 1969). Though references to elevation permeate the convention minutes, the following provided excellent examples of the black leadership's concern in this area: 1830 Constitution and Convention Minutes, p. 9; 1831 Minutes, pp. 13 & 15; 1832 Minutes, pp. 11, 32, and 35; 1853 Minutes, p. 7.

[8]Edward Randolph Carter, **Biographical Scketches of Our Pulpit** (Atlanta: E.R. Carter, 1888), p. iv.

[9]Thomas Oscar Fuller, **Twenty Years of Public Life, 1890-1910** (Nashville: National Baptist Publishing Board, 1910), p. 5.

[10]Daniel W. Culp, **Twentieth Century Negro Literature**, pp. 5 & 6.

[11]J.W.E. Bowen and I. Garland Penn, Editors, **The United Negro: His Problems and His Progress** (Atlanta: D.E. Luther Publishing Co., 1902), p. iii.

[12]Daniel W. Culp, **Twentieth Century Negro Literature**, pp. 115 ff., 167 ff., 330 ff.

[13]Edward R. Carter, **The Black Side: A Partial History of the Business, Religious and Educational Side of the Negro in Atlanta, Georgia** (Atlanta: E.R. Carter, 1894), p. vi.

[14]Albert W. Peques, **Our Baptist Ministers and Schools** (Springfield, Mass.: Willey and Co., 1892), p. 16.

[15]William J. Simmons, **Men of Mark: Eminent, Progressive and**

Rising (reprint ed., Chicago: Johnson Publishing Co., 1970). pp. 1-3.

Many other authors and leaders such as James T. Haley (*Afro-American Encyclopedia*, 1896), W.H. Mixon (*History of African Methodist Episcopal Church in Alabama*, 1902) and Charles H. Phillips (*From the Farm to the Bishopric*, 1932) did not always use the word uplift specifically in their writing or speaking but clearly conveyed their acceptance of the concept in stating the purposes of their books and their lives. These men sought to encourage black people. They wanted their people to know that they could move beyond the degradation of their present circumstances, whatever they were.

[16]E. Franklin Frazier, *The Negro Church in America* (New York: Schocken Books, 1964), p. 46.

[17]James Cone, *Black Theology and Black Power* (New York: The Seabury Press, 1969), p. 104.

[18]*Ibid.,* pp. 105-106.

[19]Gayraud Wilmore, *Black Religion and Black Radicalism* (Garden City, New York: Doubleday and Co., Inc., 1972), p. 132.

[20]Cecil Cone, *The Identity Crisis in Black Theology,* (Nashville: The African Methodist Episcopal Church, 1975), p. 61.

[21]*Ibid.,* p. 71.

CHAPTER 1
THE BLACK MINISTER:
UPLIFTED TO UPLIFT

When Elijah P. Marrs was born into slavery in January, 1840, on the Robinson farm in Shelby County, Kentucky, about twenty miles from Louisville, no one could have predicted that he would become one of the elite black ministers of the South, an exemplary and powerful model of clerical leadership. A brief glance at the life of Elijah Marrs is to sense the complex interweaving of accommodation and possibility in the program of the black clergy. It is to become aware of the irony in their gospel of uplift. For indeed preachers like Marrs who advocated uplift were accommodationists. They saw a need for the freedmen to become a part of the broader society and to share the values of the culture. In their vision of the future, no other pathway seemed open. And they saw no need to take another path, for they accepted the claim that America was the most civilized nation on earth. They accepted prevailing American standards of moral and ethical behavior, adopted the American ideal of education, and believed in the essential worth of the American political and economic system. Yet their call for accommodation was no simple demand for submission or acquiescence. Their insistent demand for assimilation also entailed the creation of a new range of possibilities for black people. Their very belief that a broken people could be uplifted was in one sense revolutionary, because it said that blacks had the potential to live in the society as equals rather than subordinates. The message of "uplift" meant the time for ending degradation was drawing near. It also implied specific goals and tasks that blacks could accomplish, given time, opportunity, and effort. The ministerial elite, then, were both accommodationists and architects of possibility. And Elijah Marrs managed to embody both sides of that ministerial dialectic. Interweaving a deep religious conviction, an intense commitment to education, and a keen interest in politics, Marrs exemplified a pattern of clerical activity that marked the black clergy throughout the South.

Separated from his free father and permitted to have only occasional contact with him, Marrs lived as a slave on the plantation with his mother until 1864. The farm apparently afforded unusual opportunities for slaves. They were allowed freedom to worship and given at least limited chances to learn to read. Kentucky had legal restrictions on the education of slaves, but Elijah began to read and write while a child. His first instructors were the white boys with whom he had contact. He later

1

received help from an old slave on the farm, who worked with him in late-night sessions.

The real change in his education came after he joined the church. Elijah was converted when he was about eleven years old after a time of "searching." His father, a man with a strong religious commitment, was influential in Elijah's conversion. After he heard his father discussing religion with a minister, he was ready to become a Christian. He accepted Christ at a protracted meeting led by Baptists and received his master's permission to join the church and be baptized. Marrs later indicated in his autobiography the way religion and education were connected on the Robinson farm.

> There was something on (the) Robinson place that was an exception to the general rule. There were forty-two in (the) family, and all members of the church who were above ten years of age, and all Baptists save one colored lady, Robinson having been a deacon in the Baptist Church for about forty years. After my conversion and baptism I was permitted to attend Sunday School and study the Word of God for myself. My master then removed all objections to my learning how to read, and said he wanted all the boys to learn how to read the Bible; it was against the laws of the State to write. We had to steal that portion of our education, and I did my share . . . . Only a few white people would let their slaves attend the Sunday School, hence I became an active member in it.[1]

The early training Marrs received in the church proved beneficial throughout his life. When the Civil War started, Marrs was able to follow its progress in the newspaper. In 1864, he decided to escape from slavery and join the Union Army. His attempt was successful and he led twenty-six men to Louisville where they all enlisted. Because he could read, Marrs was quickly promoted to the rank of sergeant. Appreciating the value of education, he arranged to get additional tutoring from some of the officers.

Elijah and his brother began a business when he returned home from the army but before long the residents of Simpsonville, Kentucky, asked him to open a school for their children. Marrs was reluctant but eventually yielded, saying later that "their persuasions . . . finally induced me to leave the corn-field and enter the school-room to labor for the development of my race."[2] Beginning with the Simpsonville experience, the education of the race became a major preoccupation for Marrs. His concern was manifested in that he opened several schools in Kentucky, culminating in the establishment of what became the Normal and Theological School in Louisville. He also sought to improve himself by attending school. He attended Nashville Institute for a year from 1874 to 1875 and later enrolled in the Normal and Theological School as a special student. Yet, education was not the only activity that attracted Marrs.

While Marrs was teaching in LaGrange, Kentucky, his growing interest in politics became evident. In 1869, Marrs wrote a political endorsement for a Republican candidate which some politicians thought would be the "Kiss of death," but the candidate won. This success led to Marrs' election as the first black president of the County Republican Club and as a delegate to the 1869 political convention. Activity by the Ku Klux Klan in LaGrange also led Marrs to join the Loyal League of LaGrange, a semi-political black organization established to protect black people in the town from Klan violence. Marrs served for a time as its secretary. Believing that preparation and unity were the best ways to deal with the Klan, Marrs started another Loyal League in New Castle, Kentucky, when he lived there in 1870.

Marrs continued his political activity in 1873, during the campaign for a local option bill prohibiting the sale of alcohol in New Castle. Although he was a resident of Shelbyville and was ineligible to vote, Marrs was a staunch advocate of Temperance. The campaign was bitter, and some of his opponents accused him of being a Democrat, because they saw the issue as a test of their rights as freedmen. Marrs attributed the bill's defeat to this reasoning. Three years later, the Temperance movement gained momentum in Shelbyville and Marrs again took up the fight. He gathered signatures and eventually "carried the day". Following the victory, Marrs was elected president of the Temperance Society in Shelbyville, and held the position for three years. The Society had black and white members, and from this office Marrs coordinated Temperance efforts in surrounding communities. He noted with a measure of pride that he was often invited to speak before mixed audiences and in white churches.

As the gains of Reconstruction eroded, Marrs, among others attempted to stem the erosion. One example of his work was his campaign against a bill before the Kentucky legislature known as "The Whipping Post Bill." Marrs organized "indignation" meetings in Shelbyville to protest the bill and drew up a petition, collecting the signatures of one hundred-fifty black men. The bill was defeated and the people of Shelbyville gave him credit for the defeat. Marrs later reflected on his opposition to the bill and wrote: "The reason that I was so bitterly opposed to this bill was, that I thought it was a sly way of re-establishing the old whipping post of our fore-fathers."[3] Marrs was not afraid to take a stand when he felt the black community was being threatened. Marrs joined one Loyal League and started another, then fought against legislation designed to undermine black dignity and progress. These events were the essential ingredients in the formula of uplift.

In addition to politics and education, religion played an important role in Marrs' life since his conversion at age eleven. Religion became even more important in 1873 when Marrs entered the ministry. Marrs wondered for some time whether he had been called to preach but was unable to decide. The pastor and deacons of the New Castle Baptist Church fostered the acceptance of his call. Convinced, he set his trial sermon for June 9, 1873, and as his autobiography shows, the occasion was not without some anxiety.

> It was a heart-rending time for my wife. She sat and cried during the services. Two things burdened her mind. First, that she might be the cause of hindering my success. Second, that she often told me that she was afraid I would be a 'Jack Leg Preacher,'a public hiss among the people . . .

> But as I traveled among the churches, and was highly esteemed by the leading members of the denomination over the state, she grew proud of me and did everything in her power to make me happy.[4]

In Marrs' opinion and that of his wife, the ministry gave a man and his family the opportunity for recognition and esteem in the community, but it also carried heavy responsibility. Evidently he carried the responsibility well, for two years later he was ordained.

Marrs combined his teaching and preaching careers for almost 5 years, but in Februrary, 1880, he helped organize the Beargrass Baptist Church, which called him to be the pastor. He accepted, and on March 16, 1880, he began a long pastoral career. Although Marrs had not been the pastor of a major church during his early years as a minister, he had been involved in denominational affairs since he first received a license to preach in 1873. He was respected by his peers and regularly elected as a delegate to the annual sessions of the General Association of Kentucky, the black Baptist state convention. Marrs also held elected offices in several denominational organizations, including treasurer of the General Association, and executive committee member and secretary of the Central District Association, which was the local Baptist organization composed of churches and ministers from Louisville and surrounding communities. As the century came to a close, Marrs could look over his life and conclude that since 1866, when he decided to teach in Simpsonville, he had indeed been engaged in the labor of "developing his race."

Elijah P. Marrs' life was an embodiment of the ideal of uplift. He had risen from the degradation of slavery to a position of acceptance in the "better" white circles and to leadership in his own community.

His life reflected a commitment to education, which he saw as a sure way to prepare black people to live as equals in the society. He taught in and founded schools, and continued to prepare himself as a teacher and minister. Marrs was committed to real progress for blacks through political involvement. Consequently, he campaigned for reconstruction as a Republican, opposed the Ku Klux Klan, fought legislation he felt would hold the race down, and supported the Temperance Movement. Undergirding everything else was Marrs' Christian commitment and his sense of calling as a minister. He believed that blacks were meant to be more than slaves, and he dedicated his life to demonstrating that through his own achievements. Marrs was one of the ministerial elite who was affected by the concept of uplift. And because he was a product of uplift, he sought to uplift others.

The story of Marrs' life and his rise to leadership is in some ways representative of the seventy-eight other ministers who form the basis of this study of the elite black ministerial leadership in the South from 1865 to 1902. All these men shared Marrs' faith in the possibility of uplifting the race, and they rose to positions of leadership and responsibility within the black community. They were united in their affirmation of "uplift" as the goal for their communities and in their belief that sound Christian principles undergirded the concept of uplift. They were all products of the black community and the black church. Yet Marrs' story also points to the diversity among the men who constituted the clerical elite. The black ministerial leadership represented a wide variety of experiences; their personal histories varied. They had different slave experiences, family backgrounds, educational opportunities, economic standings, and denominational affiliations. This is important because their diversity reflects the diversity in the black community of their day: the ministerial elite belonged to the broader black community. They had not been isolated from the rich diversity of experiences that characterized the post-slavery black community. They belonged, but paradoxically their role as ministers also separated them from their community; as ministers they were both part of and apart from the black community. The black clergy assumed power in part because they were like their parishioners. A quality of shared experiences was one prerequisite for leadership. Yet the role of the minister also set the clergy apart from the people.

1. THE DEVELOPMENT OF THE INSTITUTIONAL BLACK CHURCH

The church was the one black institution that began in and survived slavery.[5] Although the black church in the South did not enjoy the freedom of its northern counterpart during slavery and was often under white auspices, it met many of the needs of the slave population. Elijah Marrs' situation was unusual but his experience documented the vitality of the Christian slave community. Fourteen of the ministerial elite were converted during slavery and had some freedom to exercise their faith prior to emancipation. Once emancipation became a reality, the black church became even more important to the freedman. Between 1865 and 1902 it was often the only institution black people controlled. The church served as the social, educational, cultural, political, and religious center in the black community. In short, it served as the focus for the uplift of the race.

As such a focal point, the church displayed the balancing of accommodation and possibility in the clerical program of uplift. To later observers, drawn to the spontaneity of slave religion in the "invisible institution" and to the themes of protest in black clerical abolitionism, the black churches after the Civil War have often seemed bland and stodgy. Such a judgement, however, overlooks the fact that the very creation of stable institutions, with budgets, continuous leadership, and organizational complexity, embodied a challenge to the prevailing white expectations in the broader culture. In becoming "respectable" institutions, the black churches did lose something of the critical edge that had marked antebellum black religion when it was most vigorous. But by creating an institution with impressive power within the black community, the clergy and laity also testified to a possibility inherent in the ideal of uplift.

Most of the black Christians — and most of their ministers — became Baptists after emancipation, following a pattern that had been established during slavery. William Hicks, in his **History of Louisiana Negro Baptists,** issued a typical report on black Baptist growth when he outlined the progress of almost four decades.

> *In 1867 we had a few small churches organized, and about 5,000 members. The ministers had just been emancipated, and with a very few exceptions they could neither read nor write. We had no day schools nor Sunday-schools. Today [1902] we have 125,000 members; 1,200 churches at an average cost of $1,000 each, making a total of $1,2000,000 worth of church property throughout the state.*[6]

Black Baptists were strong throughout the nine southern states. The 1890 census study of religion in the United States revealed that among blacks in the South the Baptist church averaged one member for every 5.32 blacks. In North Carolina the average was better than 1 in every 4 blacks. Florida was the only one of the nine states where Baptists had fewer than 50,000 members. In five of the states Baptists had more than 100,000 members: Georgia, 200,515; Alabama, 142,437; Mississippi, 136,647; North Carolina, 134,445; and South Carolina, 125,572. Of the 1890 total of 1,348,989 black Baptists in America, 930,821 were in nine southern states. Baptist ministers operated from a position of strength because of their great numbers.[7]

Once churches were established, black Baptists began to organize local associations and state conventions, designed to help the local congregation do its work and give Baptists a forum for discussion. Black Baptist ministers took the lead in organizing them, beginning with the North Carolina state convention in 1866. In 1868 some twenty-seven Montgomery congregations established the Colored Baptist Convention of Alabama. When the convention met in 1890, "one hundred and fifty churches and forty associations, besides Sunday School conventions and Sunday Schools, were represented by two hundred messengers."[8] Kentucky black Baptists formed their state convention in 1868 and two years later the movement spread to Georgia and then to Louisiana in 1872.

The growth of the state conventions paved the way for the first thriving national black Baptist conventions. The Foreign Mission Convention of the United States of America was founded in 1880, the American National Baptist Convention in 1886, and the Baptist National Education Convention in 1893. Two years later the three conventions merged to form the National Baptist Convention, U.S.A.[9] Again it was black ministers who spurred the movement toward the national conventions. W.W. Colley issued the call that led to the organization of the Foreign Mission Convention and William J. Simmons played a major role in the formation of the American National Baptist Convention. Albert W. Peques was instrumental in the formation of the Education Convention and was prominent in the movement that resulted in the 1895 merger. Once the conventions began to function, the same ministers assumed the leadership positions. Even though the conventions derived their support from local congregations, and even though lay-people provided that support, the ministers were in charge when the conventions met. Of the forty-two Baptist ministers in this study, twenty-nine of them held an office in at least one of the local, state, or national conventions or associations.

The black Baptist ministry was characterized by a wide range of skills and abilities because standards for licensing and ordaining a man to the ministry varied greatly. A Home Mission Society study in 1895 revealed the enormous differences within the ranks of black Baptist ministers.

> *Many are noble, high-minded, upright, God-fearing, unselfish, sincere, self-sacrificing, who honor their high calling. Of a great number, however, it must be said in sorrow, that their moral standards are not in accord with those of the New Testament for the ministry. They have grown up in an environment unfavorable to the production of a high type of character. The development of a Christian conscience is a fundamental need.*[10]

The local autonomy of each Baptist congregation was largely responsible for the differences. Each congregation was free to choose its own pastor and often did so without any assistance from other churches or ministers. Furthermore, a man who felt "called" to preach who could not secure a church could always start his own Baptist church with little difficulty.

The Baptist minister was usually the pastor of more than one church. A small percentage served only one church, usually located in the towns and cities. Such a pattern of leadership was attributable in part to the fact that there were only 5,468 men serving over 12,000 congregations in 1890. In the rural areas where three-fourths of the black population lived between 1865 and 1902, black Baptist ministers usually served between two and four churches, in each of which they preached as infrequently as once a month. The Home Mission Society reported that "of 12,000 churches in 1895, probably not 1,000 have preaching every Sunday. Except in the larger and more progressive churches, ministers do very little pastoral work."[11]

George W. Dupree, a pastor in Kentucky and a member of the ministerial elite, was one person who served several churches at the same time during most of his career. But the majority of the Baptists in the ministerial elite did not fit the typical Baptist pattern. At least thirty of the forty-two Baptists served only one congregation at a time most of their careers.

The Home Mission Society report recognized the shortcomings of the black church and the black ministers in the Baptist denomination, but it also had to recognize the growth that had occurred since emancipation. The credit for that growth in large part went to the black Baptist ministry:

> . . . in these [churches] are sincere,
> devout souls, in whom the Spirit of God seems
> to have wrought a genuine work and to whom
> He has given singularly clear views of truth.
> The process of emancipation from the old
> order of things is going on . . . Numerous
> churches maintain most orderly services,
> have good Sunday-schools, and young people's
> societies, and are interested in missions.
> Thousands of Church edifices, some well
> equipped and very costly bear witness to
> the zeal and devotion of the people, and to
> the persuasive power of their religious
> leaders.[12]

The black Baptist ministry, though laboring against great odds, still provided the leadership that led Baptists to an almost two-to-one edge over all Methodist Church memberships combined in the early years of the twentieth century.[13]

Understandably, the counties with the largest black population often had the greatest number of black Baptist churches and the largest total number of members, but this was not always the case, as an examination of two Louisiana parishes shows. Orleans Parish, which included New Orleans, had a black population of 64,491 in 1890 and had 25 black Baptist churches with a total membership of 2,665. Webster Parish in the northwest section of the state, with a black population of only 7,289, had 52 black Baptist churches with a total resident membership of 3,684.[14] Further study shows that among Baptists, the average membership per church in urban counties often exceeded that for churches in rural counties. In Charleston County, South Carolina, (which included the city of Charleston) the average membership for the eight black Baptist churches was 326 persons. The Baptist churches in the more rural counties of Edgefield in the West and Beaufort in the extreme southeastern corner, where Baptists were particularly strong, however, averaged 186 and 233 persons respectively. But this apparent show of urban strength could not always be presumed. In the urban Alabama counties of Jefferson and Mobile (which incorporated Birmingham and the port city of Mobile) the average black Baptist membership for the 51 and 31 churches respectively was 84 and 105 persons. The rural predominantly black Alabama County of Dallas, however, had 87 black Baptist churches with an average membership of 137 members. The largest black churches were not neccessarily found in the cities. The apparent balance of Baptist strength between urban and rural counties may have been a contributing factor to the demographic diversity represented by the black ministerial elite, which itself was a mix between rural and urban, large and small churches.[15]

The theology of black Baptists was basically Calvinist, although they did not devote much time to the old theological arguments that had plagued the white church in earlier centuries. They accepted the fallenness of humanity and believed that in Jesus Christ humanity had a saviour. Yet black Baptists believed that humanity maintained some freedom to accept or reject the salvation available through Christ. They maintained that justification and regeneration occurred when a person accepted Jesus Christ as Lord by faith, but full sanctification and glorification were not attainable in life. Nevertheless, black Baptists expected Christians to keep striving toward fuller obedience to God in this life, as a loving response to God's prior love for humanity. Even disobedience, however, was not enough to rob a person of salvation. Though black Baptists may have doubted the salvation of anyone whose behavior was out of line, they trusted in the permanence of true salvation; once saved always saved. The question for Baptists was not whether they could lose their salvation, but whether a person had been saved once and for all.

The African Methodist Episcopal Church (AME) was the second largest denomination in the black community, and thirteen of the men in this study were affiliated with that church. The AME Church held its first General Conference in 1816 in Philadelphia, thus making it the earliest black denomination. Soon thereafter the church attempted to establish itself in the South. This early effort had to be abandoned in 1822 when South Carolina authorities began suppressing the church after they determined that several leaders of Denmark Vesey's insurrection were associated with the Hampstead AME Church of Charleston.[16] Forty-one years later the AME Church returned to the South at the request of a minister of the Methodist Episcopal Church in South Carolina who felt that in the wake of the Union Army victories there was a need for itinerant ministers who would:

> . . . care for the moral, social and religious
> interest of the freedman of South Carolina,
> who were then as sheep without a shepherd,
> left in that condition by their former white
> pastors, who had fled before the advancing
> and conquering army of the Union.[17]

In response to this request and after receiving assurances that the missionaries would be protected, the AME Church sent James Lynch and James Hall to South Carolina in May, 1863, to begin organizing AME churches. Lynch was a minister from the Baltimore Conference and was described as a skillful organizer, always hopeful and rather bold. Hall, on the other hand, from the New York Conference, was more the follower, somewhat timid, and often fearful.[18] Despite their different personalities, they worked well together and planted the seeds that led to the growth of their church in the South. When the AME's established the South Carolina Conference in 1865, the member churches had almost three thousand communicants, spread throughout South Carolina, Georgia, and Florida. When the war ended, black Methodists defected en masse from the white-controlled Methodist Episcopal Church, South, swelling the ranks of African Methodism. By 1868, blacks in Georgia and Florida had organized separate conferences. The church continued its steady growth so that by 1890 the AME Church had 307,580 communicants, or 1 member for every 16.1 blacks in nine states. As could be expected they were strongest in South Carolina (88,172) and Georgia (73,248). Alabama and Mississippi had 30,781 and 24,439 members, with the other five states having AME memberships ranging between 13 and 23 thousand each.[19]

The organization of the AME Church was a major distinguishing mark of that church. The church was organized into episcopal districts that were presided over by bishops. Bishops were elected by vote of the ministers who were eligible to participate in the General Conference of the Church, which was held once every four years. Several smaller geographical units, called Annual Conferences, formed the episcopal districts. Once a year delegates to each Conference would meet to carry out their business. The bishop of the episcopal district presided at the annual meetings, at which time ministers were admitted to the conference, transferred to other conferences or districts, and assigned various work within the conference.

Bishops in the AME Church had enormous authority; once a man was elected to the bishopric, his authority was virtually absolute. Four of the thirteen AME ministers in this study were bishops between 1865 and 1902 and a fifth was elected to the office shortly after 1902.

The episcopal organization of the AME Church helped it move into the South and stimulated its early growth. The establishment of AME churches was more systematic than that of their Baptist brethren, resulting in less overlapping and duplication of ministries. This in part accounts for the fact that it was not unusual to find that the average membership of AME churches was larger than that of Baptist churches located in the same counties. A comparison of four urban counties in Georgia and two rural counties in Mississippi reflects a general pattern. Baptists had 137 churches in the four counties of Fulton, DeKalb, Chatham and Richmond in 1890. The average church membership in the four counties was 176, 76, 231, and 190. There were far fewer AMEs in these four counties and there were only 16 churches, but the average membership for each church was at least twice the Baptist average. AME churches in Fulton had an average membership of 645; DeKalb's churches had 152 members; there was an average of 524 per church in Chatham; and the one AME Church in Richmond County claimed 601 members. In the rural Mississippi counties of Lowndes and Holmes, Baptists had 146 churches with an average membership of 124 people in Lowndes and 79 members in Holmes. The AMEs had only one church in Lowndes with 162 members and 4 churches in Holmes that averaged 215 members each.[20] Rather than a proliferation of smaller congregations, the AMEs seemed to concentrate on a few large congregations. At least theoretically, this gave individual AME pastors a larger audience and possibly a greater base of support and power than their Baptist counterparts. Whether this was the case or not, it is difficult to say. However, the total Baptist strength in a given area may have lessened the apparent advantage an individual AME pastor may have derived from a large congregation.

The 3,321 ministers in the AME Church in 1890 benefited from the episcopal government in another very practical manner. Once they were admitted to a conference they were virtually assured of a place of service. This gave a Methodist minister more security than his Baptist brother. The early career of Theophilus Gould Steward was typical. Transferred to the South Carolina Conference from the New Jersey Conference in May, 1865, by Bishop Payne, Steward became an elder and went to Beaufort, South Carolina, where he organized a mission church in June. He became ill less than a month later and had to leave the field to recover, but when he returned to the conference in October, 1865, he was sent to Georgetown, South Carolina. The area already had an established church, so Steward asked for and received a new assignment. The new field was extremely poor and could not support a church, so Steward once again asked to be reassigned. This time he was sent to Marion, South Carolina, where he remained until the Annual Conference of May, 1866. Although ministers in the conference were not always satisfied with their places of service, a sense of security came from knowing that the denomination would provide a place.

The AME Church also had a strong sense of racial pride, because it was the earliest black-controlled institution in America. Through such leaders as Richard Allen and Morris Brown, the church had taken strong stands in support of the race. As a result, southern whites frequently accused the AMEs of being a political church, especially after Denmark Vesey's abortive rebellion in Charleston. The charge was a source of irritation to AME ministers, who denied it. Wesley Gaines, a Georgia minister and bishop who wrote the history of the AME Church in the South, reflected a prevailing opinion when he said that the fear of the AME Church as being a "political church" was behind the creation of the Colored Methodist Episcopal Church by the Methodist Episcopal Church, (ME) South.

> *It was the political influence of the North that made that church (M.E. Church, South) organize this Colored Methodist Episcopal Church of America. They felt that the African Methodist Episcopal Church was a political church in sympathy with the North. They made a mistake. While the AME Church believed fully in the freedom of the race and appreciated those who brought about that freedom, this church is not, and never has been a political church no more than is any other Christian church.[21]*

The tensions between the AME and CME churches, which continued throughout the nineteenth century, resulted from the AME position that there was no need for the CME Church even to exist.

AME theology generally reflected the theological heritage of Methodism; the church had not been founded as a result of any theological controversy within the Wesleyan tradition. AMEs were Arminian in their understanding of the freedom of the human will, and they affirmed the ability of the sinner to either accept or reject the salvation offered in Jesus. Like other Methodists, AME preachers also taught that saved persons could lose their salvation by faithlessness. As a result, they emphasized Christian holiness. African Methodists were encouraged to cultivate a desire and longing for complete sanctification in this life. The AME Church believed that perfection was attainable in this life, and that "glorification" occurred after death.

The African Methodist Episcopal Zion Church was the third largest predominantly black Christian denomination during the thirty-seven year period after the end of the Civil War. Like those of the AME Church, the roots of the Zion Church were northern. AME Zion missionaries arrived in the South during the Civil War. James W. Hood, later a bishop, was the first regular AME Zion missionary in the South. Appointed in 1863, he arrived in North Carolina in January, 1864, and his work was so successful that by December the church organized a North Carolina Conference with nearly three thousand members. It was said that Hood founded some 600 churches, most of them meeting in their own buildings. He swept through North Carolina like an army, and then raided southern Virginia and northern South Carolina as well.[22] In 1890 the AME Zion Church had only slightly less overall strength than the AME group. In nine states of the South the Zionites had 295,473 communicants, or 1 member for every 16.76 blacks in the population. Despite the fact that the Zion Church had only 8,000 fewer members in the nine states than the AME Church, the Zion Church did not have a balanced distribution. Its strength was in North Carolina, with 111,949 members, followed by Alabama with 79,231 members and South Carolina with 45,880. Almost half of the South Carolina total was in three northern counties, Lancaster, Spartanburg, and Chester that were close to the North Carolina border. Those three states accounted for over 79% of the total AME Zion membership in the nine states; the Church was clearly regional. Furthermore, AME Zion strength was not concentrated in urban areas. Except in North Carolina, where the church was strong throughout the state, and possibly Alabama, where a good percentage of the Zion membership lived in counties dominated by cities and large towns, AME Zion strength appears to have been in smaller agricultural counties. The Zion Church had entered the deep South later than the AMEs and had to go where there was less competition. Outside North Carolina, Alabama, and the three counties in South Carolina, the 1,565 AME Zion ministers found themselves working in small communities, often some distance from other colleagues in their communion.[23]

The major points that differentiated the AME Zion Church from the AME Church were the strength of the episcopacy and the involvement of the laity. The Zion structure allowed for more lay participation and curtailed the bishop's power to act unilaterally. Zion ministers still benefited from the denominational structure, as did the AME ministers. Both denominations screened men before they were given full ministerial acceptance in the church. A man could not function in either denomination until he was admitted to a conference, and both the AME Zion and the AME Church turned down applicants who did not meet minimal moral and educational standards.

The AME Zion Church occupied the same theological ground that was held by the AME Church. There was no theological dispute between the two bodies: both accepted Arminian suppositions about the will; both believed that Christians could backslide; both called for sanctified living.

The Colored Methodist Episcopal Church[24] (CME) was the smallest of the major black denominations. Unlike the other black Methodists, the CME Church had its roots in the Methodist Episcopal Church, South. In 1861 there were about 207,000 black communicants in the ME Church, South, but by 1866, defections reduced that number to 78,000. Most blacks had joined one of the two African Methodist bodies or the Baptists, with a few uniting with the Methodist Episcopal Church, North, which was also attempting to grow in southern soil. In order to prevent the further erosion of its black membership, the ME Church, South, in 1866 authorized separate annual conferences for blacks, a move welcomed by blacks who had remained in the ME Church, South. Blacks responded by establishing five annual conferences by the time the General Conference of the Southern Church met in 1870. Representatives of the five black annual conferences then called for the formation of a separate General Conference for their communicants, which was approved by the General Conference of the parent church. The process culminated with the organization of the Colored Methodist Episcopal Church in December, 1870, at a meeting in Jackson, Tennessee; representatives from eight annual conferences took part in the organizational meeting.

Throughout the remainder of the century, the CME Church had a close relationship to the ME Church, South; a relationship that other black denominations, especially the African Methodist Episcopal Church, often used to discredit the CME Church. Charles Phillips, a bishop in the CME Church, complained of the problems that faced the early CME clergy over this issue.

> *No easy field lay before these consecrated men. The church was in its infancy; it was maliciously misrepresented, wantonly maligned, and frequently calumniated by stronger religious denominations. The relation of our church to the Methodist Episcopal Church, South, was the prolific cause of most of the misrepresentations that were heaped upon us. The church was called a 'rebel Church', 'Democratic Church', and 'the old Slavery Church.' These were powerful weapons used against us, for the reason that our people were naturally credulous, especially concerning anything that might be said about those who had kept their forefathers in slavery for more than two centuries. Some were odiously inclined to the Church, South; others refused social relations with those who in any way affiliated with that church. Thus the credulity of the ignorant was played upon with ease, and they joined in the rabble cry: 'Demolish the new church! - the 'Democratic Church'.[25]*

Though much of the early criticism against the CME Church was no doubt the result of anger occasioned by the refusal of the Colored Methodists to join one of the African churches, and also stemmed from some jealousy of the financial assistance the CME Church received from White Methodists, some of the criticisms had more substantial grounds. The Colored Methodists and the African Methodists often argued over property ownership. Before the formation of the CME Church, black congregations that had been part of the ME Church, South, sometimes defected to one of the African Methodist denominations, usually bringing church property into the African Church. After the CME Church was formed, either the ME Church, South, or the CME Church would sometimes attempt to reclaim the property so that the CME congregation could use it. If a legal battle ensued, the White Methodists often assisted the Colored Methodists, a fact that did not endear them to the African Methodists. The Colored Methodists also used the discipline of the ME Church, South, and purchased Sunday School literature from them.[26]

Despite the damaging criticism of the CME Church and its obvious ties to the ME Church, South, CME membership grew during the period, albeit at a rate much slower than that of the other black denominations. In 1890, the CME Church had 1,800 ministers (more than the AME Zion) and 129,383 communicants in the United States; 103,553 members were in the nine states of the South. The average of 1 member for every 47.83 blacks in the nine-state area was far below the average of the other three black denominations. Like the AME Zion Church, a large percentage of the CME membership was located in a relatively small area. Over 75% of the CME strength was confined to Georgia, with 22,840 members, Mississippi with 20,107, Tennessee with 18,968, and Alabama with 18,940. All the remaining five states had less than 10,000 members; three of these, South Carolina (3,468), North Carolina (2,786), and Florida (1,461), having fewer than five thousand members. Furthermore, very little CME strength was exhibited in urban counties. In Tennessee, for example, the urban county showing the greatest CME strength was Shelby County in extreme southwest Tennessee. With Memphis as its population center, the county had a black population of 61,613 in 1890. The CME Church there had 1,601 members in 13 congregations.[27] In the agricultural and rural counties of Madison and Gibson, also located in western Tennessee, there were 25,006 blacks in the 1890 census. Yet, the CME Church had 47 congregations (almost one-fourth the total CME Churches in the state) with a membership of 5,097. The same rural strength was apparent in Georgia, Alabama, and Mississippi.[28] Like the AME Zion Church, the CME group suffered because they started their work later than the Baptists and the AMEs. The CMEs, no doubt, also suffered from their relations with the ME Church, South in the urban counties, where blacks tended to affiliate with the more independent Baptist or AME churches.

Though the CME Church had a small membership, it had almost as many congregations as the two African Methodist bodies. In the nine southern states the CME Church had 1,312 congregations while the AMEs had 1,358 and the Zion Church had 1,333 (the Baptists had 8,751). This meant that the average membership of the CME congregation was only 78 members compared with an average of 226 members and 221 members per congregation for the AME and AME Zion churches respectively (Baptists had an average of 106 members per church). CME ministers, therefore, did not benefit from the overall strength of the Baptists or enjoy the power and security derived from serving sizable congregations. It is not an exaggeration to say that the CME Church was far weaker than the other black denominations between 1865 and the turn of the century.

The CME minister did have the benefits (and trials) of episcopal church government. CME ministers shared power with the bishops and could overrule them in the General Conference, but generally they went along with the bishops recommendations, for the bishops appointed the ministers to their various positions. Most ministers in the CME Church were from the South, especially the church's leaders. It is fitting that three of the four CME men in this study came from western Tennessee, and that three of the four were also converted in the ME Church, South. Near the end of the century, though, the leadership came from men like Charles H. Phillips who had been converted within the CME Church. Such men maintained historic ties to the ME Church, South, but they were not bound to it by personal experience.

The vast majority of black Christians in the South held membership in black denominations between 1865 and 1902. Such predominantly white denominations as the Presbyterians and Congregationalists, did start churches among blacks, and despite their relative numerical weakness, some of these communions provided the black community with distinguished leaders in the crusade for "uplift." But antagonism between the ministers in the black denominations and those in the white denominations sometimes reached high levels. Frequently the feuds centered on the question of who had done the most for the improvement of the race.[29] Thirteen of the seventy-eight men in this study were ministers in "white denominations." Four came from the Methodist Episcopal Church, four from the Presbyterian Church, and four from the Congregational Church; the remaining minister was ordained by the Disciples of Christ. All but one of them were highly educated men; eight held seminary degrees and two held doctorates.

The growth of the church in the black community after 1865 attested to its unique standing in the black community. In his classic work, **The Souls of Black Folk,** W.E.B. Dubois referred to the census data to show the strength of the black church.

> *The census of 1890 showed nearly twenty-four thousand Negro churches in the country, with a total enrolled membership of over two and a half million, or ten actual church members to every twenty-eight persons, and in some southern states one in every*

> *two persons. Besides these there is the large*
> *number who, while not enrolled as members,*
> *attend and take part in many of the activities*
> *of the church. There is an organized Negro*
> *church for every sixty black families in the*
> *nation, and in some states for every forty*
> *families, owning, on an average, a thousand*
> *dollars worth of property each, or nearly*
> *twenty-six million dollars in all.*[30]

The figures, used by DuBois, increased by nearly a third by 1902. Whatever the denomination, the black church was the fulcrum of the black community and the attempt to uplift the race had to start with it.

2. THE BLACK MINISTER AS PART OF HIS COMMUNITY

As the leader in the church, the black preacher held an exalted position which gave him high visibility and influence, as Elijah Marrs noted. The minister had the potential to become the visible example of "uplift." But he first had to be accepted by the community. To inspire the community, the ministerial leader had to know its suffering, deprivations, and hopes. The elite clergy met that requirement. They could claim an affinity with the community that gave legitimacy to their rhetoric of "uplift."

The affinity was evident by the biographies of the prominent ministers which reflected the diversity within the broader community. A slight majority of the leading clergymen had been slaves. Of the seventy-three men who were born prior to emancipation, at least forty-one were born into slavery.[31] And like the black population in general, the ministers had a variety of slave experiences. No identifiable peculiarity of their lives as slaves can explain their later prominence in the church. To select individual stories is to discover not so much a common pattern as to find a diverse array of experiences. William E. Holmes, a Baptist minister and teacher in Georgia, a leader in the Georgia Missionary Baptist Convention, and a trustee of several black schools, including Spelman Seminary and the Atlanta Baptist College in Atlanta, had a relatively mild slave experience. His father lived on a separate plantation and could not visit regularly, but his mother was able to hire herself out. The man for whom she worked had no children of his own, so Holmes became a sort of household pet.

> *His home was a pleasant one. Books*
> *and papers were not kept from him, or indeed*
> *anything which was elevating and ennobling*
> *in its tendencies. His mother being able*
> *to read, early inspired him with a love for*
> *books, and taught him to read simple paragraphs*
> *with some degree of ease. During the last*

*years of the war, she sent him every day
to school, carefully concealing his books
under his clothes to avoid arrest.*[32]

But other men, like T.W. Coffee, an AME minister and editor in Alabama, knew no such advantages under slavery. When he was eight years old, Coffee was taken from his mother and made to wait on his mistress. Growing up in "one of the most benighted regions of Alabama," Coffee had a master who believed in whipping his slaves.[33] After one beating, Coffee escaped to the Union Army lines. He was returned to his master because the Union had not established a procedure for dealing with runaway slaves in 1863. Undaunted, Coffee escaped again, and was never re-enslaved.

Some of the ministers lived in families that had not been broken by slavery. Wesley J. Gaines, an AME minister, elected as a bishop in 1888, was one of fourteen children in a family that was not separated during slavery.[34] Ten other ministers had Gaines' good fortune. But stability of family life did not invariably mark the childhood experience of the leading ministers any more than it did that of other blacks. George W. Dupree helped organize twelve or thirteen churches in Kentucky and served as the Moderator of the Baptist General Association in Kentucky. He was among the most successful pastors of his region. Yet in slavery, he was sold several times, and lost all knowledge of his family after the death of his mother.[35] No fewer than nineteen of the ministerial leaders in this study were separated from their families during slavery.

Even in "racial" background and in the places where they had been slaves, the ministers shared in the diversity that characterized their parishioners. Most of them had black parents, but James J. Durham represents the slaves who were children of their white masters. Durham was born in South Carolina as the son of a rich white planter and a slave woman. Though he went on to serve in leadership positions in the Sunday School Convention in South Carolina as a missionary for the American Baptist Publication Society, he worked as a field hand on his father's plantation and received the same treatment as any other salve.[36] Bartlett Taylor, on the other hand, had gentler treatment from his master-father and remained with him until economic decline forced his father to sell him.[37] Of the forty-one men who had been slaves, the majority came from the deep South states. A total of thirty came from Mississippi (2), Alabama (6), Georgia (9), Louisiana (5), and South Carolina (8). The remaining eleven came from North Carolina (1), Tennessee (2), Kentucky (5), Virginia (2), and Florida (1). With the exception of the figures for Virginia, North Carolina and Mississipi, the number of ministerial leaders from each state corresponds closely to the relative size of the black population in each state.

The variety of experiences surely helped the ministers, as a group, relate themselves successfully to the larger black community. The ministers could uplift because they were part of a slave people. Yet black ministerial leadership was not limited to former slaves. Eight of the seventy-eight leaders were born free while slavery was still legal, and five others were born after emancipation. Edward M. Brawley, the son of free parents in Charleston, South Carolina, spent the early years of his life there. Brawley, later, became an educator, missionary, pastor, and editor, holding positions of responsibility in South Carolina and Tennessee.[38] J.C. Price, an educator and leader of the AME Zion Church, was also born free, owing to a North Carolina law that attributed the status of the mother to the child regardless of the father's status: his mother was a free woman.[39] John J. Morant, who spent many years as a minister in Mississippi,[40] and Thomas D. Fuller, an outstanding Baptist Leader in North Carolina and Tennessee,[41] were both born after the Civil War ended.

The ministers shared not only the backgrounds of most other blacks, but also lived in their stable, immobile geographical location. The black population was not highly mobile between 1865 and 1902. While there is evidence of substantial intra-state black migration immediately following emancipation, there was not much inter-state black migration.[42] The same can be said generally for the black ministerial leadership. Although the Methodists often transferred their ministers from one state to another, twenty-five of the elite ministers lived and served in only one state. Another eighteen lived in two southern states; often adjacent ones. Edward R. Carter, born in Clarke County, Georgia, served in Athens and Stone Mountain and attended school in Atlanta before accepting the invitation to become the pastor of the Friendship Baptist Church in Atlanta. As a vice-president of the Georgia State Baptist Sunday School Convention, he traveled extensively, but he never lived outside the state of his birth.[43] Like Elijah Marrs, Daniel A. Gaddie spent his entire life in Kentucky, where he was not only recognized by black Baptists in the state but was also elected as treasurer of the American National Baptist Convention.[44] Only seven of the group were born outside the South. Although twenty-one men spent some time outside the area, nine of those merely attended school outside the South and returned to the region after their schooling. Like the freedmen they served, the black ministerial leaders were a part of their communities because most of them were born and lived in those communities all their lives.

The leaders were also part of their communities financially. Almost all the limited personal wealth in the black community between 1865 and 1902 was found in property ownership: houses or land or both. In 1900, blacks owned approximately 1/6 of the private family homes they occupied in the nine southern states—209,455 homes were owned out of 1,223,906 private family units occupied by blacks. A little over half of the total were farm homes (114,366).[45] This was an amazing accomplishment for a people who had been slaves only thirty-five years earlier, but the vast majority of blacks had little in the way of real or personal wealth. And although the ministerial leadership preached upward mobility, they shared in the community's impoverishment. Peter Kolchin has shown that in Alabama "most black clergymen owned little or no property and those who did were rarely wealthy men. With some exceptions,the new black clergymen were a group close to the black masses."[46] Kolchin's conclusions hold outside Alabama; the same claim could be made about the ministerial elite in the other southern states. The prominent ministers clearly felt that home ownership and savings were goals of uplift. Yet, even at the close of the century, very few leading ministers had anything vaguely approaching wealth. Of the seventy-eight men in this study, W.D. Chappelle, a businessman, teacher, AME preacher, and editor in South Carolina,[47] and Joshua Jones, another AME pastor in the same state,[48] were reported to have had assets in excess of $10,000 in the 1890's, though it appears that Jones accumulated his wealth after leaving South Carolina. The Reverend Preston Taylor, born a slave in Louisiana in 1849, was a contractor in Kentucky before becoming a Disciple of Christ pastor in Tennessee, where he soon owned a funeral business, a two-story house, eighteen horses and seven carriages,[49] and the Baptist William R. Pettiford, a pastor, bank president, publishing company president, and property owner in Alabama also had assets valued at more than $10,000.[50] Four other clergymen in our group managed to accumulate assets ranging between $3,000 and $5,000. But most of the ministers were, it seems, men whose wealth did not distinguish them from other ordinary workers. Methodist bishops in this period did not always receive the full amount of salary authorized by the General Conference; Baptist ministers often relied on uncertain collections, only to be repeatedly disappointed. At the turn of the century, R.P. Wyche, a leading Presbyterian minister in North Carolina could write:

> *The financial status of the pulpit, under existing conditions, may be considered comparatively good. It had been made what it now is by industry, economy and self-denial, and stands as an object lesson for the benefit of those wishing to better their condition. The salaries paid Negro preachers are usually small, even less than the wages of mechanics. But these small earnings are carefully saved and wisely invested. As a result many of the Negro preachers have comfortable homes, while others of them have small bank accounts. The Negro minister has learned the dignity of labor and does not hesitate to labor with head and hands in order to attain to the position of usefulness and influence in the world. The people are taught in this practical manner the lessons of industry and economy more forcibly than in any other way, and they are thus led to secure homes, to enter into business and to educate their children.[51]*

Like most of the freedmen they served, most black ministers had to work themselves up from harsh poverty.

Black ministerial leaders were often involved in manual and professional work outside the church. Fifty-three of the seventy-eight had vocations outside the ministry. In the 1900 census, only .4% of the black population listed themselves as ministers. According to the same census, 52.7% of the black population were employed in an occupation directly related to agriculture and another 25.4% were non-agricultural laborers, servants, and waiters.[52] The work of the ministers outside the church brought them in touch with the community they sought to uplift, precluding their isolation from the black masses. Bartlett Taylor in Kentucky, for instance, was a butcher whose earnings enabled him to purchase his freedom in 1840; most of the ministers with extra-ecclesiastical duties were teachers and educators (33), but others had skills ranging from farming (2) to painting (1), business (3) to smithing (1), and from shoemaking (2) to newspaper work (5). Two men were medical doctors and three others were politicians; some of the men, such as Edward M. Brawley, a Baptist minister from South Carolina, were trained in one field but devoted their career to another one. Trained as a shoemaker, Brawley was a teacher for most of his adult life.

Some of the ministers also joined benevolent and fraternal organizations. At least ten of the seventy-eight held leadership in the social organizations—a token of respect. Edward R. Carter was Grand Worthy Chief Templar for the State of Georgia; George Washington Dupree was Grand Master and Senior Warden of the Masons in Kentucky; Preston Taylor served as the State Grand Chaplain for the Masons and State Grand Master of the Odd-Fellows in Tennessee; while C.C. Vaughn, a Baptist minister, held high rank in both the Odd-Fellows and Good Samaritan organizations in Kentucky.[53] Some ministers saw the societies as "great brotherhoods, mighty in their cohesive power . . . the result of man's social instinct, which not only leads individuals to associate with each other, but leads them to associate for the purpose of mutual protection and helpfulness."[54] But J.W. Hood, who was not opposed to the societies in principle, exhibited some clerical sensitivity about the power of the societies.

> *If they claim soul-saving efficiency, encroach upon religious duties, or claim the time or talents which belong to the church, they are guilty of usurpation, and are a curse to mankind.*[55]

Still other black ministers opposed the fraternal and secret societies in principle, fearing laxity in their moral standards.[56] Despite the limited protests, however, the societies were strong, and leading ministers often joined them.

Unlike the clerical class that developed in New England in the 18th and 19th centuries, the ministry in the black community was not the exclusive property of a few families; there were no families of priests

21

who passed the mantle to their heirs automatically. Any male member of the community had a chance to become a minister. Only four men in the group of seventy-eight were the sons of fathers who had been ministers; the vast majority had no relatives in the ministry. And blacks of all sorts and all ages could become members of the elite clergy. George W. Clinton was converted at ten and began preaching at age twenty in the AME Zion Church.[57] Charles T. Walker, a pastor, State Sunday School Convention leader, editor and treasurer of the American National Baptist Convention, was converted at fifteen and was licensed to preach three years later.[58] Alexander Walters from Bardstown, Kentucky, started his climb to the AME Zion bishopric with his conversion at age twelve followed by licensing at nineteen.[59] At least thirty-five of the seventy-eight were converted and ordained before they were twenty-five. Other men who rose to leadership were older when they began to preach. William H. Heard was twenty-nine when he was converted and began to preach a year later.[60] Paul Kennedy, who later became an author, publisher, and Baptist pastor in Kentucky was ordained to the ministry when he was twenty-eight which was some three years after his conversion.[61] Mansfield Tyler, a Baptist leader in Alabama, was not converted until he was twenty-nine, and although he began preaching almost immediately, he was not ordained until he was forty-two.[62] Thirty-five of the elite ministers were twenty-five or older when they were ordained.

The black minister, then, was clearly a product of the black community and represented the broad spectrum found in that community. His identification with it and its identification with him allowed him to become the very symbol of uplift. Yet the ministerial leadership in the South was also apart from the community in a special sense. Paradoxically, this apartness further enhanced the ministers' role as the personification of uplift for the race.

3. THE BLACK MINISTER AS SEPARATE FROM HIS COMMUNITY

The key to understanding the paradox of the separateness of the preachers from their communities is found in the position a man assumed when he became a minister in the black community: as a minister, he was set apart. W.J. Gaines, a bishop in the AME Church and a longtime organizer and leader in Georgia, lectured on the ministry at such schools as Wilberforce University, Gammon Theological Seminary, and Tuskegee Institute. In his lectures he pointed, in conventional terms, to the unique self-understanding of the ministers.

> *The ministry is not a profession, but a calling . . . the high and holy functions which belong to it can be discharged only by the man who has been set apart to it, anointed by the Holy Ghost and divinely endowed for its peculiar and special*

responsibilities.[63]

Furthermore, "coincident and confirmatory proof is furnished of the call to the ministry, by a consensus of impression on the part of the church and community."[64] The call to the ministry and the confirmation of that call by the community placed the minister in a high place of influence that had consequences for his activity in uplifting the race. Gaines admonished the minister to understand that as a public figure held in high esteem, he had a sacred trust. "And in proportion as he is faithful to his trust will he mould the thought and shape the sentiment and elevate the religious life of those who hear him."[65] George W. Clinton, an AME Zion bishop, revealed his own sense of the social importance of the black minister in his comments on his predecessors.

> *In the very beginning the Negro pulpit had the leadership and the enlightenment of the race in spiritual and intellectual knowledge thrust upon it, when it was neither qualified nor regularly organized. Despite the disability within and the disadvantages without, the Negro pulpit became the pioneer in the first movements to better the condition of the race by lifting it from the degradation and disorganized state in which it was left by slavery.*[66]

The minister, in the black community, was in a unique position of leadership and he knew it.

The elite clergy thought that ministers were responsible for setting a proper example for the people. In accord with this ideal, Bishop William Henry Miles, a senior bishop of the Colored Methodist Episcopal Church, vigorously opposed allowing a minister who had married a divorcee to serve as a delegate to the General Conference of that Church in 1886. In a letter written to the Conference after the minister had been admitted, he stated his case.

> *Whereas H. Reid has married a woman that has been divorced from her husband; and whereas my conviction is that he has rendered himself unfit for the ministry and unfit to serve as a delegate to legislate for this Church; and whereas I believe that the decision of this General Conference in admitting said Reid is damaging to the morals of our Church; and whereas I believe it to be the duty of this General Conference to raise high the standard of morality among our people, I hereby protest against such*

> *decision as will allow a preacher to marry*
> *another man's wife and recognize him as*
> *a suitable man to legislate for the Church*
> *of God.*[67]

Bishop Miles' argument transcended any strictly legal aspects of the case. Rather it struck at the moral implications that this particular minister's action had for the Colored Methodist Episcopal Church and for the race. That the delegates did not agree with his assessment of Reid's credentials did not indicate that they did not agree with Miles' evaluation of the minister's role. John B.L. Williams, a leader in the Methodist Episcopal Church and a teacher in Georgia and Florida, echoed Miles' concern several years later when he wrote an article on the topic, "To What Extent is the Negro Pulpit Uplifting the Race?"

> *The Christian pulpit has ever been*
> *acknowledged to be a great power for good*
> *among all people. Coming as it does divinely*
> *commissioned and bearing to man a divine*
> *message, it has a claim upon the attention*
> *and the acceptance of mankind . . . . The*
> *Christian pulpit is peculiarly and inseparably*
> *interwoven into the social life, moral*
> *deportment and religious growth of the people.*
> *In its character it is to be the representation*
> *of the highest standard of ethical deportment*
> *and the best example of religious life. From*
> *it the people are to receive their inspiration*
> *for that which is pure, exalted and ennobling.*
> *To the Christian pulpit the people look for*
> *the loftiest ideals of life. In this respect*
> *the Negro more than any other people has*
> *been largely dependent upon the pulpit.*
> *Emerging as he did more than a quarter of*
> *a century ago from the thraldom which fettered*
> *his body and imprisoned his intellect and*
> *buried him in ignorance, it was the Christian*
> *pulpit represented at that time by the good*
> *old fathers of those dark and trying days*
> *. . . they it was who saved their people from*
> *conditions which would have been (vastly)*
> *more deplorable but for such moral and*
> *religious instruction as they were able to*
> *impart.*[68]

The minister had the responsibility of leading the black community by setting a high example. As J.W. Hood said in a sermon directed towards his fellow ministers, "Brethen, we are to be lights in this benighted land."[69]

4. THE CONCEPT OF UPLIFT AND THE MINISTERIAL LEADERSHIP

There is an ironic side to the clerical concern for uplifting the race. To the extent that they were successful, the ministers would inevitably undermine their own position of unique power and leadership. Any direct threat to their power was minimized by the fact that the church was the only free black institution. The early hope of free access to all the benefits of society was shattered, and the church remained the center of black life in the South throughout the nineteenth century. But insofar as the ideal gradually became a reality, leadership in the black community did become more diffuse.

The concept of uplift was important to the black ministerial leadership on two distinct but related levels. On the one hand, the ministers were keenly aware of the deficiencies resulting from slavery and limited opportunity. On the other hand, the ministerial leaders saw uplift as the way to eliminate prejudice, which, they often suggested, was based in part on the deficiencies in the black community.

Throughout the period, the ministers worked to enable the freedman to be more competitive in society. Hence, Elijah Marrs gave up farming because he believed he could do more to uplift the race as a teacher. T.G. Steward, an AME minister, was convinced that without the gospel of uplift, blacks would condemn their children "to be hewers of wood and drawers of water."[70] Black ministers at the end of the century could feel good about the progress the race had made, but they were quick to remind their people how far they had to go. An essay written by M.C.B. Mason, an ex-slave from Louisiana who held a doctorate from Syracuse University and was a denominational executive with the Methodist Episcopal Church at the turn of the century, wrote of both the progress and the needs of the freedman.

> From this humble beginning of a generation ago when he had absolutely nothing he has begun to acquire something of this world's goods. He has been getting for himself a home, some land, some money in the bank, and some interest in stocks and bonds. His industry, thrift, and economy are everywhere in evidence and he is bravely and consciously struggling toward the plane where his vindication as a man and a citizen is what he is and what he had acquired.[71]

Yet Mason observed:

> There is still, however, much room for improvement, and to this perhaps, more than any one thing, the race must now turn

> *its attention. Some questions regarding his*
> *inability to learn have all been settled by*
> *the remarkable achievements which he has*
> *made in all lines of intellectual endeavor,*
> *but it must still be confessed that in the*
> *field of morals and manners, the charge is*
> *still made, and that not without some*
> *semblance of truth, that evidences of the*
> *essential quality of sturdy and manly character*
> *are not as clearly manifest among us as they*
> *should be.[72]*

Mason was proud of the achievements, but he knew that the future security of black people depended on their recognition of lingering inadequacies, which others saw as the key to eliminating prejudice.

At the conclusion of the Negro Young People's Christian and Educational Congress, which brought nearly 7,000 people to Atlanta in 1902 and was acclaimed the greatest gathering of the race, the ministers who organized the meeting issued a "Public Declaration to the American People," pointing to some of the problems of black people in America. But rather than focus on the responsibility whites had to eliminate the injustices, it called on blacks to eliminate the basis for racial prejudice.

> *Whatever of burdens we may still have*
> *to endure, of adjustments which are yet to*
> *be made, we throw ourselves upon the justice*
> *and fair play of the American people, North*
> *and South, and declare our unreserved*
> *conviction that right in the end will prevail.*
> *Consequent to the work of making ourselves*
> *worthy of present opportunities and obligations*
> *growing out of them, rather than plead our*
> *wrongs and grievances, we deliberately and*
> *resolutely turn our attention.[73]*

The Declaration stressed the need for the youth to receive Christian education, and it concluded with another call for blacks to make themselves worthy of the advantages of freedom.

> *We are cognizant of the civic and political*
> *inequities under which our people are suffering;*
> *nevertheless we urge our people to continue*
> *to strive to shape their conduct that they*
> *may prove themselves deserving of any right*
> *and privilege now enjoyed by every other*
> *American citizen.[74]*

Uplift was essential if the race was to eliminate racial prejudice. In a sermon delivered before the Second Battalion of the Governor's Volunteers on the fourth Sunday in July, 1884, E.R. Carter, the pastor of Friendship Baptist Church in Atlanta, compared the fate of blacks to that of the Jews in England.

> And now what do I mean by telling this bit of history of a despised race but to show you what is true of one race may be true of another, especially when its men will do their whole duty, and have for their sole object the <u>elevation</u> of the people. Benjamin Disraeli did not come to honor by incendiary speeches and teaching his despised race anarchy and rebellion, but by being a loyal citizen himself, and teaching his people the same, and playing the man for them. What we want are men.[75]

The irony was that such a notion saddled the victims of prejudice with the responsibility for it. But it was far easier for the ministers to work for the uplift of black people than it was to effect the changes in the way whites related themselves to blacks.

If uplift was successful, most leading ministers believed blacks could earn the good will of well-meaning whites. In his opening address to the 1902 Congress, Bishop Gaines suggested that the conference could help prove that blacks were interested in their own elevation, and that would encourage whites to look more favorably on black people:

> They (whites) are in control of the country, its finances and educational enterprises, its social and industrial life. How vital, then, is our relation to our white neighbor and how important the question of his attitude toward us, whether it be one of friendliness or hostility![76]

By 1902, faced with political setbacks and Jim Crow statutes, Gaines' attitude was understandable; it was the path of least resistance, and it was also the most practical path. Other ministers like E.R. Carter of Atlanta believed that the prejudice against blacks was natural and in time would fade as blacks began to show their abilities.

> But, my brethern, we are not the only creatures of God's great creation that have to meet and encounter and struggle for the place they will occupy on this mighty, prolific and progressive globe. All things have to struggle with all their might and main for the point of eminence for which they are striving to reach . . . . It seems to be the order of nature and the plan of Providence

> to develop and improve a nation of people
> through this method of discipline, and its
> subjects have only to wait for the fruits of
> its operation.[77]

A few men like L.H. Holsey, a CME bishop, and H.M. Turner, an AME bishop, both of whom spent much of their lives in Georgia, had reservations about whether uplift alone would eliminate prejudice. They affirmed uplift but doubted that it would eliminate white hatred. Holsey stated his position in an essay published in 1902.

> In this country the Negro is despised
> and rejected, simply because he has a black
> skin, and social traits that distinguish him
> from other races . . . . As a race, the Negro
> cannot enjoy in this country, like the
> Anglo-Saxon, the immunities and privileges
> guaranteed to him by the constitution. The
> civil rights, the ample protection and the
> broad and liberal sentiment that protect
> and inspire the white people, are nowhere
> in America accorded to the black man. He
> is everywhere proscribed, because he is a
> Negro. No matter how much culture and
> refinement he may possess, he does not receive
> at the hands of the prejudiced whites that
> respectful consideration to which his culture
> entitles him.[78]

For a few men, like Turner and Holsey, uplift was valuable and necessary but it could not be called upon to eliminate prejudice by itself. Most of the ministers were more optimistic.

Uplift entailed moral, social, economic and educational development. It included a sound family life and pride in ownership of property; it involved the adoption of moral standards and behavioral patterns that conformed to the norm in American civilization. The norm was correct not because it was American or white, but because any civilized society operated on such principles. As L.H. Holsey said in his 1902 essay,

> Civilization means culture and
> refinement. The American type of civilization
> is somewhat different from the European
> and Asiatic; but, in the main features or
> characteristics, the world's great civilizations
> have always been the same in tone and
> design.[79]

America's achievements were evidence of the height to which conformity to the principles of uplift could take a people.

Despite the fact of prejudice, which was recognized and hated by all the ministers, almost all of the seventy-eight black clerical leaders in this study believed in America. Even critics like H.M. Turner, who by 1902 felt emigration to Africa was the only way blacks would be able to realize their potential, had to concede, "the United States has the highest form of civilized institutions that any nation has had."[80] Edward R. Carter represented the typical viewpoint that was even more lavish in its praise.

> We are living in one of the grandest countries on the face of the globe; none like it anywhere. Whatever we may think of it, because of our attitude and situation in it, of course, protection of life, property, liberty, friends, and all the other civil rights are of the first and highest importance with the people of the government. . . . We can own all we can pay for. So far as our standing, walking and acting are in the bounds of the law, and when I say this, I am not blind to nor ignorant of the troubles, drawbacks, hindrances and mighty resistances which, as a part of this grand republic, we have to encounter.[81]

The ministers appreciated America; they wanted to be Americans; they called for the inclusion of black people into the mainstream of American life; and they believed it would happen. It would happen through uplifting the race and they would lead the effort.

The elite black clergy in the South in the period of 1865 to 1902 were committed to the concept of uplift and were confident of their ability to uplift the race. They were leaders of the church; the one institution that was controlled by black people. They were part of their community by way of their experiences, hopes and aspirations; their diversity mirrored the diversity of the black community. Yet, they also were apart from their communities in their roles as ministers which gave them the leverage they needed to point to the higher goals and lift their people. I.D. Davis wrote an essay in response to the question, "To What Extent is the Negro Pulpit Uplifting the Race?", that was published in 1902. His reply reflected a consensus among the ministerial leaders.

> The influence of the Negro pulpit on the race is immeasurable. . . . At the close of the War when the Negroes were in darkness, the Negro preachers were the first to come forward to lead them to the light, and whatever may be said to the contrary, the Negro preachers have done more for the Negro's

> uplift since his emancipation than any other
> class of persons. We delight to boast that
> the Negroes pay taxes on $400,000,000 worth
> of property, that they have thousands of
> well-educated men and women, that their
> illiteracy has been reduced forty-five percent,
> that they have hundreds of newspapers, that
> they have four hundred or more skilled
> physicians who are making good money, that
> they have hundreds of men who are engaged
> in business enterprises, that they have
> thousands of honest, sober, upright Christian
> men and women.
>
> Now, to whom are we more indebted for
> all this than to the Negro preachers, who
> have faithfully taught their people to save
> their money and buy homes and lands, who
> have constantly advised them to send their
> sons and daughters to the schools, who have
> urged their people to patronize Negro business
> enterprises and Negro physicians and lawyers,
> who have shown their people the importance
> of taking Negro papers, who have enjoined
> them to be honest, sober, industrious
> citizens.?[82]

Davis's statement captures the essence of what uplift meant; it also illustrates the balance of accommodation and possibility. Leading black ministers accepted the symbols of success valued by the dominant society. They equated uplift with such things as the purchasing of a home, the literacy of the masses, the growth in the number of black professionals, and the development of solid black American citizens, who worked hard and paid their taxes. Like Bishop Gaines, some were even willing temporarily to accept white prejudice as long as blacks could become a part of what America was about. But even as they advocated American ideals, they also spoke of a possibility for blacks to gain equality. In calling for uplift they denied the white society's charcterization of blacks as ignorant, lazy, and inept. They rejected the white society's attempt to place blacks at the bottom of the social structure and keep them there. The message of uplift presupposed the acceptance of American values and Western Christian morality, but it also entailed the creation of black institutions that would overcome the heritage of slavery. The black ministers saw themselves as persons who had been uplifted, and they sought to move into the mainstream of American life. But they viewed their uplift as incomplete until they had uplifted others.

ENDNOTES

[1] Elijah P. Marrs, *Life and History of the Rev. Elijah P. Marrs* (Louisville, Kentucky: The Bradley and Gilbert Company, 1885; reprint ed., Miami: Mnemosyne Publishing Co., Inc., 1969), p. 15.

[2] *Ibid.*, pp. 77-78.

[3] *Ibid.*, p. 114.

[4] *Ibid.*, p. 98.

[5] Although benevolent and social organizations were formed during slavery, these functioned outside the South. The one place in the South where a large free black population developed some of the above mentioned organizations was New Orleans. (See John W. Blassingame's *Black New Orleans 1860-1880* (Chicago: The University of Chicago Press, 1973).

[6] William Hicks, *History of Louisiana Negro Baptists and Negro Baptist Beginnings in America.* (Nashville, Tenn.: National Baptist Publishing Board, 1914), pp. 28-29.

[7] The figures cited are based on an analysis of the information presented in a special study of churches in the United States. See, Department of the Interior, Census Office, *Report on Statistics of Churches in the United States at the Eleventh Census: 1890* (Washington, D.C.: Government Printing Office, 1894), pp. xxi, 45-47, 172-176.

[8] Charles Octavius Boothe, D.D., *The Cyclopedia of the Colored Baptists of Alabama* (Alabama Publishing Company, 1895), p. 50.

[9] The development of the national conventions is a fascinating story. For a brief summation of those developments, see Edward L. Wheeler, "Beyond One Man: A General Survey of Black Baptist Church History," *Review and Expositor* (Volume LXX, No. 3, Summer 1973), pp. 314-19.

[10] W.E.B. DuBois, ed., "The Negro Church," *Report . . . And Proceedings of the Eighth Conference for the Study of the Negro Problems* (Atlanta: Atlanta University Press, 1903), p. 122.

[11] *Ibid.*

[12] *Ibid.*, p. 123.

[13] This conclusion is based on census figures that were published in 1915, but which used information on religious bodies from 1906. According to those records in 1906 there were 2,354,789 black Baptists in 19,833 reporting organizations. Of that total, 2,261,607 were in 18,492 organizations affiliated with the National Baptist Convention. In the same year, there were 1,182,131 black Methodists in 13,447 reporting organizations. The majority of that total were in four different Methodist organizations as follows: Methodist Episcopal Church 308,551 in 3,682 organized units; African Methodist Epsicopal Church (AME) 494,777 in 6,608 units; African Methodist Episcopal Zion (AME Zion) 184,542 in 2,197 units; Colored Methodist Episcopal Church (CME) 172,996 in 2,381 units. (U.S. Department of Commerce, Bureau of the Census, Bulletin 129, **Negroes in the United States** (Washington: Government Printing Office, 1915), pp. 204-5. Although the 1906 numbers are higher than the membership numbers for denominations in the 1890 study of religion, Baptists had approximately the same ratio of almost more than 2 to 1 for all Methodists combined.

[14] Church membership figures were gathered from the **Report on Statistics of Churches,** pp. 45-47 and 172-76. General population figures used were found in U.S. Department of Commerce, Bureau of the Census, **Negro Population, 1790-1915** (Washington, D.C.: Government Printing Office, 1918), pp. 776-86.

[15] See **Report on Statistics of Churches,** pp. xxi, 45-47, 172-176.

[16] See Daniel A. Payne, **History of the African Methodist Episcopal Church** (Nashville, Tennessee: Publishing House of the AME Sunday School Union, 1891; reprint ed., New York: Arno Press, 1969), p. 45.

[17] Ibid., p. 467.

[18] Ibid.

[19] See **Report on Statistics of Churches,** pp. 544-549.

[20] Ibid.

[21] Wesley J. Gaines, **African Methodism in the South or Twenty-five Years of Freedom** (Atlanta: Franklin Publishing House, 1890), pp. 21-22.

[22] James W. Hood, **The Negro in the Christian Pulpit, or The Two Characters and Two Destinies, As Delineated in Twenty-One Practical Sermons** (Raleigh, NC: Edwards, Broughton and Company, 1884), p. 5.

[23] Statistics for AME Zion Church are found in **Report on Statistics of Churches,** pp. 46, 560-562.

[24] Although organized as the Colored Methodist Episcopal Church, that body is now known as the Christian Methodist Episcopal Church.

[25]Charles H. Phillips, *The History of the Colored Methodist Episcopal Church in America* (Jackson, TN: Publishing House Colored Methodist Episcopal Church, 1898: reprint ed., New York: Arno Press, 1972), pp. 71-72.

[26]*Ibid.*, pp. 46-51.

[27]Davidson County (Nashville) had 4 CME Churches with a total of 318 members and Hamilton County (Chattanooga) had one church with 31 members. Only 18 of the 206 CME churches in Tennessee were in the three urban counties.

[28]Statistics for the CME Church were gathered and analyzed from material found in *Report on Statistics of Churches,* pp. 46, 605-607. Information on black population was taken from *Negro Population 1790-1915,* pp. 776-786.

[29]See Daniel Culp, ed., *Twentieth Century Negro Literature* (J.L. Nichols & Company, 1902; reprint edition, Miami: Mnemosyne Publishing Co., Inc., 1969), pp. 356-369. The three essays by John W. Whittaker, George F. Bragg, and O.M. Waller illustrate what might be considered the "denominational chauvinism" of some black ministers in predominantly white denominations. Daniel Culp's response to Whittaker's essay is no less instructive of the enthusiasm that characterized Baptist and Methodist claims of their contributions to black uplift.

[30]*Three Negro Classics* (New York: Arno Books, 1965), *The Souls of Black Folk,* by W.E.B. DuBois, p. 341.

[31]Information regarding twenty-five men in this study is inconclusive. The evidence strongly suggests that the majority had been slaves at one time or another but the evidence is not strong enough to include those figures in the tabulation.

[32]William J. Simmons, *Men of Mark: Eminent, Progressive and Rising*(reprint ed., Chicago: Johnson Publishing Co., Inc., 1970), p. 384.

[33]I. Garland Penn, *The Afro-American Press and Its Editors* (Springfield, Mass.: Willey and Co., Publishers, 1891; reprint ed., New York: Arno Press and the New York Times, 1969), p. 266. For additional information on Coffee see W.H. Mixon, *History of the African Methodist Episcopal Church in Alabama, with Biographical Sketches* (Nashville: AME Church Sunday School Union, 1902).

[34]Wesley J. Gaines, *The Gospel Ministry: A Series of Lectures* (Atlanta: W.J. Gaines, 1899), pp. 1-13 and Edward R. Carter, *Biographical Sketches of Our Pulpit* (Atlanta: Edward R. Carter, 1888), pp. 22-23.

[35]Simmons, **Men of Mark,** pp. 599-606, also Albert W. Peques, **Our Baptist Ministers and Schools** (Springfield, Mass.: Willey and Co. Publishers, 1892), pp. 175-83 and James T. Haley, **Afro-American Encyclopedia** (Nashville, TN: Haley and Florida, 1896), p. 611.

[36]Simmons, **Men of Mark,** pp. 622-4 and Peques, **Our Baptist Ministers and Schools,** pp. 183-7.

[37]Simmons, **Men of Mark,** pp. 430-32.

[38]Culp, **Twentieth Century Negro Literature,** p. 254; Simmons, **Men of Mark,** pp. 645-7; Peques, **Our Baptist Ministers and Schools,** pp. 78-82.

[39]Simmons, **Men of Mark,** pp. 529-31.

[40]John J. Morant, **Mississippi Minister** (New York: Vantage Press, 1958), pp. 1-13.

[41]Thomas Oscar Fuller, **Twenty Years of Public Life, 1890-1910** (Nashville: National Baptist Publishing Board, 1910), p. 6.

[42]See Peter Kolchin, **First Freedom: The Responses of Alabama's Blacks to Emancipation and Reconstruction** (Westport, Conn.: Greenwood Press, Publishers, 1972), Chapter One. Census studies on the nativity of blacks living in the South, at the turn of the century, show that 6 out of 7 blacks, living in the nine states in the study, were living in the state of their birth. Furthermore, it is somewhat ironic that the two states with the highest black out migration had the lowest percentage of blacks in their population (Kentucky and Tennessee). (See **Negro Population, 1790-1915,** p. 71).

[43]Edward R. Carter, **Biographical Sketches,** pp. vi-vid; A.W. Peques, **Our Baptist Ministers and Schools,** pp. 113-7.

[44]Simmons, **Men of Mark,** pp. 445-7; Peques, **Our Baptist Ministers,** pp. 206-9.

[45]Department of Commerce and Labor, Bureau of the Census, Bulletin 8, **Negroes in the United States** (Washington: Government Printing Office, 1904), 188-9.

[46]Kolchin, **First Freedom,** p. 117.

[47]Culp, **Twentieth Century Negro Literature,** p. 63.

[48]Ibid., p. 83.

[49]Simmons, **Men of Mark,** pp. 189-92; Haley, **Afro-American Encyclopedia,** pp. 215-20.

[50]Boothe, *Colored Baptists of Alabama,* pp. 183-7; Culp, **Twentieth Century Negro Literature,** p. 469; Peques, **Our Baptist Ministers,** pp. 381-85; Simmons, **Men of Mark,** pp. 305-9.

[51]R.P. Wyche, "To What Extent is the Negro Pulpit Uplifting the Race?", Culp **Twentieth Century Negro Literature,** p. 123.

[52]*Negroes in the United States,* pp. 57-8; 176-187.

[53]Edward R. Carter, *The Black Side: A Partial History of the Business, Religious and Educational Side of the Negro in Atlanta, Georgia* (Atlanta: E.R. Carter, 1894), p. 246; Haley, **Afro-American Encyclopedia,** pp. 217-8, 611, 619; Peques, **Our Baptist Ministers,** p. 116; Simmons, **Men of Mark,** pp. 191, 507, 606-7.

[54]J.A. Bray, "The Effect of Secret and Benevolent Societies," J.W.E. Bowen and I. Garland Penn, editors, **The United Negro: His Problems and His Progress** (Atlanta: D.E. Luther Publishing Company, 1902), p. 191.

[55]J.W. Hood, "A Desirable Consummation," in **The Negro in the Christian Pulpit,** p. 246.

[56]See "The Model Church," in Haley, **Afro-American Encyclopedia,** pp. 417 ff.

[57]Culp, **Twentieth Century Negro Literature,** p. 115; Haley, **Afro-American Encyclopedia,** pp. 118-20; Penn, **Afro-American Press,** p. 309.

[58]Carter, **Biographical Sketches of Our Pulpit,** p. 65; Peques **Our Baptist Ministers,** p. 508.

[59]Alexander Walters, **My Life and Work** (New York: Fleming H. Revell, Co., 1917), Chapter Three; Simmons, **Men of Mark,** p. 221.

[60]William H. Heard, **From Slavery to the Bishopric in the AME Church: An Autobiography** (Philadelphia: The AME Book Concern, 1924; reprint ed., New York: Arno Press and the New York Times, 1969), pp. 64-72.

[61]Haley, **Afro-American Encyclopedia,** p. 613; Peques, **Our Baptist Ministers,** p. 311.

[62]Boothe, **Colored Baptists of Alabama,** pp. 209-10; Peques, **Our Baptist Ministers,** pp. 493-5.

[63]Gaines, **The Gospel Ministry,** p. 7.

[64]*Ibid.,* p. 14.

66George W. Clinton, "To What Extent is the Negro Pulpil Uplifting the Race?", Culp, *Twentieth Century Negro Literature,* pp. 115-6.

67Phillips, *The History of the Colored Methodist Episcopal Church in America,* pp. 137-38.

68John B.L. Williams, "To What Extent is the Negro Pulpit Uplifting the Race?", Culp, *Twentieth Century Negro Literature,* pp. 120-21.

69Hood, "The Earliest Gospel Symbol," in *The Negro in the Christian Pulpit,* p. 118.

70Theophilus G. Steward, *Pioneer Echoes: Six Special Sermons* (Baltimore: Hoffman and Co., 1889), p. 15.

71M.C.B. Mason, "Did the American Negro Make in the Nineteenth Century Achievements Along the Lines of Wealth, Morality, Education, Etc., Commensurate With His Opportunities? If So, What Achievements Did He Make?" Culp, *Twentieth Century Negro Literature,* p. 35.

72Ibid., p. 37.

73J.W.E. Bowen and I. Garland Penn, editors, *The United Negro: His Problems and His Progress* (Atlanta: D.E. Luther Publishing Company, 1902), p. 493.

74Ibid., p. 496.

75E.R. Carter, "Let Us Play the Man" in *The Black Side,* p. 288.

76Bowen and Penn, *The United Negro,* p. 9.

77Carter, "Let Us Play the Man," *The Black Side,* pp. 285-6.

78L.H. Holsey, "Will It Be Possible for the Negro to Attain in This Country, Unto the American Type of Civilization?", in Culp, *Twentieth Century Negro Literature,* p. 46.

79Ibid.

80H.M. Turner, Ibid., pp. 44.

81Carter, "Let Us Play the Man," *The Black Side,* pp. 284-5.

82I.D. Davis, "To What Extent is the Negro Pulpit Uplifting the Race?", in Culp, *Twentieth Century Negro Literature,* p. 124.

CHAPTER 2
"OF ONE BLOOD": A
THEOLOGY OF UPLIFT

Lucius H. Holsey was a highly respected bishop in the Colored Methodist Episcopal Church when he published his **Autobiography, Sermons, Addresses and Essays** in 1898. Though he was not the first black minister to publish an autobiography or a volume of sermons, Holsey's book was important because of his position in his denominational hierarchy and because his sermons illustrated an ideal of "theological preaching" that prevailed among the prominent clergy.

One of the ministers who took part in the birth of the denomination in 1870, Holsey was elected to the bishopric three years later. He assumed numerous positions of leadership within the church; a clear token of acceptance. But during his early career he was not considered a great popular preacher, because of his weak voice, his reserved style of delivery, and the "philosophical" content of his sermons. He worked to improve both the strength of his voice and his delivery, but he maintained the philosophical and theological flavor of his sermons because he was convinced that blacks needed sound doctrinal sermons; sermons that taught as well as inspired the congregation. He hoped that the publication of his **Autobiography,** containing some of what he considered the best sermons he had preached over the ten preceding years, would encourage others to write and to memorialize the contributions men of color had made to the black race and to humanity by preaching the gospel. He also hoped that the sermons would demonstrate the theological insights of the black pulpit.

Holsey's sermons indicate that he stood within the mainstream of nineteenth-century conservative Protestantism. In this, he reflected the prevailing theological views among the leading black clergy. For the most part, they had the same theological conviction as their white counterparts.[1] Yet the black ministers sounded a distinctive note when they asserted that their notion of uplift was grounded in their theological suppositions. Hence, they preached and occasionally wrote that the possibility for uplifting the race rested on the Christian understanding of humanity and its relationship to God. Holsey and the black clerical elite argued that because "God had made of one blood all nations of men for to dwell on all the face of the earth" and had redeemed man through His Son Jesus Christ, the full humanity and value of black people had been divinely affirmed.[2] God's creative and redemptive activities embraced black men and women and made them as capable of uplift as all other human beings.

Holsey articulated a theological foundation for uplift in his sermon on the "Fatherhood of God and the Brotherhood of Man."

> *Human nature is found by experience as well as by history and philosophy to be the same in quality and essentials, in all ages, states and conditions. . . .*
>
> *Every man is made by the same hand, according to the measure, mental contour and personal and original endowments. Neither can racial distinctions, color, climatic or geographical situation of birth and growth make any difference in the characteristics of his real manhood. This proves the unity of the race of man, the oneness of interest, origin and destiny. What, therefore, is possible for one man is possible for all men under the same conditions and circumstances. All are made in 'the image of God', after the same pattern, in the sublime fundamentals of the original.[3]*

For Holsey, God as the creator of all life had endowed each human being with the qualities that made humanity unique. People differed from one another only in accidental ways, for all humanity shared one goal. The soul was the evidence that all men and women were created in the image of God, and from the soul came their highest qualities. The ministers, then, believed that when their black parishioners were given the same opportunities as whites, they could achieve the same results; they could be uplifted.

The preoccupation with uplift resulted in an intriguing eclecticism in the theology of the black ministerial elite. On the one hand, they retained the doctrines and images of an older evangelical tradition; they preached of heaven and hell, the blood of Jesus, the atonement on the cross, and the need for repentance and salvation. On the other hand, they adopted the rhetoric of other nineteenth-century Protestants who were by no means theologically conservative. Their sermons—like Holsey's address on "The Fatherhood of God and the Brotherhood of Man"—sometimes bore titles, and expounded themes, that were familiar among northeastern Unitarians and urban modernists from university divinity schools. Their penchant for combining disparate patterns of Protestant language might have seemed incongruous had it not been for the unifying theme of uplift. For they did not unthinkingly adopt the rhetoric of other Protestants alongside their older vocabulary; they used the rhetoric of other traditions for their own purposes and integrated it with the older rhetoric in their own way.

1. THE OLD-TIME RELIGION

The black ministers stood in the revivalistic tradition of southern Protestantism. Like their white counterparts, they preached on the themes of justification, salvation, and moral living that were so prevalent in the camp-meetings of the antebellum revival South. In the more than one hundred twenty sermons and addresses published by the seventy-eight ministers, one finds an outline of a traditional Protestant theology that could have characterized almost any conservative congregation in the southern Bible Belt.

The preachers had a traditional concern for the "soul," and its salvation. J.C. Price, whose death in 1893 at the age of thirty-nine robbed the AME Zion Church and blacks of a temperance leader, college president, respected preacher, and advocate of uplift, tried to define the soul in his sermon, "The Value of the Soul."

> *The soul is that immaterial, immortal, living substance in us that wills, feels, and moralizes and is the seat of our personalities. The soul then is the man and the body is but an instrument under its control.*[4]

Though Price intended to define the soul, his definition alludes to three closely related ideas about the soul that reappeared continually in the essays and sermons of the ministerial leader. First, they insisted on a dualism of soul and body. The soul, not the body, was the "essence" of the self. For that reason the ministers preached that the material world could not satisfy the soul's desires and that the body was a source of restriction and limit.[5] Second, they asserted a doctrine of the soul's immortality: death freed the soul from bodily limits. In death the soul could find true peace, wrote George Clinton, an AME Zion bishop and editor, for in death the soul found freedom.[6] And finally—the most important theme—the soul reflected the divine image. In the words of James Hood, the leader of the AME Zion Church in North Carolina, the soul "in its purity is the divine image, and possesses kinship to Deity."[7] The significance of salvation for life in the world, in fact, was precisely that regeneration restored the "image" that had been manifest prior to Adam's fall.[8] The soul of the humblest tenant farmer could embody an inner harmony akin to that of the life of God. But even before the moment of regeneration, the soul still bore the divine image, however deformed by sinfulness it might be. Every soul was created in the "image" of God; every soul was therefore precious.

While the black ministers preached that the soul bore the image of God, however, they also insisted that all men and women—all souls—had fallen into sinfulness. Although they rarely tried to describe the details of Adam's fall, they believed that "that Gospel is founded on the depravity of human nature."[9] Adam's sin had destroyed the unity of creation and damaged all his posterity. Harrison Bouey, a Baptist minister in South Carolina and Alabama and a missionary to Africa, preached, in typical fashion, that Adam had been created holy, free, and intelligent without the tendency to sin but with the power to do so. His fatal choice condemned all mankind to punishment—a spiritual death in separation from God.[10] Emmanuel King Love, a founder of the black Baptist state convention in George, outlined the consequences of Adam's fall: "Man by nature is not disposed to do right. Sin has depraved his disposition, poisoned his affections, spoiled his taste for righteousness, and made his mind diseased. He is a rebel against God, and hates his law."[11] Few themes appeared more often in the sermons of the black ministers: human beings were corrupt, fallen, and lost.[12] And they were sinful by nature, not merely by reason of their vices. Humanity shared in the consequences of Adamic sinfulness.

Despite the accent on weakness and insufficiency, however, the ministers rarely suggested that depravity had utterly bound the will; they assumed, on the whole, a measure of volitional freedom. The Methodists, especially, emphasized the centrality of freedom; they aligned themselves with the broader transition from an accent on free grace to an insistence on free will that was becoming characteristic of other Wesleyan theologians in the predominantly white denominations.[13] Bishop James Hood of North Carolina, argued that sinners had to choose to consecrate themselves to God: "The right way is made plain, and if we walk not in it, it is because we will not."[14] Hood acknowledged the weakness of the will and its inability to choose the right without some assistance: "Mankind is so weak and helpless, so under the reigning power of sin, that he cannot come to Christ until drawn by cords divine. He cannot savingly believe until God helps his unbelief."[15] But weakness was no excuse for stiffnecked resistance: "The consent of the will is what he [God] demands. An entire surrender of soul and body to him, a sacrifice of self."[16] Because God was continually trying to attract sinners, preachers agreed that those sinful creatures had to accept the responsibility for not accepting God's way. The various Methodist ministers agreed that Christians had to attune their wills to the divine will and that each Christian could do so.[17]

Even the Baptist clergy, who often held on to the more deterministic language of an older Reformed tradition, moved cautiously toward an affirmation of the human ability to accept or reject salvation. W.G. Parks, whose sermon was reprinted in an anthology designed to demonstrate the competence of the black Baptist pulpit, argued that each person could respond to the gift of grace; each person who failed to respond bore the responsibility for that choice.[18] The Baptists agreed with their Methodist counterparts that stubborn resistance merited damnation; a grateful response did not exactly merit salvation, but it certainly was the precondition of salvation. The older disputes between Wesleyans and Calvinists over the minutiae of volitional freedom was simply not a concern for many of the leading black clergy in the later nineteenth century. African Methodists and Presbyterians, Colored Methodists and Baptists all joined in the call for a decision. They did not dissect the will; they appealed to it.

Of course, even the Methodists, like their Reformed colleagues, viewed freedom as a gift of a sovereign God. James Hood insisted that the initial work in the process of salvation was always an act to divine mercy. The Baptist E.K. Love put it this way: "It is the spirit who urges our acceptance of the plan of salvation. . . . Our initial turning to God is his work, and any succeeding graces that may spring up are his fruit."[19] Again, the ministers ignored the earlier debates over the fine points of the order of salvation. They agreed simply that salvation was an act of the Spirit, even though it also presupposed a free response.

Because nothing men or women could do on their own could effect their salvation, the clergy said, everyone stood in need of a saviour. And they insisted, in traditional terms, that Christ had bridged the gap between God and humanity that had been opened by Adam's sin. Joseph C. Price, the president of Livingstone College, an AME Zion school in North Carolina, told his readers that "the soul and its ruins so moved the Father as to give His Only Begotten to restore it to a state of grace, that it might return to that happiness from which rash transgression had driven it."[20] The Baptist H.N. Bouey preached that Jesus restored men and women "to that image which we lost in Adam's fall."[21] Or the African Methodist Alexander Newton expressed a consensus when he said that "Christ came on a special mission, the saving of the lost, the saving of man. He is therefore represented as the Lamb that taketh away the sins of the world."[22] Occasionally the ministers adverted to the older technical controversies. In an address to the American National Baptist Convention and the Baptist Foreign Mission Convention, Micheal Vann of Tennessee insisted that Christ's atonement was "universal"; salvation was available to all, because Christ had died for all.[23] And A.J. Stokes resorted to the older controversial language of Reformed theologians when he insisted that justification occurred when the righteousness of Jesus was "imputed" to humanity.[24] But these allusions to earlier controversies were not typical. Most of the black ministers preached simply that Jesus had paid the debt. They did not worry about the fine-points of the bookkeeping.[25]

Jesus was also an example. He was the perfect man who transcended all who came before and after him. He was the example of what men and women were created to be in their moral character. But with Bishop George Clinton, the black preachers agreed that no man or woman could follow Christ's example without aid. Unless Christ provided the ability and power, his perfection simply served to mock human imperfection: "We cannot live righteously," said Clinton, "we cannot live like Christ except as we have been saved from our sins by the sacrifice of Christ."[26] Christ had to remove the penalty of sin; only then could he serve as

41

an example to be followed.

Jesus had died on the cross, been resurrected from the grave, and ascended into heaven. Since that ascension, he acted as a mediator and intercessor. As the Beloved Son, he advocated the cause of humanity before the throne of God. He was the mediator through whom his followers prayed; he was the intercessor; he was the divine and supernatural advocate before a heavenly court.[27] The imagery was Biblical and traditional. Christ was a sacrifice, an example, an intercessor. The black clergy spoke from within the boundaries of an older evangelical Protestantism when they described the work of Christ.

In like manner, they also affirmed a traditional view of Christ's Person. Although they did not devote much time to explaining the unity of the two distinct natures, they did proclaim that the human and the divine were one in Jesus. G.W. Raiford, a Baptist who published a sermon in **The Negro Baptist Pulpit,** advanced a common theme:

> *Christ alone was truly human and divine, and his power to save lies in the fact that he possessed both the divine and human nature. Divine and human, Jesus assumed the mighty task. Clad in human form, he came to earth, and by his obedience unto death vindicated the divine law, and made it possible for man to be saved.*[28]

God broke into history in the form of a man—Jesus—who was God incarnate. Hence, E.R. Carter in Atlanta could proclaim that God condescended to become a man in Jesus; or M.W. Gilbert in South Carolina described Jesus as God in the flesh; or J.C. Price spoke of Christ's pre-existent divinity; or Bishop Holsey spoke of Christ as co-eternal with God: "He is identified with the creation of the world."[29] Yet Jesus was fully human. A.H. Newton warned against so accenting the divinity as to forget the humanity; George Clinton preached that Jesus was both God and man; Bishop Hood insisted that Jesus' humanity found vivid expression "when he hung upon the cross, when the rays of the divine glory were wholly withdrawn from our view, and his lifeless body hung between the heavens and the earth."[30] Once again, the message was familiar, traditional, orthodox.

Christ came to offer salvation, and for the black clergy, to speak of salvation was to speak of heaven and hell. Their belief in a literal heaven and a literal hell illustrated still again their allegiance to the old-time religion characteristic of the South. In the imagery of their sermons and essays, hell was a place of eternal torment, devoid of God's presence, reserved for all who did not accept the Lordship of Jesus. Hence, they admonished their hearers to live in the full awareness of hell and its sufferings: "Men will see more clearly than they see here their mistakes and sins and losses," wrote S.W. Anderson of Nashville.

Nothing, he added, will be there forgotten: "A rejected Christ, a neglected gospel, and slighted prayers will stare men in the face."[31]

Heaven was the abode of all who accepted Jesus, and although the ministers often confessed that the joys of heaven were "unspeakable," they nevertheless had quite a bit to say about them. In heaven, they said, the soul could know God "more completely"; in heaven, the reborn assembled in a spiritual kingdom.[32] A.H. Newton spoke for his peers when he contrasted the joys of heaven to the sorrows of both earth and hell:

> *No dens to rob men and women of their virtue, no pitfalls or saloons and gambling hells to lead astray the holy inhabitants of that land of rest, none of these things are to be found there! The ungodly rich man, the oppressor of the poor, the robber, the thief, these are all cast into the lake where the worm dieth not and the fire is not quenched. There is the place of our Eternal Rest. It is a mountain where heavenly pastures grow and the rivers of life gently flow.[33]*

Death for the Christian was therefore the doorway to the joys promised by God. Some of those joys could be experienced in this life, but they could not equal the joys of the next. Heaven meant freedom from oppression, rest from toil, liberation from sin, the completion of holiness, and fellowship with God.

The clergy, however, did not lose sight of the earthly obligations that accompanied salvation. A.H. Newton warned his congregation that much had to be done on earth as a prelude to the rewards of heaven:

> *Frequently Christians get the idea that salvation is to bring them at last to Heaven; well, that is in a manner true, but remember that is the last work of salvation, bringing us to heaven. Salvation deals with thousands of things in our lives here, before we are ready for Heaven.[34]*

The ministerial elite did not let the hope of heaven obliterate the reality of earth. But the reality of heaven also gave reason for hope on earth.

The leading black preachers also proclaimed the coming kingdom. They taught that Christ would return in glory. Just as their depiction of heaven was vivid and literal, so their eschatology was colorful and dramatic. Christ was coming.[35] But the ministers rarely tried to guess—or calculate—when he would return. It was more important for them to say that the Church—their churches, in fact—embodied the beginning of the Kingdom on earth. Bishop Hood likened the church to an earthly "City of God" and proclaimed that in the midst of the world's upheaval, occasioned by sin, "the Church, the body of believers in Christ Jesus, shall still enjoy abundant peace, consolation, joy and gladness."[36] A.H. Newton preached that the church was "the receptacle of truth" and its task was to perpetuate his Kingdom until his return.[37] According to the preaching of Bishop Clinton, God "set up his church . . . to be a saving power and sway among men."[38] The ministers had no doubt of the ultimate triumph of the Kingdom because the resurrection was conclusive proof of God's victory over Satan and the sinful world. Yet the defeat of Satan and the imposition of the Kingdom would only occur in God's own time.[39] The Kingdom was both present and yet to come; human activity would not bring its consummation. The Kingdom of God could not be equated with any present society, even though the Kingdom was present in every society.

Hence, in broad outline the black elite clergy proclaimed a traditional Protestant theology. They stood in the mainstream of conservative Protestant culture, and they had no reservations about the supernaturalism and other-worldliness that had marked that older tradition. To overlook their pietism and theological traditionalism is to ignore a religious vocabulary that shaped their preaching and their activity as ministers. Yet the black ministers used other concepts which, despite their being rooted in a conservative theology, had currency well outside the bounds of the old time religion.

2. THE FATHERHOOD OF GOD AND THE BROTHERHOOD OF MAN

When Lucius H. Holsey proclaimed the Fatherhood of God and the Brotherhood of Man in the sermon published in his **Autobiography,** he was using a vocabulary with a long, albeit elusive, history. Sometimes used separately, but often paired, the two phrases had appeared in the writings of eighteenth and nineteenth century abolitionists, Unitarians, and late nineteenth-century liberals. The phrases had been associated with various Scriptural citations: the creation story, passages from the Gospels, and the Pauline letters. But the most frequent Biblical association was with Acts 17:26: "[God] hath made of one blood all nations of men for to dwell on all the face of the earth."[40]

When the ministers spoke of the fatherhood of God and the brotherhood of man, they could have been mistaken for Victorian Unitarians or liberals of the Social Gospel variety. Certainly the associations engendered by the phrases would have made it unlikely that they would have been embraced by evangelical Protestants in the mainline white churches of the South. Hence, the frequent repetition of the imagery by the black preachers has a surprising, even jarring, quality; the language seems illfitting when it appears in juxtaposition with the traditional evangelical vocabulary. Where did the language about the fatherhood of God and the brotherhood of man come from? What function did it serve?

The imagery of divine "fatherhood," of course, had Biblical roots and a lengthy history in western Christendom. It had not occupied a prominent place in American theology, however, until the anti-slavery movement of the late eighteenth century thrust it to the fore. The Puritan jurist, Samuel Sewall, had written in his **Selling of Joseph** (1700) that the sin of the first Adam, the sacrifice of the second, and the "fatherhood" of God combined to ensure the unity of humanity.[41] The Quaker, John Woolman, had argued in a similar way in 1754 that slavery could and should not last because "all men" were to be treated "as becometh the sons of one father."[42] Both Woolman and Sewall accepted the prevailing notions of black inferiority, but they taught that God's "fatherhood" precluded the exploitation of the slave system.

It was the Unitarian movement, however, that after 1819 elevated the theme of divine "fatherhood" to a position of special honor. William Ellery Channing had spoken of God's fatherhood in his 1819 ordination sermon that popularized the Unitarian revolt against Calvinism: "To give our views of God, in one work," he said, "we believe in his Paternal character. We ascribe to him not only the name, but the dispositions and principles of a father."[43] Channing later observed that the paternal title had been applied to God in the New Testament more frequently than had any other: "In the New Testament God is made known to us as a Father; and a brighter feature of that book cannot be named. Our whole religion is to take its character from this view of the Divinity."[44]

Theodore Parker had carried Unitarian theology into abolitionist reform by accenting the notion of God's fatherhood: "there is one thing I cannot fail to trust," he wrote in 1851. "That is the Infinite God, Father of the white man, Father also of the white man's slave."[45] Few Unitarians, however, were so bold. Most maintained their distance from the abolitionist crusade. But they affirmed the notion of God's "fatherhood," and by the end of the century their belief in "the Fatherhood of God, the Brotherhood of Man" was close to the center of what it meant to be a Unitarian.[46] And the close association between "fatherhood" and "brotherhood" had by that time become well-established: the "brotherhood" that was confirmed by the divine "fatherhood" referred not only to oneness of humanity but also to the human potential to achieve the high morality set by Jesus of Nazareth. All persons were "brothers" in the sense that they could grow and develop in response to God's love.

The social implications of the concepts of fatherhood and brotherhood made them useful for the antebellum black abolitionists who advanced theological arguments in the debates over slavery. When Henry Highland Garnet spoke to the National Negro Convention in 1843 in Buffalo, he called for slaves to give their allegiance to God rather than to their masters.[47] By 1848 he was informing his audiences about the mercy and wisdom of the "Universal Father,"[48] and he was drawing the moral conclusion that slavery was intolerable. Speaking to the House of Representatives, Garnet chastised the apologists for slavery:

> But others, their fellow-men, equal before
> the Almighty, and made by him of the same
> blood, and glowing with immortality, they
> doom to life-long servitude and chains. Yes,
> they stand in the most sacred places on earth,
> and beneath the gaze of the piercing eye of
> Jehovah, the universal Father of all men, and
> declare, 'that the best possible condition of
> the Negro is slavery'.[49]

In short, the notion of "fatherhood"—as both a theological and moral theme—assumed enormous importance among the antebellum black clerical abolitionists.[50]

By the late nineteenth century, the theme of the fatherhood of God and the brotherhood of man had become firmly established in the theology of Protestant liberalism. The liberals liked to talk of God's "paternal" character and to emphasize the "solidarity of the race."[51] The classical work of American Theological liberalism, William Newton Clarke's **Outline of Christian Theology** (1894), codified a liberal consensus when he insisted that "the truest name of God in his relation to his creatures is Father,—a name that has Christ's authority."[52] By 1888 the Universalists inaugurated their series of apologetic publications with a volume on **The Fatherhood of God,** in which they argued that the divine fatherhood made "a single family of the whole human race."[53]

The themes of divine fatherhood and the brotherhood of man had been prominent in three religious movements by the late-nineteenth century: the Christian anti-slavery crusade, the Unitarian revolt, and Protestant theological liberalism. So important were these themes that the Social Gospel advocate, Washington Gladden, believed them to be two of the ruling ideas of the age.[54] When the black clerical elite of the period used those themes—as they did repeatedly—they never specified their sources. It was clear only that they were incorporating a vocabulary that was not standard within the southern white churches that proclaimed the evangelical message which the black clergy otherwise found so appealing. The black clergy reached outside the boundaries of their regional tradition when they caught hold of the imagery of fatherhood and brotherhood and made it serve social ends.

No theme appeared more often in the writings and sermons of the black clergy than did the theme of God's fatherhood. It became a ground for evangelical endeavor; it signified God's creative power; it pointed to God's redemptive activity; it revealed God's love.[55] The AME Zion bishop, George Clinton, expounded on the theme in accents redolent of liberal theology:

> Christianity takes up all that was purest
> and best in the Jewish idea of God, amplifies
> and enlarges it immeasurably. It brings God

46

> *into human life and reveals him to us as Father,*
> *a Father who loves, and whose love prompts*
> *him to suffer with, and for, his children, that*
> *he might redeem them from sin and bring*
> *them to the perfection of life.*[56]

Or the black ministers associated paternity with power: "Whether he speaks to us as Father, Master or Ruler," wrote L.H. Holsey, "we are his subjects and are bound to obey."[57]

The black ministerial elite believed that brotherhood was the logical consequence of God's fatherhood: the fatherhood of God had its corollary in the concept of "Universal Brotherhood."[58] E.W.D. Isaacs, a leader in the Negro Young People's Christian and Educational Congress, assured seven thousand delegates that "the brotherhood of man is as much an integral part of Christianity as the fatherhood of God. Whoever denies either is an infidel."[59] Throughout the 1870's and 1880's, the imagery of fatherhood and brotherhood reappeared continually in regional conferences and local sermons.[60] Bishop Daniel Payne informed the AME bishops in 1888 that their task was to harmonize the races in obedience to Christ and "make all live in one common brotherhood."[61] Ernest Lyons, the pastor of a black Methodist Episcopal Church, reminded a 1902 Congress in Atlanta that the fatherhood of God and the brotherhood of man entailed the unity and equality of humanity.[62] In sermon after sermon, address after address, the black ministers hammered on the theme: if divine fatherhood was real, so was human brotherhood.[63] M.W. Gilbert, a South Carolina Baptist, summarized the consensus in an essay published in 1902:

> *A true believer in the Scriptures must*
> *be equally a believer in the fatherhood of*
> *God and the brotherhood of all men. For the*
> *divine record declares that God 'hath of one*
> *blood created all nations of men for to dwell*
> *on the face of the earth.' Language, physiology*
> *and psychology confirm the truthfulness of*
> *Scripture on this issue. The mission of*
> *Christianity to preach the Gospel over the*
> *inhabited world is based upon this great idea.*
> *Science and Holy Writ assert the intellectual*
> *quality of all men of whatever race or color,*
> *so far as real capacity and possibilities are*
> *concerned.*[64]

Brotherhood in this sense was not something that began after the "second birth" or resulted only from the saving work of Christ; neither was brotherhood optional. It was rooted in the oneness of creation. It meant that the differences between people were circumstantial rather than essential. And it was not far from believing in equality to the belief that, given the opportunity, black people could be uplifted.

*into human life and reveals him to us as Father,
a Father who loves, and whose love prompts
him to suffer with, and for, his children, that
he might redeem them from sin and bring
them to the perfection of life.*[56]

Or the black ministers associated paternity with power: "Whether he speaks to us as Father, Master or Ruler," wrote L.H. Holsey, "we are his subjects and are bound to obey."[57]

The black ministerial elite believed that brotherhood was the logical consequence of God's fatherhood: the fatherhood of God had its corollary in the concept of "Universal Brotherhood."[58] E.W.D. Isaacs, a leader in the Negro Young People's Christian and Educational Congress, assured seven thousand delegates that "the brotherhood of man is as much an integral part of Christianity as the fatherhood of God. Whoever denies either is an infidel."[59] Throughout the 1870's and 1880's, the imagery of fatherhood and brotherhood reappeared continually in regional conferences and local sermons.[60] Bishop Daniel Payne informed the AME bishops in 1888 that their task was to harmonize the races in obedience to Christ and "make all live in one common brotherhood."[61] Ernest Lyons, the pastor of a black Methodist Episcopal Church, reminded a 1902 Congress in Atlanta that the fatherhood of God and the brotherhood of man entailed the unity and equality of humanity.[62] In sermon after sermon, address after address, the black ministers hammered on the theme: if divine fatherhood was real, so was human brotherhood.[63] M.W. Gilbert, a South Carolina Baptist, summarized the consensus in an essay published in 1902:

*A true believer in the Scriptures must
be equally a believer in the fatherhood of
God and the brotherhood of all men. For the
divine record declares that God 'hath of one
blood created all nations of men for to dwell
on the face of the earth.' Language, physiology
and psychology confirm the truthfulness of
Scripture on this issue. The mission of
Christianity to preach the Gospel over the
inhabited world is based upon this great idea.
Science and Holy Writ assert the intellectual
quality of all men of whatever race or color,
so far as real capacity and possibilities are
concerned.*[64]

Brotherhood in this sense was not something that began after the "second birth" or resulted only from the saving work of Christ; neither was brotherhood optional. It was rooted in the oneness of creation. It meant that the differences between people were circumstantial rather than essential. And it was not far from believing in equality to the belief that, given the opportunity, black people could be uplifted.

3. THEOLOGICAL FOUNDATIONS FOR UPLIFT

Southern white theologians—and northern ones, too, for that matter--could speak about fatherhood or even about brotherhood, though few linked them together as part of a theological argument for racial justice. Even a moderate like Atticus Haygood, who elicited the wrath of the racial conservatives when he published his **Our Brother in Black,** did not carry his imagery to the point of affirming racial equality.[65] In a period when some white extremists were arguing that blacks had neither souls nor moral ability, that God "could not be the Father of black," that black people were in fact "beasts" rather than people, the themes of God's fatherhood and human brotherhood had explosive social implications.[66] By combining their traditional theology with these notions of fatherhood and brotherhood, the black clergy were issuing a challenge to a white social consensus while at the same time continuing to address their own people in a vocabulary that allowed them to appropriate the social message. They were standing apart from the southern white way of thinking theologically.

The black ministers believed that the manifest inequalities in the society were attributable to a lack of opportunity; given the chance, they thought, blacks would achieve as whites. E.R. Carter preached that uplift of the race was possible precisely because "all races are naturally, essentially and constitutionally the same, and therefore bear unmistakable resemblance to each other in every essential particular."[67] Or E.N. McEwen, an Alabama Baptist, wrote that since black people had been created in the image of God, just as whites, the "noble qualities" of the race should be visible to anyone who happened to look.[68] The potential for elevation was clear; its ground was the fact that all persons were "brothers" and God was a "father" of all.[69]

The ministers did not appeal merely to theology when they made their arguments about uplift. They could look, as well, to their own first-hand experience. Most had known the degradation of slavery; all had experienced discrimination. Yet they had risen to positions of prominence. Their number included businessmen, educators, editors, and denominational executives. In a period when almost 45% of the black population was illiterate, the ministers were educated, and hence they embodied the dream of uplift through education. All of the ministers were literate; most had formal schooling. Three held doctorates and two had completed training as physicians. By seizing the few opportunities opened to them, they had proven the capacity of black people. M.W. Gilbert expressed their conviction, born of their own experience, that uplift was possible:

> *Whenever failure is recorded against the Negro it is not due to his lacking the mental endowments equal to that of the white man, but because a white man's opportunity is denied him. Equality of opportunities and equality before the laws should be cheerfully granted*

him. Criticism against him is savage and un-
christian, if those doors are closed against
him.[70]

Gilbert saw in the very resistance to blacks a proof that whites were aware of black capacities, which they feared.

Although they could point to their own experience, the black clergy more often returned to their theological foundation. The themes of God's fatherhood and human brotherhood undergirded their belief that opportunity would surely be forthcoming eventually. The clergy believed that Christianity had transforming qualities that could change even human nature and make it conform to the nature of Christ, who recognized God as Father and all persons as his brothers.[71] Once the influence of Christianity took hold in the culture, whites would see blacks in a new light.

On occasion the ministers lost faith in the possibility of transformation. Near the end of the century, Holsey ceased to hope that white attitudes would change sufficiently to allow blacks living in his own day to realize their potential as persons. But most ministers trusted that the universal fatherhood of God ensured the inevitablility of the transformation. E.W.S. Isaacs voiced that confidence in an address to the Negro Young People's Christian and Education Congress in 1902. He spoke as an officer of the National Baptist Convention's training union for youth; but more important, he spoke as the representative of a widespread hope among the leaders of the black churches in the South. Christianity, he said, taught "that all men are children of one Father; that all men are made in his image, and redeemed by his love," and it also taught "that of one blood God hath made all the nations to dwell on the face of the earth." Isaacs concluded that the one great question that had to be resolved through practical experiment in the United States was: "how are the sons of God to live together in one great brotherhood."[72] Neither Isaacs nor any other of the black ministers ventured to say exactly how the issue would be resolved. But except for L.H. Holsey, W.H. Heard, and Henry M. Turner, who concluded that the best opportunities for blacks in the immediate future were to be found in emigration to Africa,[73] the ministers believed that the reality of God's fatherhood and of human brotherhood would eventually be manifest in mutual respect between the races.

Butler Harrison Peterson, a Baptist minister who taught at Tuskegee Institute, expressed the optimism of his colleagues when he wrote:

We hail with joy the rapidly approaching time,
under the sunlight of civilization and Christian-
ity, when the color of the skin and the texture
of the hair will not be badges of reproach,
humiliation, degradation and contempt. True
merit will yet be the worth of the man, under

*the wise and just government of a beneficent
God and Father, who 'of one blood made all
nations for to dwell upon the face of all the
earth'.*[74]

Other prominent clergy expressed the same optimism in speeches and essays throughout the period: the day of equality and justice was approaching.[75] The optimism can be partly understood against the backdrop of the enormous progress blacks had made in uplifting themselves since emancipation; partly in the light of the special success of the individual black clergymen who found hope in their own rise to prominence; and also partly in view of a faith that the fatherhood of God and the brotherhood of all persons under God would inevitably issue a change in the concrete relations among black and white people in America.

The theology of the black ministers—at least, of the elite clergy—stood within the mainstream of American, and to some extent, even southern, Protestantism. Yet that theology also addressed the particular needs of a people trying to etch out a niche for themselves in American society. Precisely because of its combination of seemingly distinctive motifs—an otherworldly traditional theology and a theology of social change—it could provide for black people a sense of their own value and worth. It permitted them to hold to the piety of their childhood while yet moving beyond it. It offered reaffirmation in the face of a hostile white society's denial of their humanity. The notions of the fatherhood of God and the brotherhood of man provided hope for uplifting the race.

The North Carolina AME Zion schoolmaster and preacher, S.G. Atkins, once replied to a query as to whether blacks should be taught differently from whites. He summarized a theological consensus among the black ministers: "There is still a higher authority for a negative answer to the question, 'Should the Negroes be give an education different from that given to the Whites?' ," he wrote. The answer was clear: "God had made of one blood all nations of men for to dwell on the face of the earth."[76]

[1]This statement should not be interpreted as being supportive of the Franklin Frazier thesis that black religion in America was simply a less sophisticated reproduction of white religion without any identifiable or traceable connection with African religious traditions. Rather, the statement is a recognition of the fact that the theological perspective of the post Civil War black church was greatly influenced by the traditional conservative Protestantism of the period.

This book does not attempt to examine the antebellum roots of the black church nor does it attempt to discover the antecedent roots of the cultural expression of black religion as found in the black church. There are several excellent studies, however, that attempt to accomplish these. The recent work of several scholars seems to adequately refute the Frazier thesis. Major contributions have been made in this area by Albert J. Raboteau beginning with his dissertation study at Yale which was refined and later published as **Slave Religion.** [See Albert J. Raboteau, "'The Invisible Institution': The Origins and Conditions of Black Religion Before Emancipation" (Ph.D. dissertation, Yale University, 1974) and Albert J. Raboteau, **Slave Religion: "The Invisible Institution" in the Antebellum South** (New York: Oxford University Press, 1978)]. Less valuable for its insight into African religious practices but supportive of the thesis that "Africanisms" existed within the southern antebellum black religious community is the work of Erskine Clarke. [See Erskine Clarke, **Wrestlin' Jacob: A Portrait of Religion in the Old South** (Atlanta: John Knox Press, 1979). Also helpful are Mechal Sobel, **Trabelin' On: The Slave Journey to an Afro-Baptist Faith** (Westport, Connecticut: Greenwood Press, 1979) and Henry Mitchell, **Black Belief: Folk Beliefs of Blacks in America and West Africa** (New York: Harper and Row, Publishers, 1975)]. **Trabelin' On** and **Black Belief** have some limitations that should be noted. Sobel is concerned with the development of Baptists, but her section on the African world view raises some important questions. Mitchell's book, though interesting, is more speculative and is written in a popular style with little or no documentation.

[2]Neither the concept that the Christian faith provided the foundation for black improvement nor the use of scripture verse from Acts 17:26 "[God] hath made of one blood all nations of men for to dwell on all the face of the earth" (KJV) originated with the post Civil War black ministerial leadership. The antebellum northern black ministers used the concept and the Scripture from Acts when they spoke of the Universal equality of man. (See Monroe Fordham, **Major Themes in Northern Black Religious Thought, 1800-1860** (Hicksville, New York: Exposition Press, 1975), pp. 139-150). The popularity of the concept and the Scriptural reference in the post War South, however, meant that far more blacks

were exposed to the theological foundation for uplifting the race, at a time and place where uplift had to occur, if it was to have any meaning whatsoever.

[3]Lucius H. Holsey, "The Fatherhood of God and the Brotherhood of Man" in *Autobiography, Sermons, Addresses and Essays* (Atlanta: Franklin Printing and Publishing Company, 1898), p. 59.

[4]J.C. Price, "The Value of the Soul," in *Afro-American Encyclopedia; or, The Thoughts, Doings, and Sayings of the Race,* compiled by James T. Haley (Nashville, Tennessee: Haley and Florida, 1896), p. 519.

[5]Edward R. Carter, "Satisfaction Not Attainable in Human Life," in *Biographical Sketches of Our Pulpit or Our Pulpit Illustrated* (Atlanta: E.R. Carter, 1888), pp. 144-7 and James W. Hood, "The Perfect Felicity of the Resurrected Saints, A Result of Conformity to the Divine Likeness," in *The Negro in the Christian Pulpit, or, The Two Characters and Two Destinies, As Delineated in Twenty-One Practical Sermons* (Raleigh, NC: Edwards, Broughton and Co., 1884), pp. 190-204.

[6]George W. Clinton, "The Enlargement of Life Through Death," in *Christianity Under the Searchlight* (Nashville, Tenn.: National Baptist Publishing Board, 1909), pp. 95-110 and L.H. Holsey, "Man an Ideal Empire in Miniature" in *Autobiography,* pp. 33-42.

[7]James W. Hood, "The Loss of the Soul," in *The Negro in the Christian Pulpit,* p. 144.

[8]L.H. Holsey, "From Repentance to Final Restitution" in *Autobiography,* pp. 111-23 and J.W. Hood, "The Perfect Felicity" in *The Negro in the Christian Pulpit,* pp. 190-204.

[9]R.B. Vandavell, "The Way of Salvation," *The Negro Baptist Pulpit: A Collection of Sermons and Papers by Colored Baptist Ministers,* ed. E.M. Brawley (Philadelphia: American Baptist Publication Society, 1890; reprint ed., Freeport, New York: Books for Libraries Press, 1971), p. 56.

[10]H.N. Bouey, "The Fall of Man," in *The Negro Baptist Pulpit,* p. 52.

[11]E.K. Love, "Regeneration," in *The Negro Baptist Pulpit,* p. 67.

[12]See George W. Dupree "Prayer," in *Afro-American Encyclopedia,* pp. 445-8; James J. Durham, "Harmony of the Law and the Gospel,: in *The Negro Baptist Pulpit,* pp. 113-5; A.U. Frierson, "Is the Negro as Morally Depraved as He is Reputed to Be?," in *Twentieth Century Negro Literature: Or A Cyclopedia of Thought on the Vital Topics Relating to the American Negro,* Daniel W. Culp (Miami: Mnemosyne Publishing Co., Inc., 1969), pp. 241-246; Alexander H. Newton, *Out of the Briars* (Philadelphia: AME Book Concern, 1910), pp. 177-223; Theophilus G.

Steward, "Adam in the Garden," in **Pioneer Echoes: Six Special Sermons** (Baltimore: Hoffman and Co., 1889), pp. 56-62 and C.S. Wilkins, "An Inheritance to All," in **Our Pulpit Illustrated,** pp. 174-82.

[13]See Robert E. Chiles, **Theological Transition in American Methodism: 1790-1935** (New York: Abingdon Press, 1965), especially pp. 165-74.

[14]J.W. Hood, "Personal Consecration," in **The Negro in the Christian Pulpit,** p. 28.

[15]Idem, "The Helplessness of Human Nature," in **The Negro in the Christian Pulpit,** p. 268.

[16]Idem, "Exemplified Attachment to Christ and the Reward," in **The Negro in the Christian Pulpit,** p. 36.

[17]See L.H. Holsey, "The Irrepressible Conflict" in **Autobiography,** pp. 33-42; George W. Clinton, "Lessons from Paul's Valedictory," in **Christianity Under the Searchlight,** pp. 113-26; Charles H. Phillips, **From the Farm to the Bishopric: An Autobiography** (Nashville: Parthenon Press, 1932), pp. 36 and 52.

[18]W.G. Parks, "The Freeness of Salvation," in **The Negro Baptist Pulpit,** pp. 660-63. See also Andrew J. Stokes, "Justification," in **The Negro Baptist Pulpit,** pp. 87-90.

[19]E.K. Love, "Regeneration," in **The Negro Baptist Pulpit,** p. 76.

[20]J.C. Price, "The Value of the Soul," in **Afro-American Encyclopedia,** p. 521.

[21]H.N. Bouey, "The Fall of Man," in **The Negro Baptist Pulpit,** p. 52.

[22]A.H. Newton, "Christ's Ascension," in **Out of the Briars,** p. 203.

[23]Micheal Vann, "The Centennial of Modern Missions," in **Afro-American Encyclopedia,** p. 477.

[24]A.J. Stokes, "Justification," in **The Negro Baptist Pulpit,** pp. 87-90.

[25]See also J.J. Durham, "Harmony of the Law and the Gospel," in **The Negro Baptist Pulpit,** pp. 113-5; L.H. Holsey, "The Fatherhood of God and the Brotherhood of Man," in **Autobiography;** James W. Hood, "The Helplessness of Human Nature," in **The Negro in the Christian Pulpit,** pp. 262-77.

[26]George W. Clinton, "Christ Our Exemplar," in **Christianity Under the Searchlight,** pp. 195-6.

[27]See George W. Dupree, "Prayer," in **Afro-American Encyclopedia,** pp. 445-48; J.W. Hood, "The Soul's Anchor," in **The Negro in the Christian**

Pulpit, pp. 122-35; A.H. Newton, "The Intercession of Christ,: in *Out of the Briars,* pp. 185-90.

[28]G.W. Raiford, "Repentance and Faith," in *The Negro Baptist Pulpit,* p. 85.

[29]L.H. Holsey, "The Perpetuity of the Name of Christ,: in *Autobiography,* p. 105. See also E.R. Carter, "Will God Indeed Dwell Here," in *Our Pulpit Illustrated,* pp. 118-29; M.W. Gilbert, "Baptism," in *The Negro Baptist Pulpit,* p. 129; J.C. Price, "The Value of the Soul," in *Afro-American Encyclopedia,* p. 519.

[30]J.W. Hood, "David's Root and Offspring," in *The Negro in the Christian Pulpit,* p. 293. See A.H. Newton, "The Intercession of Christ," in *Out of the Briars,* pp. 185-90; George W. Clinton, "Christianity Under the Searchlight," in *Christianity Under the Searchlight,* pp. 20-24.

[31]S.W. Anderson, "The World to Come," in *The Negro Baptist Pulpit,* p. 186. See also Winfield Henri Mixon, "Mysteries," in *History of the African Methodist Episcopal Church in Alabama, With Biographical Sketches* (Nashville, Tenn: AME Church Sunday School Union, 1902), pp. 172-91; J.W. Hood, "Personal Consecration," "Why Was the Rich Man in Torment," and "A Desirable Consummation," in *The Negro in the Christian Pulpit,* pp. 20-32, 61-78, and 236-46; L.H. Holsey, "The Irrespressible Conflict," in *Autobiography,* pp. 43-56; and J.C. Price, "The Value of the Soul," in *Afro-American Encyclopedia,* pp. 522-23.

[32]See S.W. Anderson, "The World to Come," in *The Negro Baptist Pulpit,* p. 181; G.W. Clinton, "The Surrendered Life and Its Reward," in *Christianity Under the Searchlight,* pp. 199-215; and E.K. Love, "Regeneration," in *The Negro Baptist Pulpit,* p. 65.

[33]A.H. Newton, "The Reward of the Righteous," *Out of the Briars,* p. 223.

[34]Idem, "There is Death in the Pot," *Out of the Briars,* pp. 212-3.

[35]See W.J. Simmons, "The Lord's Supper," in *The Negro Baptist Pulpit,* p. 149; L.H. Holsey, "Christianity Shiloh's Empire," in *Autobiography,* pp. 76-78.

[36]J.W. Hood, "The Streams Which Gladden God's City," in *The Negro in the Christian Pulpit,* p. 178.

[37]A.H. Newton, "Acquaintance With God," *Out of the Briars,* p. 179.

[38]G.W. Clinton, "Christianity Under the Searchlight," in *Christianity Under the Searchlight,* pp. 80-81.

[39]L.H. Holsey, "Christianity Shiloh's Empire," **Autobiography,** pp. 67-78.

[40]Acts 17:26.

[41]Samuel Sewall, **The Selling of Joseph** (Boston: Bartholemew Green and John Allen, 1700; reprint edition, New York: Arno Press, 1969), pp. lff.

[42]John Woolman, "Some Considerations on the Keeping of Negroes," **The Works of John Woolman** (Reprint ed., New York: Arno Press, 1969), pp. 278-9.

[43]William Ellery Channing, "Discourse at the Ordination of The Rev. Jared Sparks," **Discourses, Reviews, and Miscellanies** (Boston: Carter and Hendee, 1830), p. 314.

[44]William Ellery Channing, "Likeness to God," **Unitarian Christianity and Other Essays,** ed., Irving h. Bartlett (New York: The Liberal Arts Press, 1957), p. 96. Numerous other references to God as father can be found in Channing. See **Unitarian Christianity,** pp. 56,66,71, 90, 96,98, 108, 111.

[45]Theodore Parker, "Speech at the Ministerial Conference in Boston, May 29, 1851" in **Additional Speeches, Addresses and Occasional Sermons in Two Volumes,** Volumne 1 (Boston: Little, Brown and Company, 1855), p. 15.

[46]See William R. Hutchison, **The Transcendentalist Ministers: Church Reform in the New England Renaissance** (New Haven: Yale University Press, 1959), p. 190.

[47]Henry Highland Garnet, "An Address to the Slaves of the United States of America," compiled and edited by Bradford Chambers, **Chronicles of Black Protest** (New York: New American Library, 1968), pp. 90-93.

[48]Henry Highland Garnet, **The Past and Present Condition and the Destiny of the Colored Race** (First Published 1848; reprint ed., Miami: Mnemosyne Publishing, Inc., 1969), p. 7.

[49]Henry Highland Garnet, "Discourse Delivered in the House of Representatives," Earl Ofari, **Let Your Motto Be Resistance: The Life and Thought of Henry Highland Garnet** (Boston: Beacon Press, 1972), p. 189.

[50]See Monroe Fordham, **Major Themes,** pp. 139-50.

[51]See Theodore Munger, "The New Theology," in **The Freedom of Faith** (Boston: Houghton, Mifflin and Company, 1883), pp. 23, 41; also

Newman Smyth, **Christian Ethics** (New York: Charles Scribner's Sons, 1892), pp. 108, 110-111, 132.

[52]William Newton Clarke, **An Outline of Christian Theology**, 8th ed. (New York: Charles Scribner's Sons, 1900), p. 139. Numerous other references are made throughout **An Outline** to both the fatherhood of God and the brotherhood of man. See **An Outline**, pp. 134,140, 159, 192, 224, 243, 268, 291, 389, & 411.

[53]J.S. Cantwell, gen. ed. **Manuals of Faith and Duty** (Boston: Universalist Publishing House, 1888), Vol. 1: **The Fatherhood of God**, by John Coleman Adams, p. 6. See also p. 43.

[54]See Washington Gladden, **Ruling Ideas of the Present Age** (Boston and New York: Houghton, Mifflin and Company, 1895), pp. 19-29, 33-60.

[55]See Micheal Vann, "The Centennial of Modern Missions," in **Afro-American Encyclopedia**, p. 477; E.R. Carter, "Will God Indeed Dwell Here," in **Our Pulpit Illustrated**, pp. 118-29, and J.W. Hood, "The Helplessness of Human Nature," in **The Negro in the Christian Pulpit**, p. 270.

[56]George W. Clinton, "Christianity Under the Searchlight," in **Christianity Under the Searchlight**, pp. 27-28.

[57]L.H. Holsey, "Why We Should Love God," in **Autobiography**, p. 165.

[58]G.W. Clinton, "Christianity Under the Searchlight," in **Christianity Under the Searchlight**, pp. 27-28.

[59]E.W.D. Isaacs, "Response to Congress' Welcome to Atlanta," J.W.E. Bowen and I. Garland Penn, editors, **The United Negro: His Problems and His Progress** (Atlanta: D.E. Luther Publishing Co., 1902), p. 53.

[60]See W.D. Johnson, "The White Man and the Colored Man as Christian Citizens," in **Afro-American Encyclopedia**, p. 367 and T.G. Steward, "I Seek My Brethren," in **Fifty Years in the Gospel Ministry** (Philadelphia: AME Book Concern, 1921), pp. 42-50.

[61]Daniel Payne, "The Ordination Sermon," delivered before the General Conference of the AME Church, May, 1888, in **Sermons and Addresses** (Nashville: Publishing House AME Sunday School Union, 1888; reprint ed., New York: Arno Press, 1972), p. 62.

[62]Ernest Lyons, "The Present Religious Status of the Negro in the United States" in **The United Negro**, pp. 90-100.

[63]See S.G. Atkins, "Should the Negro Be Given an Education Different From That Given to the Whites?," and Lucius H. Holsey, "Will It Be Possible for the Negro to Attain, in This Country, Unto the American Type of

Civilization?," in **Twentieth Century Negro Literature,** pp. 80-83 and 47. Also see S.A. Peeler, "What Improvements Should Be Made in the Religious Worship of the Churches," in **The United Negro,** pp. 146-49.

[64]M.W. Gilbert, "Did the American Negro Prove, in the Nineteenth Century, That He is Intellectually Equal to the White Man?," in **Twentieth Century Negro Literature,** p. 287.

[65]Atticus G. Haygood, **Our Brother in Black: His Freedom and His Future** (New York: Phillips and Hunt and Nashville: Southern Methodist Publishing House, 1881). Haygood wrote charitably of blacks and of their potential. He called for whites to respect black rights, including the right to vote, and saw education as a way to reduce the ignorance that held the freedman back. Yet Haygood wrote about blacks in such a manner as to clearly show he was superior to his brother in black. Haygood's vision of a South free of strife and prejudice was not based on black and white equality, but on a mutual respect for the place of blacks and whites in the Society. It almost goes without saying that white superiority, in Haygood's opinion, would keep them in a position of leadership.

[66]See H. Shelton Smith, **In His Image, But. . . .: Racism in Southern Religion, 1780-1910** (Durham: Duke University Press, 1971), p. 108 and I.A. Newby, **Jim Crow's Defense** (Baton Rouge: Louisiana State University Press, 1965), p. 96. Smith's book deals extensively with the attitudes of white southern Christians during the period under consideration. Newby's work, though informative, focuses more on the attitudes of the early twentieth century and therefore has less direct impact on this book.

[67]E.R. Carter, "Can the Negro Attain What Other Races Have?," in **Our Pulpit Illustrated,** p. 80.

[68]I.G. Penn, **The Afro-American Press and Its Editors** (Springfield, Mass.: Willey and Co., Publishers, 1891; reprint ed., New York: Arno Press, 1969), p. 304.

[69]See W.D. Chappelle, "The Work of the AME Church for the Race,: in **The United Negro,** pp. 77-83 and W.J. Gaines, **African Methodism in the South or Twenty-Five Years of Freedom** (Atlanta: Franklin Publishing House, 1890), p. 108.

[70]M.W. Gilbert, "Did the American Negro Prove, in the Nineteenth Century, That He is Intellectually Equal to the White Man?," in **Twentieth Century Negro Literature,** p. 290.

[71]L.H. Holsey, "Why We Should Love God," in **Autobiography,** p. 161.

[72]E.W.D. Isaacs, "Response to Congress' Welcome to Atlanta," in **The United Negro,** p. 52.

[73]See Culp, **Twentieth Century Negro Literature,** pp. 45, 442-45 and Edwin S. Redkey, ed., **Respect Black: The Writings and Speeches of Henry McNeal Turner** (New York: Arno Press and The New York Times, 1971), pp. 52-9, 76-80, 83-4, 135-64, 167-71.
P

[74]B.H. Peterson, "Is the Negro as Morally Depraved as he is Reputed to Be?," in **Twentieth Century Negro Literature,** 240.

[75]See W.J. Gaines, "Introduction to the Negro Young People's Christian and Education Congress," in **The United Negro,** pp. 8-11 and Sterling N. Brown, "How Can the Friendly Relations Now Existing Between the Two Races in the South Be Strengthened and Maintained," in **Twentieth Century Negro Literature,** pp. 68-71.

[76]S.G. Atkins, "Should the Negro Be Given an Education Different From That Given to the Whties?," in **Twentieth Century Negro Literature,** p. 81.

CHAPTER 3
THE UNFULFILLED
PROMISE OF UPLIFT:
POLITICS AND THE
MINISTERIAL ELITE

Henry McNeal Turner was born on February 1, 1833 or 1834, in Newberry Court-House, South Carolina.[1] Born free, Turner nevertheless knew hardship as a child. Though he dreamed of being a leader of his people, his youth gave few indications that the dream would be realized. But Turner did become a leader in the AME Church, and his involvement in politics typified the activity of several leading black ministers during Reconstruction.

Their theological traditions pointed to a possibility for uplift, but without indicating how uplift would be achieved. In the early years after emancipation many clerical leaders, including Turner, thought politics would be the instrument to realize new possibilities. They accepted traditional political structures and worked within the traditions of party politics, but they hoped to use those structures and traditions for their own purposes. As Reconstruction ended, however, fewer ministers could continue to believe in politics. In its place they substituted an allegiance to the temperance movement. Such a shift displayed obvious tendencies toward accommodation. But ministerial support for temperance was not without a paradoxical quality. Temperance was not an end in itself but rather a means to the end of fulfilling black possibility. Turner's career illustrates the interweaving of accommodation and possibility as the ministers sought to uplift the race through political means.

Turner's mother, the major influence in his formative years, was a free-born black; his father, who was of German lineage, had no contact with his son. As a child Turner worked in the cotton fields beside slaves and as an apprentice blacksmith on a plantation. Though receiving no formal education as a child, he took advantage of several informal learning opportunities. His earliest teacher was a white play-mate who taught him the alphabet and some spelling. Later, after he and his mother moved to Abbeville, South Carolina, Turner continued learning under the guidance of the young lawyers in the law office where he was employed. Turner was able to round off his education by studying English Grammar, Hebrew, Latin, Greek, and German while he worked as an AME missionary in Baltimore a few years prior to the outbreak of the Civil War. This training proved helpful as he assumed leadership during the War.

During the early part of his career, Turner was able to combine his devotion to the church with a commitment to politics. Having joined the Methodist Episcopal Church, South in 1848, he was licensed to preach by the Connection in 1853. Disappointed by the lack of opportunity to participate fully in the activities of the denomination, Turner developed an interest in the African Methodist Episcopal Church in 1857, following a trip to an AME meeting in New Orleans. The next year, at the General Conference in St. Louis, he was admitted to that denomination as an itinerant minister. His first assignment was as a missionary to Baltimore, but in 1860 he was ordained a Deacon and assigned to a church in Washington, D.C. Here, he nurtured relationships with political leaders that proved beneficial later. In 1862 Turner was ordained an Elder, and the next year President Lincoln appointed him Chaplain of the First Regiment, United States Colored Troops; he was the first black chaplain to be commissioned. He was mustered out of the service after the War but President Andrew Johnson immediately reappointed him as a chaplain in the Regular Army and assigned him to the Freedman's Bureau in Georgia. Accepting the assignment, Turner went to Georgia in 1865 and immediately began the work of organizing the Republican party in the state and of establishing the AME Church on southern soil. Desiring more time for both his political and religious work, Turner soon resigned his commission in the Army. At the first Annual Conference of the South Carolina Conference of the AME Church in 1866, Bishop Payne recognized Turner's valuable work by appointing him Superintendent of the Church's work in Georgia.

Turner's work on behalf of the Church and the Republican party continued until 1871, when he resigned his position as pastor of a Savannah church. In an address to his Savannah congregation in 1871, Turner recalled that he was responsible for having brought "nearly forty thousand souls" into the AME Church through his ministry in Georgia.[2] By that time he was recognized as the most important AME minister in the state. But in the same address, delivered when he was about to withdraw from active involvement in party politics, Turner also spoke of his contributions to the Republican party.

> It is well known to everyone that I have done more work in the political field than any five men in the State. . . . I first organized the Republican party . . . and have worked for its maintenance and perpetuity as no other man in the State has. I have put more men in the field, made more speeches, organized more Union Leagues, Political Associations, Clubs, and have written more campaign documents that received larger circulation than any other man in the State has.[3]

Though others assisted in the work in Georgia, even Turner's critics did not dispute the contributions he made to the Republican party. He served as a delegate to the Constitutional Convention in Georgia in 1867 and was elected to the Georgia Legislature in 1868. He was appointed as the Postal Inspector in Macon in 1870, and after moving to Savannah he accepted an appointment as Customs Inspector. Yet despite the offices he held and his efforts on behalf of the party, Turner's experience in politics eventually led him to the conclusion that blacks would not get justice in America through political means, and his hope for political uplift ended. The 1871 speech was one of the last he gave that was supportive of the political process.

Turner's political problems began soon after he arrived in Georgia and started organizing the Republican party. Though he was never physically harmed, he was often the target of Democratic threats and white Republican jealousy. He was jailed on a few occasions and accused of dishonesty, though nothing was ever proven. The major disillusionment, however, came at what should have been his greatest hour of political triumph: the 1868 Georgia elections. In that year, two blacks were elected to the Georgia Senate, and Turner and twenty-four other blacks gained seats in the House of Representatives. The state was still controlled by the Democrats, however, and the blacks were denied their seats in both chambers, solely because of their color. After three weeks of arguments and recriminations, Turner addressed the House. His speech not only voiced an ethical and theological basis for seating the elected black officials, but it also indicated Turner's early disillusionment with the political process, a disillusionment that increased in the next thirty years. "Never, in the history of the world," said Turner, "has a man been arraigned before a body clothed with legislative, judicial or executive functions, charged with the offense of being of a darker hue than his fellowmen."[4]

> *The Negro is here charged with holding office.*
> *Why, sir, the Negro never wanted office.*
> *I recollect that when we wanted candidates*
> *for the Constitutional Convention, we went*
> *from door-to-door in the 'negro belt,' and begged*
> *white men to run. . . . They told black men,*
> *everywhere, that they would rather see them*
> *run; and it was this encouragement of the*
> *white men that induced the colored man to*
> *place his name upon the ticket as a candidate*
> *for the Convention. . . . Now, however, a*
> *change has come over the spirit of their dream.*
> *They want to turn the 'nigger' out; and, to*
> *support their argument, they say that the*

black man is debarred from holding office
by the Reconstruction measures of Congress.[5]

Turner concluded his speech with a claim that the offense was "a thrust at the God of the Universe," because as Turner saw it, the whites in the Legislature were guilty of accusing God of "making a man and not finishing him; it is simply calling the Great Jehovah a fool."[6] Turner's protest, however, fell on deaf ears. Only the intervention of the federal government eventually secured the black legislators' seats.

Black emigration of Africa was an idea that Turner entertained soon after the close of the Civil War. But it was not until the increased repression of black civil rights and the political reverses of the 1870's and 1880's that Turner, who was elected a Bishop in his church in 1880, became an outspoken advocate of African Colonization. In a series of letters written in 1883, Turner argued against such northern churchmen as Benjamin Tanner who believed African emigration was a dead issue. He articulated his growing belief that the possibilities of political uplift were all but gone in America. His letter of January 25, 1883, represented his position.

> *Do you know of any instance in the world's history where a people shut out from all honorable positions, from being kings and queens, lords, dukes, presidents, governors, mayors, generals and all positions of honor and trust by reason of their race, ever amounted to anything. . . . People must have one like them on high to inspire them to go high. Jesus Christ had to take upon himself our very nature before his plan of redemption was a success. . . . And till we have black men in the seat of power, respected, honored, beloved, feared, hated and reverenced, our young men will never rise for the reason they will never look up. . . . There I maintain that African colonization should be encouraged.*[7]

The purpose of African emigration was to give black people a chance to have models of leadership they could emulate. This was essential for uplifting the race. The chance that America would allow blacks to have their own political heroes was, according to Turner's assessment of the times, very remote. Consequently, the chances for uplifting blacks in America were diminished.

The events of the next decade reinforced Turner's negative view of political opportunity for blacks in America. By the 1896 presidential elections most blacks in the South had been disfranchised; blacks faced racially motivated legal barriers designed to subjugate the race; and there were dramatic increases in the number of incidents of violence against black people. Looking at these unpleasant facts, Turner wrote an article in the AME publiction, **The Voice of Missions,** in October, 1896, that referred to the upcoming contest between William Jennings Bryan and William McKinley. His advice to blacks who could still vote was for them to cast their ballot for whatever would kill "this rotten shame of a nation." "What time," wrote Turner, "has the fool Negro to bother with the gold or silver side either, while he is lynched, burnt, flayed, imprisoned, etc., two-thirds of the time for nothing. Vote any way in your power to overthrow, destroy, ruin . . . and fragmentize this nation, until it learns to deal justly with the black man."[8] As his commentary on the election indicates, by 1896 Henry McNeal Turner had completely reversed his earlier hopes for the political system. He had changed from being a staunch supporter and organizer of the Republican party immediately following the War to being a man who rejected politics as a tool for black uplift.

To use Turner as representative of a shift in attitudes toward politics by the black ministerial elite is not to suggest that all the ministers arrived at the same conclusions. But the ministers' reactions followed the pattern that marked Turner's career—optimism, followed by disillusionment, culminating in a rejection of the idea that political means would uplift the race. The one political issue that remained alive for the ministerial leadership was Temperance. It was kept alive for the sake of uplift; temperance crusades substituted for other political activities that seemed unlikely to produce the uplift of the race. Though no substitute for justice, the Temperance movement offered the black ministers a meaningful struggle that could be won. In the midst of the political defeats, that was perhaps a worthy undertaking.

1. THE HOPE OF RECONSTRUCTION

The Civil War lasted longer than either side anticipated, but as the War continued the Union forces slowly gained and pressed the advantage. As the probability of a Union victory increased, two related issues took on increased importance for the Union leadership. One was the question of how the rebellious states would be restored to the Union. The other was the question of how and with what rights the almost four million freedmen would be incorporated into the post-War American society. Two very different solutions to these problems were proposed; one by President Lincoln and his successor; the other by some members of Congress who had been ardent abolitionists.[9] The victory of the Congressmen gave many blacks a false sense of security about the uplifting potential of the political process.

Lincoln had argued from the beginning of the War that the States were organically united to the union and therefore secession was technically impossible. He claimed that individuals, not the states themselves, were in rebellion against the Union. This position informed his Proclamation of Amnesty and Reconstruction in 1863. According to this edict, all but a few high ranking military officers and civil servants of the Confederacy were eligible for amnesty if they took an oath of allegiance to the Union and accepted the Emancipation Proclamation. Furthermore, Lincoln's plan provided for the reorganization and full recognition of any state once ten percent of those eligible to vote in 1860 took the oath of allegiance. Known as the "ten percent" or "presidential plan" of Reconstruction, these provisions permitted Tennessee, Louisiana, and Arkansas, as well as the rump government in Virginia, to be recognized before the end of the War. The plan readmitted States to the Union, but it said nothing about the status of freedmen within those states, and it made no provision for black suffrage.

When Lincoln died in 1865, opponents of the presidential plan hoped to attract the support of the new president and to make the re-admission of the seceded states more difficult. Andrew Johnson indicated, however, that he planned to keep the Lincoln plan with only minor modifications. He accepted the four states that had been admitted under Lincoln's proposals and issued both an amnesty and a political reconstruction proclamation for North Carolina. These proclamations closely resembled the earlier presidential plan, but with one alteration. Johnson excluded more ex-confederates from participation in the new governments. In any case, the North Carolina plan became the model for the way the other Confederate States were treated. By December, 1865, all the states of the old Confederacy had been reconstructed under the Lincoln-Johnson Plan, and the Thirteenth Amendment to the Constitution, abolishing slavery, had been ratified. But because no provisions had been made to protect the freedman's rights, Congress rebelled.[10]

Lincoln's strength as a war president had insured support for his plan for reconstruction, but from the beginning several "Radical" Republicans, led by Charles Sumner in the Senate and Thaddeus Stevens in the House, had views of the secession quite unlike Lincoln's. Sumner claimed that the States had committed suicide when they seceded from the Union and that Congress had the right to establish harsh requirements for their re-admission; one of which would be the extension of the franchise to the freedman. Contrary to the belief (common during the first half of this century) that political concerns were the primary motivations behind Republican support for Sumner and Stevens, the more recent work of John and LaWanda Cox indicates that these men were committed to protecting the rights of the freedmen by securing them the right to vote, even though they risked losing voter support.[11]

As early as July, 1864 the Radical Republicans had passed their own reconstruction legislation, the Wade-Davis Bill. Drafted as a counter-measure of Lincoln's reconstruction plans, the bill would have permitted the reorganization of States when half of the eligible voters in a state took the oath of allegiance. It barred anyone who had served in the Confederate military or who had held an elected post in the Confederacy from participation in government. Lincoln vetoed the measure.

Following Lincoln's death, Congress asserted itself more forcefully. Under the leadership of Sumner and Stevens, a joint committee of fifteen began to investigate the legitimacy of the reconstructed governments before their elected Representatives and Senators took their seats in Congress. This delay protected Republican control of Congress but it also gave the Congress an opportunity to discover that the southern states were not only ignoring the rules that barred certain Confederate officials from leadership but also excluding blacks from participation through a variety of measures known as "black codes." These effectively reduced the freedman to a state of semi-servitude. Radical Republicans were convinced that the new system meant that the Union victory had changed very little. They were determined to make the victory meaningful for both the freedman and the Republican party.

On April 9, 1866, Congress passed a Civil Rights Act over President Johnson's veto. The Act secured certain rights for the freedman that were denied by the "black codes." Later that month, the joint committee presented its report, which insisted that statehood be denied any Confederate state that failed to accept certain guarantees established by Congress for the protection of blacks. Accepting the report, Congress approved the Fourteenth Amendment in June. Ratification of the Amendment, which incorporated the major feature of the Civil Rights Act, was made a precondition for admission to statehood. Tennessee approved the Amendment and was admitted to the Union on July 24, 1866, but the other southern states rejected it.[12]

The fall elections of 1866 turned into a test of strength between President Johnson and the Congress. Congress won.[13] With a solid majority supporting the Radical Republican position, Congress dismantled the Lincoln-Johnson plan and replaced it with its own version, often over the veto of the president. The Congressional plan, passed in 1867, organized the South into five military districts and dissolved all existing governments. The major aid to black political aspirations, however, was the mandate that new elections had to be held, with black suffrage. The elections would select men to draft new state constitutions for the new state governments. Ratification of the new constitutions, drafted in accordance with federal laws, would be the precondition for returning to the Union. With such legislation, and with the ratification of the Fifteenth Amendment guaranteeing black political rights, many believed that the freedman was adequately protected with what Michael Les Benedict has described as a minimum of federal intervention in what was rightfully the domain of state governments.[14]

Though the black ministerial elite had no influence in the formulation of either the Presidential or Congressional Reconstruction Plans, the ministers had to respond somehow to the changed political conditions. To be sure, few of them were engaged in political activities. In fact, prominent black Methodists denied that churches were interested in politics.[15] Refuting the charge that the CME Church was a tool of the Democratic party, C.H. Phillips-a denominational official-claimed that the denomination had no connection with any political party. As a bishop in the CME Church, Lucius Holsey informed the readers of **The Independent** that "as ministers of the Gospel," the preachers in his branch of Methodism, "make no stump speeches and fight no battles of the politicians. We think it better," continued the bishop, "to let the dead bury the dead, while we follow Christ."[16] Such AME leaders as William Gaines also denied that their Church was "political," although Gaines added that the AME Church had an interest in whatever affected people.[17] Bishop Daniel Payne of the AME Church criticized the political activities of three southern AME leaders: he said that Richard H. Cain of South Carolina "damaged his usefulness as an ambassador of the Cross, so also, did Pierce in Florida, and so also did Turner in Georgia."[18] Payne was not opposed to politics; he was worried that the political involvements of the three men took time they should have devoted to the church.

It is clear, however, that a few of the black ministers did develop intense political interests. Payne suggested one reason for their political activities.

> *The only apology which can be made for them is that for intelligence and organizing power their equals could not be found in the laity, hence politics laid hold of them and by a kind of conscription forced them into the army of politics.*[19]

Ten of the seventy-eight elite ministers held elected or appointed political offices between 1865 and 1902, most of them serving before 1877. At least ten others, who never held any political office, were actively involved in partisan politics, and no less than seven others worked for Temperance laws and against "Jim Crow" legislation. One third of the clerical elite, therefore, became involved, directly or indirectly, in some phase of the political process.

The ministers who were involved in the political process did not seek to change the political structures. They worked within the established political framework. From this perspective they can be seen as accommodationists. In another sense, however, the very fact that blacks sought to participate in the political structures signaled a change in those structures. It meant that blacks could successfully encounter whites as equals through the political process. The ministerial elite were convinced that blacks could use politics to further their own ends, just as whites had done.

Before the congressional Reconstruction in 1867, the black ministerial leaders had limited political experience. Some worked to organize the Republican party in the South. H.M. Turner's work with the party began in Georgia in 1865. Jesse Freeman Boulden, who moved to Natchez, Mississippi, in 1865 to promote Baptist work, petitioned Congress in 1866 requesting that it guarantee blacks the right to vote. He also helped organize the Republican party in Northeast Mississippi, and in 1867 he served as a delegate to the first Republican State Convention in Mississippi.[20] Others met with black groups trying to voice their political interests and grievances. In North Carolina, Bishop James Hood of the AME Zion Church participated in the "Colored Convention" that met in Raleigh in 1865. During the gathering, Hood sounded the theme of black equality and called for the extension of the vote to the freedman.[21] Still others inserted political themes in their sermons and addresses. Theophilus G. Steward, an AME minister who served in South Carolina and Georgia, gave thanks in his 1866 Thanksgiving Day Sermon in Charleston for "the return of Peace and the triumph of the holy cause of Freedom in the Fall elections."[22] Steward was aware that the Radical Republican victory made the future of the freedman more promising than it would have been had Johnson's supporters won. But as important as these early involvements were, it was not until after Congressional Reconstruction began that the ministers could enter the mainstream of political activity.

The second phase of ministerial politics began during the elections of delegates to the new constitutional conventions. The elections were held in 1867, with black suffrage, and the Conventions began to meet later that year.[23] Three of the seventy-eight ministers served as delegates to their state conventions: James Hood in North Carolina in 1867, Henry M. Turner in the 1867 Georgia Convention, and Richard Cain of Charleston in the 1868 South Carolina Convention.

The work of Richard Cain in the South Carolina Convention illustrated the new style of ministerial activity. Born free in Virginia in 1825, ordained in the Methodist Episcopal Church, Cain became an AME in 1859. An educated man, having received a Bachelor of Arts degree from Wilberforce University, he was transferred in 1865 from his church in Brooklyn to a congregation in Charleston, South Carolina. While serving in this position, he became state Superintendent over his denomination's missionary efforts. He also joined the Republican party and was elected to the 1868 Constitutional Convention in Charleston.[24] There Cain distinguished himself with oratory and a passion for the freedman and poor whites. He fought to secure the rights of blacks in the new constitution and gave special attention to education and land reform for the poor. When he sponsored a petition to Congress for a grant of one million dollars for the state to purchase land for redistribution, an acrimonious debate erupted. Cain defended his position by appealing to the theme of brotherhood. "The true principle of progress and civilization is to recognize the great brotherhood of man," said Cain, "and a man's wants, whatever he may be, or whatever clime he comes from, are as sacred to me as any other class of men."[25] But he also spoke specifically of the dreams of his black constituents.

> I want to see a change in this country. Instead of the colored people being always penniless, I want to see them coming in with their mule teams and ox teams. I want to see them come with their corn and potatoes and exchange for silks and satins. I want to see school houses and churches in every parish and township. I want to see children coming forth to enjoy life as it ought to be enjoyed. This people know nothing of what is good and best for mankind until they get homesteads and enjoy them.[26]

Without using the phrase, Cain advanced the themes of the program of "uplift." He wanted to move the freedman from a position as a beggar and consumer to the status of being an owner and producer. Like some other ministers, he was confident that the redistribution of land brought from previous owners at a fair price would help achieve that goal. Land ownership would teach people pride in themselves and their country and eliminate their dependence on the Freedman's Bureau. After a long debate, the Convention voted to endorse Cain's position and send it to Congress.[27]

The general elections of 1868 marked the beginning of a third phase of political activity: several of the preachers ran for elected office, received governmental appointments, and worked for the Republican party. By 1868, Theophilus G. Steward, the pastor of an AME Church in Macon, Georgia, was an organizer and stump speaker.[28] After working for the Republicans in the November election, he again used a Thanksgiving Sermon to express his optimism over the outcome—an optimism shared by other ministers, some of whom were elected to offices never before held by black men. Steward wrote that he was grateful for: the movement toward the permanence of the peace and the spread of equality and opportunity to all people in the land; the impeachment of President Johnson; the advance of reconstruction; and the election of Grant, under whose administration, "we may hope to see our rescued country permanently settle upon the basis of a righteous peace."[29] Blacks had the vote for the first time and they had exercised their freedom in a meaningful way. The optimism of the ministerial leadership was understandable.

Seventeen of the seventy-eight ministers were active in politics after 1868. Most of those clerical politicians were native southerners. Only three (J.W. Hood, T.G. Steward, and Jesse Boulden, who was born in Delaware and whose parents had been slaves) were born outside the South, and only two others (William J. Simmons and Hiram Revels) had spent any appreciable time outside the old Confederacy before they began their political careers. G.W. Gayles of Mississippi was typical of the clerical politicians. Born into slavery in Mississippi, he had left the State only during the time he served in the Union Army. In 1867 he was ordained to the ministry in the Baptist church, and in 1868 he established a church in Bolivar County, Mississippi. The following year he accepted an appointment to the District Board of Police. In 1870 he was appointed Justice of the Peace and later that year he received an appointment as district Supervisor for his district. Gayles then ran for and won a State House Seat in 1873. Following this he ran for the State Senate in 1877 and again was elected. He served ten years as a State Senator. He also served on the executive committee of the state Republican party. Though he was actively involved in politics, he continued serving as the pastor of the church he organized. Indeed, his career demonstrated that involvement in politics certainly did not result in ostracism by ministerial peers. He was elected to several leadership positions in the Baptist State Missionary Convention of Mississippi, including the presidency in 1870.[30] He also edited the black Baptist state paper, **The Baptist Signal**, and was described by a fellow journalist as "a dignified and practical writer," who believed "in laying before his readers that which . . . [was] of solid benefit to them in their progress through life."[31]

The educational achievements of the politically active clergy varied, but all seventeen who were active after congressional reconstruction had attained to a level of literacy above that of the average freedman. Five held at least a Bachelor's degree. William J. Simmons who was a county campaign chairman for the Republican party in Florida before moving to Louisville in 1879 received his degree from Howard University. Thomas O. Fuller had earned both the Bachelor's and Master's degrees from Shaw University before he served in the North Carolina Legislature in the 1890's.[32] Typical of the twelve men who had more limited formal education was W.H. Mixon, an AME minister from Alabama, a self-taught man who did some formal work at Selma University.[33] The white criticisms of "ignorant blacks" in politics were not accurate descriptions of these seventeen political clergymen.

At least half of the seventeen men had been slaves, while six are known to have been born free. But the men of free birth did not stand in isolation from the slave population. For instance, H.M. Turner, born free, had worked beside slaves for many years. A.H. Newton had been born free in North Carolina by virtue of his mother's status, but his father had been a slave, and Newton's experiences had not been very different from those of slave children.[34]

Most of the clerical politicians were ministers in the Baptist or

71

African Methodist Episcopal Church. Eight Baptists and six AME ministers were politically active, while only one of the seventeen came from the ME Church, North, one preached in the AME Zion Church, and one was a minister in the CME Church. The numbers reflected the relative strength of the southern black denominations. But the preponderance of ministers from two denominations also reflected the independence of the local congregations within the Baptist tradition and the historic involvement in politics by AME ministers. Baptists had no structure outside the local congregation that could dictate their actions; and in any case, political involvement was no bar to denominational approval and recognition. The AME Church did have a structure that could demand obedience from its ministers. Yet even when the bishops disapproved of political involvements, they and the denomination gave black Methodist ministers considerable freedom to become active in politics. The doctrine of the "spirituality of the church," or the position that the church had no right to speak on issues of political justice, had emerged into prominence in the South's predominantly white churches during the struggle over slavery, when white theologians had used it to defend themselves from northern critics. The policy of non-involvement became a mark of white southern Protestantism after the War, despite occasional breaches when consistency seemed harmful. But the black churches had no historic reason to maintain such a policy, with the exception of the Colored Methodist Episcopal Church whose close ties to the M.E. Church, South may have influenced its non-political stance.[35] As indicated earlier, some of the black clergy criticized political activity by the churches, but their criticisms did not prevail.

The twenty-seven politically active ministers were all Republicans during Reconstruction, and they served as sheriffs, probate judges, state Senators, Representatives, Justices of the Peace, and school board members. One was a U.S. Senator. They also held important positions within the party, contributing to it in a variety of ways as state executive committeemen, delegates to the National Conventions, stump speakers, organizers for state and local party organizations, and writers supporting the party in denominational and secular publications. As long as the Republicans held the balance of power in the South, the ministers believed their future was secure and the goals of uplift were attainable. As the balance of power shifted and the Democrats regained control, the ministers found that much of their political power, real and imagined, disappeared. The hope that politics would help uplift the race also faded. The politically active ministers soon discovered that their allegiance to the Republican party carried an expensive price tag. The return of the Democrats to power forced some ministers to re-evaluate their traditional ties with the Republican party, while other like H.M. Turner wondered about the chances of political uplift under either party.

2. DEMOCRATIC GOVERNMENTS: DEFEATS AND DISILLUSIONMENTS

Just as Reconstruction had taken years to implement, the Democrats did not return to power all at once. The process that led to their return to power began at the same time as the process that placed the Republicans in control of the South.[36] Surely the most important factor that led to the eventual return to power of the Democrats was the party's identification with southern whites. Despite the Republican victory in the elections of 1868, the Democrats were still the party of the majority of southern whites, who viewed the Republicans as the party of blacks, carpet-baggers, and scalawags. From the beginning of Reconstruction, the Republicans had to rely on the disenfranchisement of many whites and the voting strength of blacks to keep them in power. Once the restrictions on former confederates were relaxed, the Democrats were in a position to control state governments again, and the restrictions began to ease almost as soon as they were imposed. By 1872, all but about six hundred confederates had been given amnesty. This helped Democrats regain control of three state governments—Tennessee, North Carolina, and Virginia—by 1870.

A second factor in the rise of the Democratic party was the successful use of white terrorism against blacks, designed to undermine black freedom and suffrage. Such groups as the White Camelias, the White League, and the knights of the Ku Klux Klan used violence as a tactic of control even when the "Black Codes" were in effect. But the violence increased as blacks became active in politics. The ministers referred continually to the viciousness of the white harassment. According to T.G. Steward, "Ku Kluxism became a terror and a power. Floggings and assasinations were frequent; leaders in politics were served notice to leave the state. Although by no means prominent as a political leader, I had attracted sufficient attention to be favored with one of these missives."[37] Steward, whose church was burned, wrote an essay in 1869 that detailed the trouble in Georgia and appealed to President Grant for help in suppressing the violence.[38] Elijah P. Marrs, who had reported Klan activity in parts of Kentucky before 1870, wrote that Klansmen were active in Newcastle in the early 1870's. After a brush with a Klan member in 1870, Marrs organized a Loyal League and "For three years . . . slept with a pistol under my head, an Enfield rifle at my side, and a corn-knife at the door."[39] A.H. Newton, a AME minister, voiced sympathy with blacks who responded in kind to Klan violence,[40] although few did. The widespread violence against the freedman helped negate the independent black vote even before the formal end of political reconstruction.

By the end of 1876, all but three southern states—Louisiana, Florida, and South Carolina—were under Democratic control. The closeness of the 1876 election meant that voters in Louisiana and South Carolina would determine whether the Republicans would retain the presidency. Both parties claimed victory in those states, but the Republicans won the victory in the Congress by making concessions that signaled the end of political reconstruction. Among these were the removal of federal troops from the region and a promise to provide financial assistance for the rebuilding of the South's economy.

Blacks were so closely associated with the Republican party that one immediate result of the Democratic victory was the decrease in the number of black elected officials. Between 1880 and 1890, G.W. Gayles, in Mississippi, was the only minister of the seventeen who was able to retain his elective office. Other ministers were defeated by the Democrats; still others decided that they would no longer seek elective office.[41] The Methodist minister Hiram Revels, who had served in the U.S. Senate and as Secretary of State for Mississippi, abandoned political life in the wake of violence even before the elections and accepted the presidency of Alcorn University. William H. Heard, an AME minister who had been an active Republican in Georgia and who also served a term in the South Carolina House of Representatives, left politics altogether in 1880 and devoted himself to the ministry. He did not engage in politics again until he was appointed as a diplomat to Liberia in 1895.[42]

Following the resurgence of the Democratic party, the ministers also began to turn away from partisan Republican activities. William J. White was one of the few who remained active in the party, serving as a Georgia delegate to the National Convention as late as 1886.[43] Most of the others who had been active dropped their ties with the party machinery. Jesse Boulden, who had helped organize the Republicans in Mississippi, left the state in 1876, returning in 1882, but apparently ceasing his work in the party. T.G. Steward left the South in 1871, convinced that politics alone would not solve the problems confronting the race.[44] In part the diminished role of blacks in the party represented a new Republican southern strategy: a retreat from support for black civil and political rights in an appeal to a broader white constituency. But the withdrawal of the black ministerial leadership also reflected a growing disinclination among blacks to rely solely on the Republicans for accomplishing their purposes.

The ministers continued to voice loyalty to the Republican party throughout much of the 1880's, but fear of the Democrats prompted much of that loyalty. Monroe F. Jamison, a CME minister expressed a common fear after the 1880 election:

> I was not afraid of the return of slavery in case the Democrats had been successful in electing General Hancock, but I foresaw a sad picture as to how the Negroes of the South would be treated. I prayed for the election of Garfield as earnestly as I prayed for the conversion of sinners. . . . The Republican party has not done all that it might have done for the Negroes, but it has done wonderfully well by them.[45]

Jamison was more fearful of Democratic rule than supportive and uncritical of the Republicans.

As it became obvious that the Democrats were going to retain their power, black ministers attempted to secure what they could. As early as 1879 the North Georgia Conference of the AME Church petitioned for state support of blind black children, noting that white children already received substantial support. When the state responded by building a new facility in Macon in 1881, W.J. Gaines observed that the Church "Should not hesitate to undertake those things that are in any way for the bettering of the condition of the race." Furthermore, he claimed that despite the racial problems in Georgia, the Democratic government had shown that, "there is . . . a great deal of justice to be found residing in human hearts."[46] At least three others—Elijah P. Marrs, C.C. Vaughn, and W.J. Simmons—devoted their political energies to the State Convention of Colored Men in Kentucky, where the focus was not on party affiliation but on addressing the needs of black people. Simmons however, used the convention to call on blacks to re-examine their ties to the Republican party at the state level. He believed that both parties at the national level were committed "to the pernicious doctrine of States Rights," compelling blacks to attend to what was actually happening in the State.

> Shall we live deluded with the hope that the general government will bring to us a panacea for all our ills? No; we must court the favors of the people of the state. We must be for progress wherever found. We must act wisely. Indeed the Republican party could not, if it would, help us. . . . Let us cast our votes for liberal men who will help us. We cannot expect those against whom we vote to do so. . . . The colored man is such a slave to party that his blind obedience has befogged his reason so that he has fought the white man's battles, secured office for him, and fought for his own rights unaided in 'Negro Conventions'. . . . Negroes attempt to do in convention what they ought to do with their votes, and are driven to it by the policy of the Republican party in the South. We should change this thing.[47]

Despite such pleas, dissatisfaction with Republican policies, and a growing black disillusionment with politics in the 1880's, the ministers who continued to vote supported the "party of emancipation." Yet black voters and black political power became less important as the decade progressed and the Democrats sought to eliminate the black vote altogether.

The return of conservative Democratic state governments did not immediately result in the disfranchisement of the black population, although the violence that accompanied the campaign and the elections of 1876 had discouraged black participation.[48] In fact, once the Democrats regained power they took a paternalistic attitude and attempted to control the black vote for their own purposes. They were only maginally successfully, and soon they recognized the danger of allowing blacks to tip the balance of political power, especially in areas with a large black population.[49] In the mid 1880's southern Democrats moved to eliminate blacks as a political force, using not only intimidation and terror but also such extra-legal methods as re-districting, ballot-box stuffing, and the multiple ballot-box system.[50] These efforts accompanied increased social subjugation of blacks.

Both trends brought protests from the leading black ministers. William Gaines reported that as early as 1880 blacks were emigrating from Georgia because of "political persecution and the poverty of the land," and two years later he complained of an attempt by whites to eject him from his first class seat on a train from Thomasville to Albany. He did not give up his seat, but the attempt angered him. "Better treatment is deserved by those of our race in the South," wrote Gaines, "who are intelligent, refined, whose behaviour is that of ladies and gentlemen, and who are constant patrons of these roads. May the Lord hasten the day when no man shall be known by the color of his skin, but by his walk."[51] In church newspapers and political conventions, William Simmons frequently criticized the disfranchisement and public abuse of blacks who exercised their rights in Kentucky. In 1886, after chairing a committee of the black convention that articulated grievances to the State Legislature, he addressed the lawmakers, demanding that they recognize black rights in the state.[52] A.N. McEwen, a former slave who settled in Alabama after preaching and studying in Tennessee, one of the few ministerial leaders who maintained his ties with the Republican party, serving on the state executive board, became editor of **The Baptist leader** and used the paper to defend the right and ability of blacks to vote and rule intelligently. In 1889 he answered the question: "Should the Negro Be Disenfranchised?" "There is as much absurdity in thinking of his disenfranchisement, as there is in thinking of placing the United States in the center of Africa," wrote McEwen. Blacks were made in the image of God and had a right to every privilege and responsibility. McEwen also opposed property qualifications for voters, reaffirming that "Justice is what the Negro calls for. Give him that, and he will prove as true a citizen as anybody. Wealth has nothing to do with a man's voting. If he can't buy a resting-place in the graveyard, if he is a citizen of the United States he has as much right to vote as a millionaire."[53]

Despite the Democratic control of the South in the 1880's and the white success in reducing the black vote, blacks retianed a measure of power. Yet as McEwen observed, the close of the decade brought an intensification of white attempts to disenfranchise blacks. The political reality that finally led to white success and ministerial disillusionment with politics came in the wake of failure in the Populist movement during the 1890's.

3.   DISFRANCHISEMENT, POPULISM, AND THE FINAL DEFEAT OF POLITICAL UPLIFT

The last decade of the nineteenth century proved disastrous to black hopes of uplifting the race through political means. Although hopes rose in the middle of the decade with the Populist victories in North Carolina, by 1902 the Populist party was dead. The ministerial elite protested against a resurgent racist politics, as they had done in the past, but to no avail. Strangely, however, even as they protested the leading ministers affirmed their hope that America would one day live up to her high ideals. Very few ministers believed it had been a mistake to accommodate themselves to the existing political systems and make them their own. Even though they had not succeeded in securing the participation of the freedman in American society, most ministers continued to believe that the American political system and its underlying principles were valid. But political setbacks convinced them that politics would not be the means by which either justice or uplift would be achieved for their people.

The 1890's began with setbacks for blacks on at least two fronts. In the fall of 1890 the U.S. Senate defeated the so-called "Force Bill," which would have authorized the use of federal troops to protect black voters, who had been threatened and harassed while attempting to vote. Through the bill was not as strong as H.M. Turner would have liked, he considered it a step in the right direction. When it appeared on the verge of defeat, Turner commented that, "weak as the bill is, it is a menace in our favor, at least. But it seems that the bill is to be defeated by Democrats, Negro-hating Republicans and a herd of Negro monstrosities."[54] The second front in the white offensive was in the states. Early in 1890, Mississippi Democrats called for a Convention to revise the state constitution. One of their intentions was to disfranchise blacks, who were in the majority in the state. They accomplished their goal by placing restrictions on the suffrage. All voters had to pay a poll tax and were required to meet residence and property qualifications. The revision also barred anyone from voting who could not read and satisfactorily interpret the Constitution. In order to protect whites, however, the laws had a number of loopholes, such as a"grandfather clause" that allowed anyone to vote whose grandfather had been eligible to vote, a provision that protected only white voters. Other states soon followed Mississippi's lead, beginning with South Carolina, which successfully revised its constitution in 1895.[55]

Even before the Mississippi Constitutional Convention blacks sensed the mood of the nation and foresaw the erosion of their rights. In response, a leading black editor issued a call for blacks to meet in Chicago on January 15, 1890, to organize for black rights. The result was the Afro-American League, organized when one hundred forty-one delegates responded to T.T. Fortune's call. Joseph C. Price, a preacher in the AME Zion Church, was elected president of the League; Alexander Walters, another AME Zion minister, assumed a prominent position. The organization disbanded in 1891, but in the face of further setbacks, Walters and Fortune helped start a new organization in 1898. Like its predecessor, the National Afro-American Council called for the protection of black rights and protested against lynchings, the convict lease system and the separate Coach laws. Walters, who became a bishop in 1892, was elected the president of the organization.

Despite the efforts of the Council and the League, disfranchisement proceeded apace, encouraged by the attitude of the United States Supreme Court. In a series of decisions dating back to 1876, the Court had undermined the protection blacks received under the 14th and 15th Amendments to the Constitution. By the middle of the 1890's it was clear to the ministerial elite that the Court simply would not protect blacks from white supremacy. The ministers complained: Turner expressed his resentment, as did others, like Thomas Oscar Fuller, a North Carolina Baptist,[56] but to no avail.

In the early 1890's a new coalition of blacks and whites challenged Democratic control of the governments in several southern states. For a brief moment, ministerial hopes rose again. But this Populist movement ended in disaster; in its aftermath, all the southern states adopted constitutional revisions to eliminate black voting.

Agrarian discontent with Democratic policies began to surface in the 1880's as part of a nation-wide movement by farmers to improve their economic situation. The unrest took political form and in 1890 a coalition of blacks and whites, old Republican supporters, and rural folk was able to elect several candidates. Bouyed by success, the Populists organized to support their own candidates in other elections. While not advocating social equality, the coalition stood for political equality and the resolution of economic problems common to black and white farmers. It had success in Georgia and North Carolina; in 1894 the Populists gained control of the North Carolina legislature. Four years later, Thomas O. Fuller was elected to a seat in the State Senate, the last member of the ministerial elite to serve in an elected office, his victory secured by black voters protected by a populist legislature. The campaign produced violence and charges of "Negro Dominance."[57] Fuller tried to reassure his constituency that the Democrats would be just, but even as he took his seat, the ruling Democrats began to consolidate their victory by eliminating blacks as a political force in the state. His eloquent pleas on behalf of his constituency fell on deaf ears. By 1900, the Constitution of North Carolina disfranchised blacks. Populism and black rights fell before the fury of white supremacy and Negrophobia.

The ministers continued to object to the subordination of blacks, but their protests were unheeded. Silas X. Floyd, a field worker for the International Sunday School Convention, deplored the nation's drift "toward the rocks of destruction" that he saw as the inevitable result of its failure to deal fairly with the black population. "All the trouble with reference to the Negro in this country," said Floyd, "is demonstrably due to the failure of the American nation to fully acknowledge and grant the equal and inalienable rights with which, as asserted as a self-evident truth in our National Declaration of Independence, all men are endowed by their creator."[58] The remedy, he said, was simple justice. W.D. Chappelle, an AME minister in South Carolina and president of Allen University, charged that in the South racial relations were peaceful only because whites had the power to enforce their will. Friendly relations, he added, depended on a mutual respect that did not exist in the South.[59] George W. Clinton, an AME Zion bishop, deplored the recent politics of reaction and applauded the Afro-American Council in its attempt "to uplift the Negro along social lines to combat the prejudices, caste regulations and other efforts to crush our race-manhood and turn back the hand in the dial plate of the Negro's progress."[60] Thomas Fuller decried the events in North Carolina as contrary to the "genius and spirit of our institutions."[61]

Even in their protests, however, the ministers affirmed the "principles of America," called on those principles to defend blacks, and expressed confidence that the nation would one day live up to them. Edward R. Carter, pastor of the Friendship Baptist Church of Atlanta, was lavish in his praise of America's principles and laws:

> We are living in one of the greatest
> countries in the face of the globe; none like
> it anywhere. Whatever we may think of it,
> because of our situation in it. . . . We can
> own all we can pay for. So far as our standing,
> walking, and acting are in the bounds of the
> law, and when I say this, I am not blind to
> nor ignorant of the troubles, drawbacks,
> hindrances and mighty resistances which, as
> a part of this grand republic, we have to
> encounter.[62]

George A. Goodwin, a Baptist minister and teacher in Georgia and Florida, thought it providential that blacks were in America where they could learn in the most advanced society on earth. Silas Floyd, though critical of America, remained loyal and reaffirmed his belief that the nation's perils would be overcome because the nation would accept its own principles. Charles H. Phillips, a CME leader, was optimistic about the country and the black community's future in it: God's hand would lead the nation to greatness and the black American would enjoy the full measure of prosperity. Even H.M. Turner conceded that "the United States has the highest form of civilized institutions that any nation has had."[63]

The leading ministers concluded in the 1890's, however, that politics could not fulfill the dream of uplift. In his sermon extolling American virtues, Carter belittled the benefits of political activity.

> There is no other way for us to live with another race but to seek mutual confidence and pursue it. We have tried politics long enough; we have looked forward to the results of political measures in hope of a resurrection from all our ills, and still we are in our graves without hope of ever living again.[64]

Charles H. Phillips announced that the CME Church had always exhibited strong opposition to political activity, and indeed the delegates to the 1894 CME General Conference voted not to establish a committee to report on the political state of the country. Thomas O. Fuller, who had once won office in North Carolina, decided that no office-seeker or professional politician could be entrusted with the future of black people. Only blacks could accomplish their task of uplift, and only outside the nation's political institutions.[65] In 1902, as the Negro Young People's Christian and Educational Congress came to a close, the President, Bishop Wesley J. Gaines of the AME Church, proudly noted that the Congress "recognized the truth that mere political agencies are powerless, to change our status or to remedy the evils of our situation."[66] Clearly the black ministerial leaders had lost hope that politics would achieve uplift. By the end of the century, only one "political" issue offered them hope for uplift. That issue was Temperance.

4. TEMPERANCE AND UPLIFT

Even before the Civil War, Temperance societies flourished in America, but the movement had not been popular in the South. Neither did it enjoy widespread southern support immediately after the War. But in the 1870's with the emergence of such groups as the Women's Christian Temperance Union, the southern attitude changed. By the end of the century, the temperance cause drew southern support across racial and denominational lines. Opposition to the liquor industry was so great that it eventually took the form of a political crusade to eradicate the great menace,[67] and black ministers frequently took the lead in the war against "Demon Rum," participating in societies, leagues, and political contests to outlaw the sale of alcohol. As many ministerial leaders concluded that politics would not uplift the race, some decided that alcohol had been an impediment to black improvement. Having always opposed excessive drinking, they turned increasingly to the temperance issue in the face of intensifying opposition to black civil and political rights. Before long they viewed temperance as a major step on the road to uplifting the race; a victory would show the world that the race could be uplifted and trusted with the responsibilities of freedom, including the franchise.[68]

In embracing the Temperance movement, the clergy adopted the dominant society's view of morality. But this was no unthinking accommodation to white morality. Rather, it reflected an earnest attempt by black clergymen to solve what they perceived as a social problem that plagued the freedman. They concluded that alcohol was a stumbling block that precluded black political equality. That the ministerial elite could work with whites in eliminating the problem was for them further proof of black equality and possibility.

Anxieties about alcohol appeared in the 1860's but temperance developed into a full-blown cause for the ministers in the 1870's and 1880's. A laissez-faire attitude gave way to a growing conviction that temperance, even total abstention, was imperative. The AME organization in Alabama, for instance, worried initially only about drunkenness, suspending a minister for that reason in 1869. In 1878 the Alabama Conference urged ministers to refrain from using alcohol so they could purchase books. Seven years later, however, the Conference gave wholehearted support to Bishop Turner's description of the temperance issue as "the greatest question now being agitated over the civilized world" and his attribution of society's ills to intemperance. The attitudes in the Alabama Conference were typical of the growing ministerial hostility to alcohol.[69]

The earliest successes of the Temperance movement seem to have come from moral suasion or what Joseph Gusfield has described as assimilative reform.[70] In 1876 Elijah Marrs, joining with white temperance workers in Kentucky, persuaded over 700 people in two towns to sign a pledge to stop drinking. Following his success, Marrs became president of the temperance organization, composed of black and white advocates for the cause. About the same time, Bishop Hood of North Carolina was preaching that intemperance was a sure sign that one was not yet a Christian, or as a Methodist might well believe, an indicator that one had "fallen from grace." His sermons were among the earliest to link Christian standing with temperance. Other preachers, like A.H. Newton, were content to proclaim that one reward of heaven would be freedom from alcohol and saloons.[71]

Despite its early successes, the temperance effort was not without opponents and setbacks, owing to an absence of denominational clarity about the issue and a fear among blacks that the movement was an attempt to limit their rights as freedmen. Not until the 1890's did the clergy resolve the problems and become consistent advocates of the temperance position.

Ministers often opposed early attempts to limit sales of alcohol—a sign that the church's position was initially unclear. One referendum on liquor evoked from James Hood the observation that "there were a number of persons, who professed to be Christians, that voted . . . to license the sale of intoxicating drinks." But even more distressing, he found "ministers, who indulge in the intoxicating cup, and who oppose the efforts that are put forth to remove it from the land."[72] Without denominational directives, connectional churches could not force compliance, while congregational polities left decisions to local congregations.

Politics also intruded in the early temperance movement. Elijah Marrs and E.R. Carter lost in efforts to limit liquor sales because blacks feared that Democrats were using the temperance issue to cut away at black freedoms. Marrs was accused of being a Democrat when he campaigned in 1873 for prohibition in Kentucky. Carter helped win the 1885 prohibition vote in Atlanta, only to lose a similar contest two years later when blacks accepted the argument that a vote for prohibition would erode black freedom. J.C. Price complained that "in all the prohibition and local option contests in the South numbers of colored men have been on the side of temperance and fought valiantly for its success. Many other would have . . . had they not been duped by misguided leaders who raised false cries of alarm, declaring that prohibition was a device to take away their dearly-brought liberty."[73] At a time when blacks witnessed the erosion of their rights as free people, the equation of temperance with that erosion was a sure way to impede the progress of the temperance movement among blacks.

The large southern white denominations began taking decisive action on temperance in the late 1880's, and soon thereafter the black churches began to express themselves more clearly. In their 1892 General Conferences, the AME and AME Zion Churches made it clear that ministers were to abstain from alcohol, not only for moral reasons but also for the sake of uplifting the race. Even while he was president of the Afro-American League, which advocated the retention of laws designed to protect black rights and objected to injustices against blacks, J.C. Price felt the church had to keep itself pure from the taint of alcohol in order to "lift up and give honor and freedom to the freedman." Through abstinence, "the race is to be uplifted morally, as well as materially and religiously."[74] With black disfranchisement, the issue was no longer whether blacks could vote for temperance, but whether temperance could regain the vote for blacks. The ministerial leaders concluded that sobriety would merit favorable treatment from powerful whites and thus enable blacks to strengthen their tentative hold on a limited freedom.

By 1902, temperance was the special cause of the black ministers. At the Education Congress in Atlanta, they spoke much more about alcohol than about politics. A panel of ministers representing the black denominations resoundingly condemned the use of alcohol as "one of the greatest hindrances to the progress and uplift of the race," and as one cause of black disfranchisement.[75]

Between 1865 and 1902, then, politics failed to "uplift the race." The temperance movement attracted black leaders because it seemed to point to a weakness in the freedman's attempt to gain confidence and power and to impress an increasingly hostile white society. Alcohol was also a topic on which blacks and whites could agree. And ministerial leaders thought that abstinence would overcome the ills that impeded the uplift of the race; it might even lead to a restoration of political rights. As the ministers adjusted to the ebb and flow of their political fortunes, they took up the call for temperance, because throughout the thirty-seven year period, one theme remained constant: the goal was to uplift the race.

[1] *The biographical data on H.M. Turner was compiled from several sources. The most important were: Daniel W. Culp, **Twentieth Century Negro Literature** (J.L. Nichols and Co., 1902; reprint ed., Miami: Mnemosyne Publishing Co., Inc., 1969), n.p.; William J. Simmons, **Men of Mark: Eminent, Progressive and Rising** (reprint ed., Chicago: Johnson Publishing Co., 1970) pp. 556-76; M.M. Ponton, **Life and Times of Henry M. Turner** (Atlanta: A.B. Caldwell Publishing Co., 1917; reprint ed., New York: Negro Universities Press, 1970).*

[2] *Henry McNeal Turner, "Speech to a Savannah Church," in **Respect Black: The Writing and Speeches of Henry McNeal Turner**, ed. Edwin R. Redkey (New York: Arno press, 1971), p. 32.*

[3] *Ibid., p. 31.*

[4] *Ibid., "On the Eligibility of Colored Members to Seats in the Georgia Legislature," p. 15.*

[5] *Ibid., p. 17.*

[6] *Ibid., p. 25.*

[7] *Ibid., "Emigration to Africa," p. 53.*

[8] *Ibid., "The Presidential Election," p. 175.*

[9] *The difficulty of comprehending and interpreting reconstruction history is attested to by the transitions in reconstruction historiography. In 1898 William A. Dunning published his **Essays on Reconstruction** which dominated the field for almost fifty years. Essential to the success of the work was the simple, straight forward, seemingly factual nature of his conclusions. He maintained that Reconstruction had been a failure and Reconstruction governments (which had been headed by blacks, scalawags, and carpetbaggers) had been corrupt, inefficient, and detrimental to the post-War recovery of the South. He further hailed the Democratic party as the Saviors of the South. He claimed they retired enormous debts, brought in industry on a basis more favorable to the South than had the Republican-Industrialists, restored order to a society that had been disrupted by black rule, and "redeemed" the South from continued interference of the federal government in its internal affairs.*

While not totally disregarding the work of Dunning and his disciples, more recent research has shown that these earlier conclusions were far too simplistic and reflective of the times in which they were written. The availability of additional source material and the refinement of various new research techniques have also raised questions about the reliability of Dunning's conclusions. The work of the revisionist historians in the last thirty years has not always produced a consensus on the specifics of reconstruction, but their writings have developed a new appreciation for the complexities inherent in the study of the period: Republicans and Democrats alike are not easily cast as villians or heroes and as importantly, revisionist writers have shown that blacks were neither the ignorant incompetents or the mere passive objects of reconstruction politics that the earlier historians had portrayed them to be.

It is this later revisionist viewpoint that informs the interpretation presented in this book. (Some of the strengths and weaknesses of revisionist historiography are clearly articulated in Herman Belz, "The New Orthodoxy in Reconstruction Historiography," *Reviews in American History* 1 (March 1973): 106-113). Though several sources were consulted and are incorporated in the discussion that follows, including several monograms and essays cited in footnotes, the most helpful were: Robert Cruden, *The Negro in Reconstruction* (Englewood Cliffs, N.J.: Prentice-Hall, 1969); Leon F. Litwack and Kenneth M. Stampp, editors, *Reconstruction; An Anthology of Revisionist Writings(* (Baton Rouge, Louisiana: Louisiana State University Press, 1969); and James M. McPherson, *The Struggle for Equality: Abolitionists and the Negro in the Civil War and Reconstruction* (Princeton: Princeton University Press, 1964).

[10]See McPherson, *The Struggle for Equality,* pp. 308-341.

[11]While the revisionist position does not overlook other factors that may have contributed to the Republican support of black voting rights, a strong case is made for the altruism of Republican support for this issue. See LaWanda and John Cox, "Negro Suffrage and Republican Politics: The problem of Motivation in Reconstruction Historiography," *The Journal of Southern History* 33 (August 1967): 303-330. Work by Glenn M. Linden examined the overall voting record of those who supported the extension of the vote to blacks to see whether they had consistently supported black rights. His conclusion was supportive of the position of LaWanda and John Cox. There was a great deal of consistency on pro-black issues in the voting records of those who supported the extension of the franchise to blacks even prior to the Civil War. Such evidence adds legitimacy to the "altruistic" theories. See Glenn M. Linden, "A Note on Negro Suffrage and Republican Politics," *The Journal of Southern History* 36 (May 1970): 411-20.

[12]Although Tennessee was re-admitted to the Union, investigations of the Memphis and New Orleans Riots, of May and July, 1866, during which eighty blacks and four whites were killed and over one hundred

and eighty-four persons were wounded, confirmed the need for major revisions in the existing plan of reconstruction in the opinion of Radical Republicans. For an extensive examination of the Congressional findings related to the riots, see: U.S., Congress, House, **Memphis Riots and Massacres,** 39th Congress, 1st session, 1866 (Washington, D.C.: Government Printing Office, 1866; reprint ed., New York: Arno Press, 1969) and U.S., Congress, House, **New Orleans Riots,** 39th Congress, 2nd Session, 1867 (Washington, D.C.: Government Printing Office, 1867; reprint ed., New York: Arno Press, 1969).

[13]See McPherson, **The Struggle for Equality,** pp. 341-66 also William L. Barney, "Johnson and Reconstruction: Swinging Around the Circle Again," **Reviews in American History** 8 (September 1980): 366-71 and Donald G. Nieman, "Andrew Johnson, the Freedman's Bureau, and the Problems of Equal Rights, 1865-1866," **The Journal of Southern History** 44 (August 1978): 399-420.

[14]In an article published in 1974 Professor Benedict argues that the Radical Republicans were Constitutional Conservatives who were not willing to broaden federal power over the states beyond the bare minimum in their attempt to protect loyal southern whites and blacks. Though he believes that the motivation was to protect Republican power in the South, his theory does not conflict with the newer "altruistic" motivation forwarded by some revisionists. More importantly, Benedict's theory provides another possible explanation for Republican willingness to restore power to the states themselves as soon as possible. See Michael Les Benedict, "Preserving the Constitution: The Conservative Basis of Radical Reconstruction," **Journal of American History** 61 (June 1974): 65-90.

[15]Because of the autonomy of the local church and the lack of a black Baptist denominational structure for much of the period, Baptist ministers were more independent of denominational pressures when it came to their involvement in politics. Furthermore, the fact that the majority of the black ministerial leadership was not actively involved in partisan politics is not as surprising as the relatively large number who were. When the involvement of black ministers is examined in light of the political activity of their southern white counterparts, the number of black ministers who were involved in politics seems very high. Rufus Spain observed that Southern Baptists "believed that Christians should exercise their political rights and privileges as individuals not collectively as denominations" and although they did not deny a minister the right to seek public office, the propriety of such was seriously questioned. (Rufus Spain, **At Ease in Zion: A Social History of Southern Baptists, 1865-1902** [Nashville: Vanderbilt University Press, 1961] pp. 42-43). According to Hunter Dickinson Farish, the Southern Methodists were also opposed to the direct involvement of the church in purely political matters and tended to discourage the involvement of Methodist ministers to an even greater degree than the Southern Baptists. (Hunter Dickinson Farish, **The Circuit Rider Dismounts: A Social History of Southern Methodism 1865-1900** [Richmond: The Dietz Press, 1938] pp. 153-58.)

[16]Charles H. Phillips, *The History of the Colored Methodist Episcopal Church in America* (Jackson, Tennessee: Publishing House CME Church, 1898; reprint ed., New York: Arno Press, 1972), pp. 71-2 and "The Colored Methodist Episcopal Church" by Lucius Holsey, *The Independent* (New York), March 5, 1891, p. 332.

[17]Wesley J. Gaines, *African Methodism in the South or Twenty-Five Years of Freedom* (Atlanta: Franklin Publishing House, 1890), pp. 21-2.

[18]Daniel A. Payne, *History of the African Methodist Episcopal Church* (Nashville, Tennessee: Publishing House of the AME Sunday School Union, 1891; reprint ed., New York: Arno Press, 1969), pp. 470-71.

[19]Ibid., p. 471.

[20]Albert W. Peques, *Our Baptist Ministers and Schools* (Springfield, Mass.: Wiley and Co., 1892; reprint ed., New York: Johnson Reprint Corporation, 1970), pp. 66-70; Carter G. Woodson, *The History of the Negro Church* (Washington, D.C.: Associated Publishers, 1921), pp. 204-5.

[21]William J. Simmons, *Men of Mark,* pp. 70-76.

[22]Theophilus G. Steward, "A Call to Thanksgiving and Praise," in *Pioneer Echoes: Six Speical Sermons* (Baltimore: Hoffman and Co., 1889), p. 43.

[23]Despite the black majority of voters in these elections, the South Carolina Convention was the only one where the majority of delegates were black. The South Carolina delegation was sixty-one percent black. In Louisiana, white and black delegates were evenly divided, but in all other state Constitutional Conventions, blacks were in the minority. White fears of "Negro Domination" never materialized either during or after Reconstruction. (See: John Hope Franklin, "The South's New Leaders" in *Black History: A Reappraisal,* ed. Melvin Drimmer [Garden City, New York: Doubleday Co., 1967] pp. 309-323).

[24]Simmons, *Men of Mark,* pp. 612-16 and Alexander Wayman, *Cyclopedia of African Methodism* (Baltimore: Methodist Episcopal Book Depository, 1882), p. 11.

[25]South Carolina, *Proceedings of the Constitutional Convention, 1868* (Charleston, SC: Denny and Perry, 1868, reprint ed., New York: Arno press, 1968), p. 421.

[26]Ibid., p. 423.

[27]Recent revisionist writings have suggested that Cain was correct in his concern for land reform. Indeed some historians have gone so far as to attribute the failure of reconstruction to provide blacks with

a permanent basis of equality on the failure to provide the freedman with land. While I agree that land reform was needed, it is somewhat of an oversimplification to attribute all of the shortcomings of reconstruction and the subsequent undermining of black rights to the lack of an extensive land reform program. Furthermore, it is somewhat unhistorical to assume what dangers could have been avoided had a particular course of action been followed. It is quite logical to think that while certain problems may have been avoided with major land reform legislation, certain other problems may have developed with unknowable consequences. See Peter Kolchin, "Race, Class, and Poverty in the Post-Civil War South," **Reviews in American History** 7 (December 1979): 515-26.

[28]Theophilus G. Steward, **Fifty Years in the Gospel Ministry** (Philadelphia: AME Book Concern, 1921), pp. 125-33. Elijah P. Marrs was also active as a stump speaker during this period. He was also elected the president of the Republican Club of Oldham County, Ky. See Elijah P. Marrs, **Life and History of the Rev. Elijah P. Marrs** (Louisville: The Bradley and Gilbert Company, 1885; reprint ed., Miami: Mnemosyne Publishing Co., Inc., 1969), p. 86.

[29]Steward, "Thanksgiving Sermon," **Pioneer Echoes,** pp. 47-55.

[30]Peques, **Our Baptist Ministers and Schools,** pp. 214-17; Simmons, **Men of Mark,** pp. 404-6; Woodson, **The History of the Negro Church,** pp. 203-5.

[31]I. Garland Penn, **The Afro-American Press and Its Editors** (Springfield, Mass.: Willey and Co., Publishers, 1891; reprint ed., New York: Arno Press, 1969), p. 144.

[32]See Thomas Oscar Fuller, **Twenty Years of Public Life, 1890-1910** (Nashville: National Baptist Publishing Board, 1910), p. 203; Peques, **Our Baptist Ministers and Schools,** pp. 439-53; Simmons, **Men of Mark,** pp. 5-19.

[33]Winfield Henri Mixon, **History of the African Methodist Episcopal Church in America, with Biographical Sketches** (Nashville, Tenn.: AME Church Sunday SChool Union, 1902), pp. 17-19; Penn, **The Afro-American Press,** pp. 201-202. Those ministers who were involved in the early phases of black political activity were also better trained than their peers.

[34]Alexander Herritage Newton, **Out of the Briars** (Philadelphia: AME Book Concern, 1910), pp. 1-10.

[35]In an essay on the history of the Methodist Episcopal Church, South published in 1911, Gross Alexander discussed the creation of the CME Church. He took time to discuss that Church's disinclination toward political issues and supposedly quoted directly from an article written by a CME bishop. "One peculiarity of the Colored Methodist Episcopal

Church," wrote Alexander, "is that 'it stands aloof from politics.' One rule of their Discipline is that their church-houses shall not be used for political speeches and meetings." While Alexander appears to be on safe ground to this point, his remaining quote from the CME Bishop (Bishop Lucius Holsey) is not accurate even if it may contain the spirit in which the bishop made his remarks. "'While exercising their rights as citizens, they endeavor to keep their religious assemblies free from that complication with political parties which had been so damaging to the spiritual interests of the colored people.'" (See Gross Alexander, **History of the Methodist Church, South,** The American Church History Series, Vol. II [NY: Charles Scribner's Sons, 1911], p. 92). Though Holsey did not say that political concerns had damaged the spiritual interests of blacks, it is obvious from his article on the CME Church, that the Colored Methodists did not represent their Church in their political activities. (For the full text of Bishop Holsey's article see Lucius Holsey, **The Independent [New York],** March 5, 1891, pp. 331-2).

[36]Although several sources contributed to the discussion of the return of Demoncratic control and the later rise of Jim Crowism, the most important sources were: Joseph H. Cartwright, **The Triumph of Jim Crow: Tennessee Race Relations in the 1880's** (Knoxville: The University of Tennessee Press, 1976); John Hope Franklin, **From Slavery to Freedom: A History of Negro Americans** (New York: Alfred A. Knopf, 3rd ed., 1967), pp. 324-343; Leon F. Litwack and Kenneth Stampp, editors, **Reconstruction: An Anthology of Revisionist Writings;** C. Vann Woodward, **The Strange Career of Jim Crow** (New York: Oxford University Press, 2nd edition, 1966). The persistency of the southern resistance to post-war change and the leaders of that resistance continue to attract the attention of historians of the period. Two examples of both their concern, and their opinion that resistance was long standing and led by a definable group of people are provided by LaWanda Cox's review of Micheal Perman's, **Reunion Without Compromise** and James Tice Moore's essay on "Redeemer" governments. (See LaWanda Cox, "Reconstruction Foredoomed? The Policy of Southern Consent," **Reviews in American History** 1 (December 1973): 541-7 and James Tice Moore, "Redeemers Reconsidered: Change and Continuity in the Democratic South, 1870-1900," **The Journal of Southern History** 44 [August 1978]: 357-78).

[37]Steward, **Fifty Years in the Gospel Ministry,** p. 128.

[38]Ibid., pp. 131-3. Also see William H. Heard, **From Slavery to the Bishopric in the AME Church** (reprint ed., New York: Arno Press, 1969), pp. 89-90.

[39]Elijah P. Marrs, **Life and History,** p. 90; also see p. 86.

[40]A.H. Newton, **Out of the Briars,** pp. 98-106.

[41]Thomas O. Fuller would not be elected to office until after 1890.

[42]Simmons, **Men of Mark,** pp.672-73; Heard, **From Slavery to the Bishopric,** pp. 39045. Others who held elected offices prior to the Democratic victories and who did not remain active in elective politics after 1880 were William Simmons, H.M. Turner, Richard Cain, James Hood, and Harrison Bouey. (See Simmons, **Men of Mark,** pp. 8-12; 70-76; 567-76; 613-616; 675-76). Turner did not seek elective office after he completed the remainder of the term during which he had been refused his Seat in the Georgia House. The early return of the Democratic party to the control of Georgia effectively curtailed black Republicanism in the state around 1870, which was much earlier than the return of Democratic party strength in most of the southern states.

[43]Penn, **The Afro-American Press,** pp. 216-22; Peques, **Our Baptist Ministers and Schools,** pp. 526-39; Simmons, **Men of Mark,** pp. 791-2.

[44]Peques, **Our Baptist Ministers,** pp. 66-70; Woodson, **The History of the Negro Church,** pp. 204-6. Others who withdrew from active participation in the party include many of those who were once elected officials as well as men like Elijah P. Marrs, W.H. Mixon and A.H. Newton. (See Simmons, **Men of Mark,** pp. 392-3; Newton, **Out of the Briars,** pp. 98-106, 155; Mixon, **History of the AME Church,** pp. 1-13). Although Mixon was not actively involved in the Republican party during the 1880's, he was elected and served as an Alabama delegate to the Republican National Convention in 1896.

[45]Monroe F. Jamison, **Autobiography and Work of Bishop M.F. Jamison, D.D.** (Nashville: Publishing House of the ME Church, South, 1912), p. 143.

[46]Gaines, **African Methodism in the South,** p. 82.

[47]Simmons, **Men of Mark,** pp. 9-10. At least one other ministerial leader was convinced that blacks had to support the best man regardless of his party. E.H. Lipscombe, a Baptist minister who was also a college professor and editor, was a Republican. However, in his paper **The Mountain Gleaner,** he gave support to a Democratic appointee who faced an uphill struggle for approval by a Republican Senate. In his editorial he wrote, "This is fair and manly, [the confirmation of Matthews as Recorder of Deeds] and should remind us that however good Republicans the colored man may naturally be, no policy of political coercion can be applied to them with success." (Penn, **The Afro-American Press,** p. 213).

[48]Racial violence occurred throughout the South but some of the most persistent and bloody violence occurred in Louisiana and South Carolina, two of the "unredeemed" states between 1874 and 1876. One of the bloodiest clashes occurred in Hamburg, South Carolina following a confrontation between black militiamen and white ex-confederate soldiers during a July 4, 1886 parade. Several black militiamen were killed after they were arrested on a charge of blocking traffic and the

ex-confederates came to insure that "injustice," was done. (See Franklin, **From Slavery to Freedom,** pp. 329-31).

[49]See Joseph H. Cartwright, **The Triumph of Jim Crow.** Although Cartwright studies race relations, he focuses on the political involvements of blacks in the decade. The study is very valuable despite two weaknesses. On one hand, he has a tendency to attribute greater political power to blacks than he demonstrates. While arguing for their independent political life, he shows that black political power was in fact dependent upon concessions from whites who controlled the poltical process. Black strength was not able to demand a share of the political leadership or prevent white exploitation of the black vote during the decade. On the other hand, Cartwright relies almost solely on white sources to determine black attitudes.

[50]An excellent discussion of this period is provided by C. Vann Woodward in Chapter 2 of **The Strange Career of Jim Crow,** pp. 31-65. Also see Joseph H. Cartwright, **The Triumph of Jim Crow** for a more detailed account of events in Tennessee. Chapter 14 in Vernon Lane Wharton, **The Negro in Mississippi 1865-1890** (New York: Harper and Row, 1965) is also instructive of a more generalized methodology adopted in the South for the elimination of the black vote.

[51]Gaines, **African Methodism in the South,** pp. 102-143.

[52]Simmons, **Men of Mark,** pp. 10-12.

[53]Penn, **The Afro-American Press,** pp. 300-305. In addition to McEwen, Penn refers to several other ministers, who in their capacity as editors defended the race and spoke out against racial injustice, including attempts to disenfranchise blacks. Two of these are part of this study: T.W. Coffee an AME who served in Alabama until 1896 and was the editor of **The Birmingham Era** and later of the Eufala, Alabama, **The Vindicator** and E.H. Lipscombe of North Carolina (Penn, pp. 210-213, 266-7). Henry M. Turner wrote several articles during the decade that protested against the restrictions placed on blacks in both the social and political spheres. Some of the more important of these can be found in Edwin R. Redkey's, **Respect Black: The Writings and Speeches of Henry McNeal Turner,** pp. 49, 52-72, 74-5. W.H. Mixon indicated that some editors in Alabama were forced to escape from Selma on account of racial conflicts. They were accused of "writing inflammatory editorials" in defense of black rights in the secular and denominational press between the 1889 and 1890 Annual Conferences of the AME Church. (See Mixon, **History of the AME Church,** pp. 89 ff.)

[54]H.M. Turner, "The Force Bill," in Edwin R. Redkey, **Respect Black,** p. 81.

[55]Discussions of the political climate of the 1890's including black disenfranchisement and populism, can be found in several sources. The

most helpful for me included: John Eighmy, **Churches in Cultural Captivity: A History of Social Attitudes of Southern Baptists** (Knoxville, Tennessee: The University of Tennessee Press, 1976), pp. 41-56; John Hope Franklin, **From Slavery to Freedom**, pp. 332-43; C. Vann Woodward, **The Strange Career of Jim Crow**, pp. 67-109.

[56]Some of the crucial decisions rendered by the Court during the period covered by this book include: 1) the 1883 decision that virtually destroyed the accommodation provisions of the Civil Rights Act of 1875; 2) the 1890 decision that permitted states to constitutionally require segregation on carriers; 3) the 1896 Plessy V. Ferguson decision that allowed "separate but equal" and 4) the 1898 decision in Williams V. Mississippi which upheld the suffrage provisions of the new constitution for Mississippi. Turner reacted immediately to the 1883 decision, calling it "barbarous." As other decisions were rendered that further destroyed black legal resistance to white supremacy, Turner published responses to all the decisions. (See Turner, "The Barbarous Decision of the Supreme Court," in Redkey, **Respect Black**, pp. 60-69). Fuller's reaction to the 1898 decision is found in his autobiography: Thomas Oscar Fuller, **Twenty Years of Public Life, 1890-1910** (Nashville: National Baptist Publishing Board, 1910), pp. 43-5.

[57]One of the most violent incidents took place in Wilmington, NC where several blacks were killed. Fuller tried to calm black fears that following the Mississippi Supreme Court decision and the Democratic violence they would be disenfranchised, but his optimism proved unfounded.

[58]Silas X. Floyd, **National Perils: An Address Delivered at Atlanta, Georgia, Monday, January 2, 1899** (August, Georgia: The Georgia Baptist Print, 1898).

[59]W.D. Chappelle, "How Can the Friendly Relations Now Existing Between the Two Races in the South be Strengthened and Maintained," in Culp, **Twentieth Century Negro Literature**, pp. 63-68. Also see S.N. Brown's article, **Twentieth Century Negro Literature**, pp. 68-71.

[60]George W. Clinton, "To What Extent is the Negro Pulpit Uplifting the Race," in Culp, **Twentieth Century Negro Literature**, p. 119.

[61]Fuller, **Twenty Years**, pp. 82-87. Other reactions by the ministerial elite to various developments during the period were numerous. Some examples can be found in Charles H. Phillips, **The History of the Colored Methodist Episcopal Church in America**, pp. 119 ff.; H.H. Proctor, **Between Black and White: Autobiographical Sketches** (Freeport, New York: Books for Libraries Press, 1971), pp. 89-108; Culp, **Twentieth Century Negro Literature**, pp. 42-45, 46-48, 442-444.

[62]Edward R. Carter, "Let Us Play the Man," in **The Black Side: A Partial History of the Business, Religious and Educational Side of the Negro in Atlanta, Georgia** (Atlanta, GA: E.R. Carter, 1894), pp. 284-85.

[63]George A. Goodwin, "Is it Time for the Negro Colleges in the South to be put in the Hands of Negro Teachers," in Culp, **Twentieth Century Negro Literature,** pp. 132-9; Silas X. Floyd, **National Perils,** pp. 3-4, 7, 9, 12-14; Charles H. Phillips, **From the Farm to the Bishopric: An Autobiography** (Nashville, Tenn: Parthenon Press, 1932), p. 119; H.M. Turner, "Will it be Possible for the Negro to Attain, In This Country, Unto the American Type of Civilization?," in Culp, p. 44. Even as Turner admitted this, however, he immediately emphasizes that those institutions have not made America a civilized nation. Other examples of respect and appreciation for American's positive qualities can be found in Culp, pp. 468-72; Proctor, **Between Black and White,** pp. viii, 108; J.W.E. Bowen and I. Garland Penn, editors, **The United Negro: His Problems and His Progress** (Atlanta: D.E. Luther Publishing Co., 1902), pp. ii-xii, 67-72, 77-83, 493-96.

[64]Carter, "Let Us Play the Man," in **The Black Side,** pp. 289-90.

[65]C.H. Phillips, **From the Farm to the Bishopric,** p. 171; Thomas O. Fuller, **Twenty Years in Public Life,** pp. 43-45.

Henry M. Turner's early doubts about political uplift have already been mentioned, but another member of the ministerial elite who had early doubts about the possibility of uplifting the race through political means was Theophilus G. Steward. He held his opinion even while he was working for the Republican party in Georgia. His clearest statement was in 1868 when he wrote a speech on the key to social reform. He did not accept the idea that politics was that key. "To elevate the blacks and place them beyond the rash of foul wrong, power, force, must be put into their hands. Yes; says one. 'The power of the ballot!' Give them the elective franchise and nothing else, and you put saddles on their backs for white politicians to ride upon, and well will they use them." (Steward, **Fifty Years in the Gospel Ministry,** p. 103).

[66]Bowen and Penn, **The United Negro,** p. 491. Further ministerial comments on the abandonment of politics as a tool of uplift can be found in Bowen and Penn, pp. 8-11; A.H. Newton, **Out of the Briars,** pp. 42-45, 46-48, 63-71, 323-25. Even the Afro-American Council under Alexander Walters did not emphasize the role politics could or should play in uplifting the race. Walters and the Council deplored the disenfranchisement, the lynching, the injustice, and the segregation forced on blacks, but politics would not eliminate those. (See Alexander Walter, **My Life and Work** (New York: Fleming H. Revell Co., 1917), pp. 109-131.

[67]While members of Southern Baptist and ME Church, South churches tried to avoid involvement in political concerns, and preferred the technique of moral suasion in promoting temperance, by the late 1880's they began to sanction the use of political methods to place legal limits on the sale and consumption of alcohol. The local option referendum was usually preferred and although the temperance crusade in the South

began by opposing intoxication and the use of hard liquor, it soon included beer and wine among those beverages that were prohibited. Furthermore, the churches moved from mildly reprimanding church members who violated the restrictions in the early years of temperance agitation to expelling members by the end of the century. A more detailed history of the attitudes of southern white denominations toward the Temperance movement of the late nineteenth century can be found in: John Eighmy, *Churches in Cultural Captivity,* pp. 49-56; Hunter Dickinson Farish, *The Circuit Rider Dismounts,* pp. 305 ff; Fufus Spain, *At East in Zion,* pp. 177-195.

[68]The idea that there was a connection between abstinence and social status is discussed in Joseph R. Gusfield's, *Symbolic Crusade: Status Politics and the American Temperance Movement* (Urbana: University of Illinois Press, 1963)--pages 61-110 cover the period following the Civil War to the turn of the century. Though Gusfield does not direct his findings to the freedmen, my conclusions about the relationship between temperance and uplift, arrived at independent of Gusfield's study, indicate that Gusfield's linkage of the Temperance movement and status is valid for the black ministerial elite who were the topic of this book.

[69]W.H. Mixon, *History of the AME Church,* pp. 47, 79. Other conferences experienced a similar increase in concern over the issue of temperance. Wesley J. Gaines makes mention of the increase in temperance concern in Georgia after 1881. Gaines himself called for total abstinence and said "The voice of every preacher must be raised against the liquor power in every form: (*African Methodism,* p. 286). The 1886 conference of the CME Church also voiced its support of the Temperance movement and thereafter the issue grew in importance (C.H. Phillips, *History of the CME Church,* pp. 138 ff.).

[70]See Joseph Gusfield, *Symbolic Crusade.*

[71]Marrs, *Life and History,* pp. 115-116; J.W. Hood, *The Negro in the Christian Pulpit, or, The Two Characters and Two Destinies, As Delineated in Twenty-One Practical Sermons* (Raleigh, NC: Edwards, Broughton and Co., 1884), pp. 33-48, 105-21; Newton, *Out of the Briars,* pp. 213-223. Other examples of temperance men among the ministerial elite during the 1870's and 80's are W.J. White who advocated temperance in the Baptist paper in Georgia (Penn, *Afro-American Press,* pp. 216-222); G.V. Clark a teacher and congregationalist minister in Georgia (James T. Haley, *Afro-American Encyclopedia; or, The Thoughts, Doings, and Sayings of the Race* [Nashville, Tenn.: Haley & Florida,], pp. 615-17); Daniel A. Gaddie, a Baptist leader and denominational organizer in Kentucky (Peques, *Our Baptist Ministers and Schools,* pp. 206-209; Simmons, *Men of Mark,* pp. 445-7); and J.C. Price who began his illustrative temperance career during the period. In 1887 Price was invited by an interracial temperance group, at the urging of C.H. Phillips, to speak in Memphis. He came and was well received. (See Phillips, *From the Far to the Bishopric,* p. 71).

[72]Hood, "The Earliest Christian Symbol," in *The Negro in the Christian Pulpit,* pp. 118, 120.

[73]Marrs, *Life and History,* p. 100; E.R. Carter, *Biographical Sketches of Our Pulpit* (Atlanta: E.R. Carter, 1888), pp. vic-vid; J.C. Price, "Temperance," in Haley, *Afro-American Encyclopedia,* p. 192.

[74]See Haley, *Afro-American Encyclopedia,* pp. 188-9, 190, 191.

[75]Penn, *The United Negro,* pp. 248-67.

CHAPTER 4
SECURING THE PROMISE
OF UPLIFT: EDUCATION
AND THE
MINISTERIAL ELITE

The Colored Baptist Missionary State Convention of Alabama was meeting in its 1873 Annual Session When William H. McAlphine offered a resolution that the Convention establish a school for the training of preachers and teachers under the direct control of the Convention. The resolution, which was not passed until 1874, indicated McAlpine's lifelong commitment to education. Even more important, McAlpine's determination to seek education, his conviction that minister needed to be trained, his concern for educating as many people as possible, and his continued close relationship to the institutional black church reflected the educational concerns of his peers among the ministerial elite from 1865 to 1902.

The ministerial elite were cognizant of the educational deficiencies of the freedman and sought to address them soon after the end of the Civil War. From a practical viewpoint, a rudimentary education was essential if the race was going to survive. But the concern for education was not only a practical matter. It was also a reflection of a theological position that made people responsible for developing their God–given abilities. The ministerial elite accepted the concepts of the fatherhood of God and the brotherhood of man—and the corresponding responsibilities, including the development of black intellectual ability. With the destruction of the political option as a means for the uplift of the race, education became even more important. In the final years of the period, education was viewed as the means by which the race would be eventually uplifted.

The examination of the ministerial concern for education as a means for uplifting the race, however, once again reveals the critical interplay of what we have called accommodation and possibility. The accommodationist tendencies are apparent in both the forms and the content of education among blacks. Yet, the demand for education was an affirmation of black possibility. Clerical leaders like William McAlpine saw themselves as exemplifying the truth that education would help blacks achieve equality even in the midst of the dominant society's denial of black humanity and possibility.

McAlpine's first exposure to formal education was experienced while he was a slave. Born into slavery in Buckingham County, Virginia in 1847, at the age of three he was sold, along with his mother and brother, to a Presbyterian minister named Robert McAlpine. Under normal circumstances McAlpine would have had little or no opportunity to receive an education while a slave, but his master's death in 1855 presented him with a unique opportunity. As part of the settlement of his former master's estate, William became the property of Rev. McAlpine's son who was a doctor. He served as a nurse to the doctor's children who received private instruction from a tutor in their home. As their nurse, William lived in the house and was exposed to whatever the children were learning. As a result, he learned to read and write and also gained proficiency in arithmetic, grammar, and geography.

William McAlpine's next encounter with formal instruction was motivated by his religious experience. Shortly before the Civil War ended, he was converted and baptized as a member of the white Baptist church at Talledega. Soon after his conversion, McAlpine became convinced that he was called into the ministry, but he refused to seek a license to preach because he felt he was not adequately trained. The necessary training being unavailable to him, he worked as a carpenter and school teacher for a few years immediately following the War's end. Seeking to acquire the training he felt he needed to enter the ministry, however, he enrolled in the newly opened Talledega College in 1868. He then sought and received a license to preach. Two years later in 1871, he was ordained. McAlpine continued in school until 1873. While in school he served as the pastor of a church in Talledega and, later, of a congregation in Jacksonville, Alabama. In addition, he continued teaching school, and, convinced that others should attend Talledega, McAlpine recruited students for the school during the summers.

Despite his leaving school in 1873, lacking only six course hours for his degree, McAlpine's commitment to education was unfaltering. Active in the black Baptist state convention since its organization in 1870, McAlpine believed that despite the work being done at Talledega College, there was a need for a black Baptist school in Alabama. This led him to propose his 1873 resolution. The resolution was delayed until a committee, appointed by the Convention, conferred with white Baptist leaders about the practicality of the proposal. The whites advised them not to start a school, but McAlpine was able to convince the 1874 Convention that the project should be undertaken. The delegates authorized him to spend six months trying to solicit funds. The school's future rested with McAlpine's work, and according to a contemporary, it could not have been in better hands: "my first impression of him was that he was a man of special mission, and I immediately sympathized with him and with the school project."[1] McAlpine must have affected others the same way for although the initial efforts were disappointing, the Convention again appointed him as the chief fund raiser. By 1877, his efforts were securing a thousand dollars above his expenses, but McAlpine began to doubt that he could solicit the necessary funds, and he declined to accept a third appointment. By that time the Convention was committed to McAlpine's dream, and the delegates to the 1877 Session voted to use the money already solicited to purchase a tract of land at Selma, Alabama, for the establishment of the school. A few months later, McAlpine was asked to serve as president of what became Selma University. He served two years before resigning the post, feeling that the president of the school ought to have more formal training.

McAlpine's resignation in 1883 did not signal an end to his concern for education or his involvement with educational institutions. Rather, it simply marked a new beginning. While continuing to serve as a pastor and a leader in the Baptist Foreign Mission Convention of the United States, McAlpine also served as the only black member of the Board of Trustees of the Lincoln Normal University. He also returned to Selma as a theological instructor under appointment by the Board of Domestic Missions of the Southern Baptist Convention. In recognition of his contributions to education and especially to Selma University, the Board of Trustees for the school awarded him an honorary doctorate. The award took on added significance because Selma's Board of Trustees was composed primarily of ministers, who were his peers.[2]

McAlpine's life demonstrated a belief that education was essential for uplifting the race. And in this belief he was joined by the other black ministerial leaders. As the century came to a close, education became increasingly important as a means of uplift. The theology of the ministers had always affirmed the race's potential for uplift. But politics had failed to bring the potential to reality. As the century ended, temperance stood alone as the last dim reminder of the bright hope that politics would uplift the race. As political solutions seemed less promising, the ministers placed more and more faith in education as the vehicle for uplifting the race. By 1902 the leading clergy were convinced that education would secure the elusive promise of uplift.

1. EARLY CONCERN FOR EDUCATING BLACKS

Among the tragic legacies of slavery was the fact that at the close of the Civil War, the vast majority of the black population was illiterate. Hampered by restrictions on the education of slaves, blacks had few opportunities to learn even the basic skills of reading and writing.[3] Some did learn to read the Bible, often as a result of their having become Christians, but even this was not common. Census figures indicate that as late as 1890, 81.9 percent of the 1.3 million blacks born before 1855 were illiterate.[4]

The educational deprivations did not go unnoticed. Between 1855 and 1902, a number of agencies, denominational societies, and private philanthropists contributed money and time to educate the freedman. Advancing into the South behind the Union Army, some organizations began their work before 1865. But once the War was over, teachers poured into the South, establishing schools for blacks and cooperating with blacks in their own institutions.[5]

The fact that white organizations and teachers were intimately involved with the freedman's early education implies that from the beginning the freedmen were exposed to the dominant society's standards and were expected to accommodate themselves to these to a certain degree. Furthermore, continued white support of institutions established by whites was frequently contingent upon the institution's conformity to acceptable norms and procedures. For the most part, blacks appeared to have few problems with accommodating themselves to these expectations, especially in the year immediately after the end of the Civil War. Even schools founded and supported by blacks reflected the educational standards and philsophy prevalent in the dominant society. But education more than any other endeavor, exemplified the way in which accommodation could have a subversive underside.

The Federal Government, through the Bureau of Refugees, Freedmen, and Abandoned Lands, had a prominent part in the education of blacks. Between 1866 and 1870, when it expended its last Congressional appropriation for black education, the "Freedman's Bureau" spent over five million dollars for black education in the South.[6] The funding, used primarily to support educational efforts of northern benevolent societies, came at a propitious time, for it helped to keep new schools functioning until the sponsoring agencies found sufficient money to keep them operating. Freedman's Bureau funds also paid teacher salaries, renovated abandoned government buildings, paid for confiscated property for use as schools, and transported teachers. The Bureau, under the leadership of General O.O. Howard further demonstrated its commitment to black education by encouraging the use of black teachers, and through the office of the General Superintendent of Education it coordinated the efforts of other organizations committed to educating the freedman.[7]

The most active private northern organization involved in the education of blacks was the American Missionary Association. Acting out its belief that blacks could be educated in much the same way as whites,[8] the AMA devoted itself to providing a non-sectarian Christian education for the freedman, and by 1872 it had established eighty-nine lower grade schools and seven chartered institutions of higher learning, including Talledega College, Fisk, and Atlanta University. At least eight of our seventy-eight ministers attended or graduated from the chartered institutions supported by the AMA.

The American Missionary Association did not stand alone. Other northern societies, linked to Protestant denominations, established schools as well as churches. The most prominent were the Freedmen's Aid Society of the Methodist Episcopal Church and the American Baptist Home Mission

Society, established in 1866, charged with the task of mission and education in the South,[10] initially worked only with blacks; by 1869 the FAS supported fifty-five elementary level schools, six colleges, and two Bible institutes all designed to promote religion and education.[11] The American Baptist Home Mission Society had been in existence since 1832, but after the Civil War most of its resources were directed toward educating the freedman. By 1890, the Home Mission Society owned and managed twelve schools of higher education employing one hundred forty-one teachers for 2,692 students. The property value of the Soceity schools exceeded $800,000.[12] The Home Mission Society also helped support other Baptist schools it did not own or control. Twenty-one of the seventy-eight ministers did at least some of their academic work at one of the schools of the Home Mission Society.

Southern denominations, led by the Baptists and Methodists, joined in the work of educating blacks after the War. Hampered by the wartime devastation, as well as by questions about black ability, the southern white denominations began later and provided less support of black education than their northern counterparts.[13] Yet, white fear of northern teachers and their egalitarian theories of education as well as the prevailing belief, forwarded by such eminent churchmen as Atticus Haygood, that black education was better off in the hands of southern whites who understood them best, led southern whites to assume some responsibility for the education of blacks.[14] The Board of Domestic Missions of the Southern Baptist Convention expressed an early interest in a Christian education for blacks through religious institues staffed by missionaries, but not until well after the northern Baptists had established a school at Augusta could the Domestic Board report any progress in the education of blacks. By the 1890's, however, the Board abandoned its attempt to start a Southern Baptist school for blacks.[15] The Methodist Episcopal Church, South, was somewhat more successful. With the rapid decrease in the number of black members after 1865, the Southern Methodists did little for black education until the formation of the Colored Methodist Episcopal Church in 1870. In the ensuing years, pleas from the CME Church for white help led the ME Church, South, in 1884 to establish Paine College in Augusta, Georgia.

Gifts from individuals helped, but black higher education in the South received a major boost in 1882 when John F. Slater, a wealthy New England merchant, established the John F. Slater Fund with a grant of one million dollars to be used for "the uplifting of the lately emancipated population of the southern states, and their posterity, by conferring on them the blessings of Christian education."[16] By 1902, the Slater Fund had given almost $700,000 to black institutions of higher learning. Though most of the money went to Hampton Institute in Virginia and Tuskegee Institute in Alabama, both of which had strong industrial arts programs, at least twenty-one other schools received Foundation funds.[17] And at least twenty-three of the seventy-eight ministers attended schools that received funds from the Slater Foundation.

The black ministers valued the contributions of whites. Several attended the schools supported by whites; some of these men later worked with white-controlled agencies concerned with black education. Fifteen preachers served on the faculties or trustee boards of the white-supported schools or served as missionaries for church-related educational agencies. The ministers acknowledged their gratitude publicly. In his book on **The Negro Baptist Pulpit,** E.M. Brawley, a Baptist minister, cited the work of the Baptist agencies and praised "men like Nathan Bishop and John P. Crozer" [who] "gave their thousands for our uplifting."[18] Brawley was grateful not only for the assistance but also for the implication that all humanity could benefit from educational opportunities—a familiar theological claim made by black ministers. M.C.B. Mason, a Methodist Episcopal minister and denominational executive, who received degrees from white-supported schools before acquiring a Ph.D. from Syracuse University, pointed with pride in 1902 to the strides blacks had made, with white help, since emancipation:

> *In addition to the work of the Freedmen's Aid Society there are the American Missionary Association. . ., the Baptist Home Mission Society, the Lutheran Evangelical Society-all of which support institutions for Christian learning for the education of the colored people throughout the South. These schools are mainly for the higher and secondary education of the Negro and have accomplished untold good.[19]*

Another minister, also writing in 1902, even felt that white leadership of predominantly black schools had been and would be desirable, because the South would prevent able blacks from accomplishing as much as white leaders.[20]

Whites made a major contribution to the education of the freedman; the ministerial elite valued those efforts. But blacks also supported their own forms of educational "uplift." The ministerial leaders, believing that education was the pathway to uplift, were among the strongest advocates of education, and they thought that education should begin with the black minister who, once uplifted, would help uplift the whole race.

2. SECURING AN EDUCATED MINISTRY

William McAlpine was literate at the close of the Civil War but most of the ministers were not. Of the forty-one clergymen born in or before 1855, twenty-three (54%) were illiterate when they were emancipated. Of the twenty-nine born before 1855 who were reared in slavery, twenty-two (76%) were illiterate at the War's end. Despite the differences, both groups could and did rise to clerical prominence. But among the younger clergy—those born after 1855—education became the mark of the denominational leaders, the authors, the subjects of biographies and histories, and the pastors of influential churches. Within a few years after the Civil War, all seventy-seven men born after 1855, twenty-two (51%) had at least a Bachelor's degree by 1902—a goal reached by only 8 (20%) of the older ministers.[21]

Undergirding the demand for an educated ministry was the fear that an untrained clergy would misinterpret the Bible and misinform the people. Daniel Payne, a patriarch of the AME Church, agreed with the negative assessment of the typical black preacher that Booker T. Washington advanced in August, 1890.[22] Developing a position espoused by A.N. McEwen, a leading Baptist preacher-editor in Alabama, Washington had complained that most black ministers, being uneducated, failed to expose the masses to the truths of Christianity. He admonished ministers to seek theological training at a variety of levels, suggesting the creation of Bible schools for ministers of average abilities. Writing to Washington almost three months later, Daniel Payne supported Washington's contention and added his own evaluation of the situation. "I say emphatically, in the presence of the great Head of the Church, that not more than one-third of the ministers, Baptist and Methodist, in the South are morally and intellectually qualified."[23] As a result of Washington's concern, Tuskegee opened its Bible school in January, 1893, stating in its catalogue that "the demand for an educated ministry is growing throughout the South, and those who expect to preach in the future must prepare themselves for the work."[24]

William Gaines, an AME, lectured for several years at Fisk University and at Gammon Seminary, stressing the importance of an education as a prerequisite for interpreting the Bible and attributing the doctrinal ignorance of black Christians to the weaknesses of ministers who did not know how to teach doctrine. "The gospel," wrote Gaines, "cannot be fully and properly presented by a man who is ignorant, and is satisfied with his ignorance."[25] A.W. Peques, a North Carolina Baptist, insisted that ministers were "set forth for one specific purpose: to preach the Word." "But they cannot preach the Word," he added, "unless they know it."[26] The elite clergy valued education. They viewed it as a necessity for interpreting the Word. Education had lifted them to positions of leadership and it had shaped their own views of the Bible. They could only believe that it could do the same for other preachers of the Word.

They also believed in the power of their own example. The uplift of the ministry would provide an example of uplift for the race, so the ministerial leaders felt that they had to be uplifted educationally if there was to be hope for the race. William E. Partee, a Presbyterian minister in North Carolina and Florida, insisted openly that the race could not rise above the pulpit.[27] The minister would be the model, the example, for others to follow. It was this idea that led Lucius Holsey, a CME bishop, to write, "we begin with preachers and teachers, carefully and patiently training and indoctrinating them in those great moral and religious principles that lie at the basis of an elevated and sound moral manhood."[28] E.M. Brawley, a Baptist, thought that he detected moral improvement in the race after an increased number of young men began training for the ministry and leading exemplary lives.[29]

Failure to educate the ministry, therefore, was sure to have an adverse effect on black people. R.P. Wyche, a moderator of the Catawba Synod of the Presbyterian Church in North Carolina, claimed that precisely because ministers were leaders, an uneducated ministry would hinder the freedman.

> The pulpit has long been recognized as a potent factor in the formation of character, and the Negro pulpit is not an exception to the general rule. Its influence may be elevating or degrading. The character and the ability of the man in the pulpit will determine its nature and extent. The office itself implies an active interest in the elevation of man from the lower to the highest stage of life. But the uneducated ministry proved itself unequal to the task of teaching and leading the people along the difficult path of true excellence.[30]

S.N. Vass, a district Secretary for the American Baptist Publication Society, was even more harsh in his education of an uneducated ministry. He claimed that the greatest factor halting the advance of Christianity among blacks was "incompetent leaders who nevertheless lead the people."[31] "An ignorant man," added William Gaines, "is placed where usefulness to him is impossible or limited to the narrowest bounds."[32] The 1880-81 catalogue of the Nashville Normal and Theological Institute asked its theological students to read and consider that "the preacher and pastor must needs be the teacher and guide of the ignorant; but how shall he guide others, from whose own eyes the scales of ignorance have not fallen?"[33] A "call" to the ministry was not enough; one had to prepare oneself to fulfill that call; preparation meant education. The minister who failed to educate himself could not provide an example of uplift for others to follow.

Given the preoccupations of the ministerial leaders, it was not surprising that the black denominations began to seek ways to improve the educational level of black ministers. With limited resources, the denominations began to reverse centuries of educational restrictions by starting schools, mainly to train ministers. The founding of Selma University by the black Baptists of Alabama was one effort made by blacks to educate ministers. Louisiana black Baptists made advances by establishing schools at the local level to teach preachers how to read and write,[34] though they also cooperated with the Baptist Home Mission Society in founding Leland University in New Orleans. Black Baptists in South Carolina, Georgia, and North Carolina started small academies and institutes that they controlled, but like their Louisiana brethren they also cooperated with the Home Mission Society in starting Benedict College, Augusta Institute (later moved to Atlanta and named Atlanta Baptist Seminary), and Shaw University. In Tennessee black Baptists gave birth to Howe Institute in Memphis. The school later received support from the Home Mission Society, but black Baptists were the major supporters of the school as well as the primary beneficiaries of its work. Thomas O. Fuller, who had been a pastor and elected office-holder in North Carolina before accepting an invitation to preach in Memphis and teach at Howe, wrote that the students there, "studied systematic theology, church history, preparation and delivery of sermons and on Friday we studied the Sunday School lesson and prepared a sermon outline for Sunday." The practical training served the congregations in the Memphis area, which in turn encouraged their pastors to seek education. According to Fuller, "the ministers went to their pulpits on Sunday with a fresh live message and their congregations were delighted and were so free in expressing their approval of their pastor's new gift, the pastor found it necessary to continue studying."[35] Schools like Howe were started in every southern state; it is impossible to know exactly how many there were. A.W. Peques indicated that in 1890 black Baptists owned and operated 46 schools with 181 students preparing for the ministry at an advanced level.[36]

The various Methodist bodies joined in the movement to develop an educated ministry by establishing black schools. The African Methodist Episcopal Church had already purchased Wilberforce University in Ohio from the ME Church in 1863 at the urging of such leaders as Bishop Daniel Payne. After the War, however, the issue of establishing institutions of "higher learning" in the South, where AME membership was rapidly increasing, emerged when some members of the Church's North Georgia Conference wanted to start a school early in the 1870's. Lacking funds, the Conference accepted Henry McNeal Turner's offer to tutor ministerial students as an interim measure. An attempt to begin a theological institute in Atlanta in 1878 failed, but the founding of Morris Brown University three years later brought to fruition the dream of establishing a school in Georgia.[37] A year earlier Allen University had been founded in Columbia, South Carolina, by the South Carolina Conference and within a few years after Morris Brown opened, AME conferences in Alabama, North Carolina, Florida, and Mississippi started their own schools, designed mainly to train ministers.

The insistence of several AME Zion ministers led that body to incorporate what later became Livingstone College in 1879. After a tenuous start, which included closing the school for a short time because of financial problems, the Board of Trustees asked J.C. Price to serve as the financial agent. His successful effort at fund raising, combined with his national and international reputation, led the Trustees to name him president of the school in 1882. Under his leadership, the school secured the finances it needed and became a primary source of trained ministers for the AME Zion Church.[38] Several other schools of importance were started in the 1890's.

Although the Colored Methodist Episcopal Church had close ties with the ME Church, South, the leaders of the denomination wanted schools owned and controlled by blacks to train black clergy. As early as the Third General Conference of the CME Church in 1874, Bishop W. H. Miles expressed a desire, as the senior bishop, that the ministers of the denomination be educated. He had already received the support of the Kentucky Conference for building a school in Louisville, and he had purchased the land. In his address to the representatives of the whole church, he challenged the church to commit itself to educating the ministers.

> *Nothing can be substituted for it, nothing can be taken in exchange or put in its place to answer the universal call of the church: not that education is all in all, but it is one of those mighty and potent means employed by God to make known his will and the revelation of his word to the benighted sons of a degraded and apostate race. . . .*

> *We may not expect to do a great deal at present in educating the masses of our people, but we can educate our young preachers that may come into the ministry from time to time.[39]*

Despite Bishop Miles' efforts to secure the money needed, the young CME Church was unsuccessful in its attempt to establish the Kentucky school. Another CME bishop, however, was just as committed to education: Isaac Lane, an ex-slave who had educated himself, led his church to found Lane Institute in Jackson, Tennessee, in 1879. Three years later the first building was erected. The school, which eventually became a college, was the denomination's largest and best-supported institution at the close of the century.[40]

Although the black denominations did not begin the work of founding schools until after emancipation, ten of the seventy-eight leading ministers received at least part of their advanced education at the new denominational schools that were controlled by blacks.[41] The list includes Livingstone student, S.G. Atkins, who served as the president of the North Carolina Teachers' Association and Secretary of Education for the AME Zion Church; Richard Cain, the South Carolina pastor-politician, who received his A.B. degree from Wilberforce; W.R. Pettiford, a pastor, businessman, and convention president for Alabama Baptists, who studied theology at Selma University; and the AME preacher, W.H. Mixon, who also studied at Selma and was an editor of an Alabama newspaper and an officer of the AME's Payne University.

Though the specifics of ministerial training varied depending on the denomination and the academic level of the students, the education that the ministers received, even in college theological departments, was rooted in biblical studies and in the practical duties of the pastor. An examination of the curriculum offered in the theology departments of the Nashville Institute (Baptist), Morris Brown University (AME), the Phelps School of Religion at Tuskegee Institute (non-denominational), and at the Gammon School of Theology, the first school established by the Methodist Episcopal Church solely for the training of ministers, illustrates these two concerns. At the Phelps School of Religion, which had been founded to provide ministers with a practical theological education, English Bible lessons were given five days a week during the first year and three days a week during the next two years. These lessons concentrated on the history, chronology, personalities, literary character, and general content of each book in the Bible. During the third year students also engaged in more specific analyses of several books. At the Nashville Institute, Bible study was part of the daily work of all the students at the school, therefore the curriculum in the two-year theological course stressed the teaching of basic Christian doctrines both years and required such practical courses as "The Construction of Sermons" the first year and "Baptist Apologetics" and "Pastoral Theology" during the second year. The pastoral theology courses included lectures on the work of the pastor, methods of church business, and ordination.[42] Elijah P. Marrs, a Kentucky Baptist, who attended Nashville Institute in 1874 was impressed not only with the courses but with the Christian attitude of the faculty.

> *I made it my endeavor to please the faculty in all things. The faculty of the Nashville College were all great Christian workers. No labor or study was entered into without first invoking the Divine blessing. It was a rare thing for a sinner to remain six months without being converted. They made it their special duty to converse with the students frequently on this all important subject.[43]*

Such attitudes provided the students with additional lessons in the way pastors ought to function. After 1892 the Nashville Institute modified its theology department, placing it within the regular four-year college course. Students who wanted to enter the ministry were encouraged to complete their undergraduate degree at the Institute and then enter the Bachelor of Divinity degree program at the Richmond Seminary in Virginia where the American Baptist Home Mission Society had consolidated its seminary level programs. From its opening in 1883, Gammon had a three-year program that led to a Bachelor of Divinity degree for students with college degrees. Students enrolled in the degree programs had to pass Greek and Hebrew language courses. Several other courses were designed to develop exegetical skills, and lecture courses in historical and systematic theology also punctuated the three-year curriculum. But despite the more academic approach to the Scriptures at Gammon, the curriculum featured courses that were designed to assist men carry out the daily responsibilities of the pastorate. Practical theology courses taught in each of the three years incorporated such elements as lectures on pastoral visiting, church management and work, and the development and delivery of sermons to adults and children. In the words of the Gammon catalogue, the aid of the school was "to do practical work in helping men towards success in the ministry," and "to teach biblical, rather than a scientific, theology; to unfold a Christ-centered theology, expressed in Scriptural terms, rather than a dogmatic theology cast in scientific phrases."[44] By 1899 Morris Brown's Theology Department was also a three-year program. The curriculum stressed Greek and Hebrew language skills and offered courses in Christian theology, church history, and systematic theology. Yet, even Morris Brown's more academic program yielded to the need to provide practical training for ministerial students in the third year with courses on pulpit rhetoric and practical theology. Morris Brown also complemented its college level courses with a Missionary Department that was designed to train less academically prepared individuals in the practical aspects of mission work and the ministry.[45] The ministers had to be trained in the Scriptures and in practical skills.

It was a testimony to the belief of the prominent pastors in education as a means of uplift that at a time when blacks had little money, experience, or security, the denominations established so many schools and cooperated in the establishment of school by whites for the training of ministers, and that the ministers made the sacrifices to attend those schools. But while the education of the ministers was given priority, the ministers also wanted to provide education for the masses for freedmen. The masses needed uplift, too, and education would uplift them just as it was uplifting the ministers.

3. EDUCATION BEYOND THE PULPIT

The push for educating ministers indicated no lack of interest in the education of other freedmen.[46] Rather, the ministers, committed to education for the massses, became in significant numbers teachers and educators. No fewer than forty-five of the seventy-eight ministers worked either as teachers or as school administrators. Some, like Albert

W. Peques at Shaw University and W.D. Chappelle, president of Allen University from 1897 to 1899, served in well-established denominational schools, while others, like Elijah Marrs in Kentucky and John Jacob Starks at Seneca, South Carolina, found themselves responsible for translating the local residents' desire for a school into a reality. A few--including John W.E. Bowen, professor and president at Gammon School of Theology, and A.U. Frierson, who held the Chair of Greek Language and Literature at Biddle University--were identified primarily by their academic activities. On the other hand, men like Richard Cain, president of Paul Quinn College, and William Pettiford, who taught in Alabama, were better known for their achievements in politics and business. Because of the wide range in educational standards, the qualifications of the ministers for teaching also varied greatly. Some were self-taught; others had college degrees. In addition to the teachers or school administrators, at least nine others served as members of the boards of directors or trustees for the various schools. No other task, except that of preaching, was so universally supported by the ministerial elite as the task of education.

One reason for the desire that the masses be educated was a clerical belief in a relationship between education and Christianity. In a sermon on "The Bible and Education" delivered at Macon, Georgia, in 1868, Theophilus G. Steward informed his AME congregation that Christians should not be children in understanding. Because the Bible was a written document, Steward suggested, Christians ought to learn to read and write as a part of their responsibilities as Christian.[47] The pastor of the Friendship Baptist Church in Atlanta, E.R. Carter, believed that the mind and soul had to be nurtured together. Education was for him the key to achieving the moral progress promised by Christianity.[48] J.S. Flipper, an AME leader in Georgia, was convinced that education issued in higher morality; it seemed logical to him that "the upper classes of Negroes, by reason of religious and educational advantages, are an improvement morally on their fathers, whose opportunities for moral improvement were very meagere, indeed." Flipper joined other ministers in believing that educated people made better Christians because education helped them understand the demands of Christianity more fully. "The higher the idea of God," wrote Flipper, "the higher is one's esteem for man and his responsibilities to family, neighbors, and country."[49] Education, in Flipper's view, produced the "higher idea of God." Using the same logic, he claimed to see little or no moral improvement among the lowest class of blacks, who he maintained had not taken advantage of available educational opportunities.[50]

Most ministers agreed about the relationship between education and the Christian life, but several had doubts. For a few it seemed that education was important but that a purely secular education was no guarantee of moral, ethical, and Christian progress. M.C.B. Mason of the Methodist Episcopal Church, pleased with the educational development of the race, worried that there had been no corresponding improvement in moral development: "it must still be confessed that in the field of morals and manners, the charge is still made, and that not without some semblance of truth, that evidences of the essential qualities of sturdy and manly character are not as clearly manifest among us as they should be."[51] In order for education to be uplifting, argued some clergymen, Christian instruction had to be a part of the educational program. Bishop Holsey of the CME Church saw a danger to Christianity if education and religion were not united. "One of the first things done by the perverted learning of man," wrote Holsey, "is to seek to disprove the truth, the authenticity, divine inspiration and originality of the Bible."[52] Bishop Gaines of the AME Church made it clear in his opening address to the Negro Young People's Christian and Education Congress in 1902 that, as the name of the Congress implied, only the combination of Christianity and education would uplift the race. Speaking as the president of the Congress, Gaines could say: "Our young people must be educated," but "it is our business to see that their education is permeated with the spirit of the great Teacher who, in the Semron on the Mount, laid down the great elemental propositions and principles upon which all education worth while is to be based and built up."[53] An education was valuable to Christians because it let them develop their God-given mental abilities and their opportunities to understand God's dealings with the creation. But without the tempering effect of piety, some ministers believed, learning would be a barrier that kept humanity from finding God's will. Only a "Christian" education could help one understand and respond faithfully to the demands of God.

Still another reason for the preoccupation with education was the belief, which grew stronger in the wake of political setbacks, that only education could protect the freedman's freedom. As early as 1868, T.G. Steward described the defensive function of education.

> *To elevate the blacks and place them beyond the reach of foul wrong, power, force, must be put into their hands. Yes, says one. 'The power of the ballot!' Give them the elective franchise and nothing else, and you put saddles on their backs for white politicians to ride upon, and well will they use them. Another says: 'Give them wealth; place capital in their hands; give them lands and put them on the open road to prosperity and respectability.' With nothing else given the colored man: How long would he be able to hold his wealth or make it contribute to his good? It is not fencing-in by law nor bracing up by favors that will elevate. No; every grant and favor detracts so much from the honor of final success. The strength must be infused in the man. He must be made strong. This will come only*

110

*from labor, study, and thought. The only way
to elevate is to increase the intrinsic worth.*

*Knowledge must be required; Knowledge of
words and things. Every fact acquired arouses
new thoughts; the mind expands; the faculties
are strengthened and the progress is onward
to manhood.*[54]

Steward did not deny the value of the ballot, nor was he opposed to the work of the Freedman's Bureau. He was, in fact, an organizer for the Republican party in Georgia in 1868, and he argued forcefully for the protection of black political rights after the legislature in Georgia refused to seat the duly-elected black legislators. Yet Steward was convinced that uplift was not a matter of improving external conditions and circumstances as much as it was developing the intellect of the freedmen so they could think for themselves and act in their own best interest. Anything less than the development of the mind was at best a temporary solution to the problems blacks faced because only the development of the mind, in Steward's opinion, gave blacks control over their destiny. Some twenty years later, E.R. Carter was no less convinced that education was the safeguard for all the other rights and privileges blacks hoped to secure. He urged blacks to make whatever sacrifices necessary to acquire an education: "I would urge with increased emphasis that we educate at the hazard of all things. Anything that the prosecution of education consumes will be ultimately restored with interest."[55] In the midst of rising Jim Crowism and the political unrest surrounding the 1898 legislative elections in North Carolina, Thomas O. Fuller, who was elected as a Senator, took the time to affirm his belief that education was the best insurer of the race's rights. Later in the same year, Alexander Walters, an AME Zion bishop and president of the Afro-American Council, cited educated as the surest means of security and uplift for blacks, even as he decried the outrages being perpetuated against his people.[56] And in 1902, Bishop Gaines said that even liberty paled in comparison to the importance of education united with religion. "For what is liberty, priceless as it may be," wrote the bishop, "unless it is safe-guarded and preserved by the enlightening agencies of learning and religion?"[57] Educationwas the only trustworthy guardian of black rights in a society that seemed arbitrarily to grant and rescind the rights of blacks.

There was little argument within the ranks of the leading preachers about the need for the freedman to be educated, but there was debate about the type of education that best suited the needs of the freedman. Some believed that the best education for blacks was a classical education, which formed the curriculum offered at most schools and colleges. The classical curriculum was designed to provide an academic education in the liberal arts that prepared students to teach an enter the professions. Extensive training in the classical languages and literature was typical of this type of education. Such men as J.C. Price, John J. Starks, J.W.E.

Bowen, and Edward M. Brawley were products of such a "classical" education, and they continued that pattern in their schools. To S.G. Atkins, the pursuit of a classical education proved that blacks could benefit from the same kind of learning that marked the ideal for whites,[58] while for E.R. Carter classical learning would keep the race from being hewers of wood and drawers of water.[59]

Others were convinced that the best education for many freedman was one that prepared them to function as independent skilled laborers in the society. This conviction led to the formation of industrial schools and the establishment of agricultural and industrial departments in existing schools. The Slater Foundation, under the direction of Atticus G. Haygood, no doubt encouraged this development by giving sizable grants to schools that had these concerns as their primary focus or were willing to incorporate agricultural and industrial departments within the classical framework. William I. Simmons saw a growing need for industrial education in the mid-1880's, believing that good industrial schools would correct dangerous misconceptions held by black youth. Lamenting the disregard for manual labor, Simmons complained that "labor is honorable, but it is fast becoming unfashionable to the colored boy or girl to seek manual labor, and rather than work, many become loafers, dissipates, and wrecks."[60] A few years later, A.W. Peques thought he saw a growing appreciation for skilled industrial training, a development he approved.[61] And no less a leader than William R. Pettiford advocated the need for a practical education that prepared blacks to advance in the world, as opposed to a theoretical education that was not marketable.[62]

The discussions of industrial and classical education formed the context for the later famous debates between W.E.B. Dubois and Booker T. Washington. But most of the ministers seemed to value both methods of education. Ministers who supported classical training could also praise the work being done at schools like Tuskegee Institute. Thomas O. Fuller wrote that "the South has much to gain from the Washington idea of the farm and country life for the masses of the race. Industrial education means intelligent citizenship, trained labor, able to know when it is doing well and treated right, with sufficient wants to demand regular employment."[63] Though a teacher trained in the classical manner, Fuller saw dignity in training a person to do a job well. Charles H. Phillips, a CME minister and medical doctor, liked Tuskegee when he visited in 1900 because he thought that while teaching the various trades the school was not neglecting intellectual development.[64] Likewise, even as he extolled the merits of an industrial education, William Simmons suggested that "the student be free from industrial trade work when he made certain grades in his classes." Simmons' rationale was that "we want good workmen and good scholars, not deluded smatterers in either department."[65] The ministers seem to have wanted to provide the classical course of instruction for some, while giving others the skills they needed to live profitable, dignified lives.

Both the industrial and the classical forms of education reflected the accommodationist tendencies of black leaders who saw education as the hope for the uplift of the race. The acceptance of manual education for the masses was an accommodation to the expectation that blacks would have to rely on manual skills. But even the acceptance of the classical education was accommodationist. The classical education advocated by many black ministerial leaders drew on Victorian culture and the values of the dominant society; it was designed to produce educated black people who could function comfortably within that Victorian culture.

Yet the crusade for education was clearly an affirmation of black possibility, an affirmation that kept accommodationism from becoming an uncritical acceptance of everything that the dominant society offered. The acquisition of the skills for manual labor heightened a sense of dignity and created skilled craftsmen who could contribute to the well-being of society as a whole. Such skills allowed even illiterate blacks a chance for uplift. And classical education provided similar opportunities for the forging of new possibilities.

4. AN EDUCATION FOR UPLIFT

The importance placed on education by the ministerial elite justifies a brief examination of the content of education in four institutions that were influential between 1865 and 1902.[66] The four schools selected, Fisk University, Nashville Institute (re-named Roger Williams University in 1883), Atlanta University, and Tuskegee Institute, had diverse programs, and they represented the scope of an education designed to uplift.

Both Fisk in Nashville and Atlanta University were founded by the American Missionary Association, but Atlanta University became an independent school in 1893. Roger Williams University was founded by the Baptist Home Mission Society and supported by blacks and Northern Baptists; Tuskegee Institute was started by Booker T. Washington, who was able to attract the support of a broad constituency, including prominent individuals and organizations, to keep the independent school alive and flourishing.

From their founding in the late 1860's, Fisk, Atlanta University, and the Nashville Institute recognized and promoted a close relationship between religion and education. Though not quite as boldly committed to the training of ministers as the Nashville institute, which stated that its "primary object" was "to prepare pious young men for the ministry; and both men and women for teachers,"[67] both Atlanta University and Fisk required regular Bible study as part of their curriculum and supported theological departments for most of the time up to 1902. As late as 1895, Atlanta University's catalogue maintained that the work of the school "broadly speaking . . . is a combined religious and educational work for the children of the Freedman,"[68] and Fisk charges no tuition for students who were preparing for the ministry. Tuskegee Institute, on the other hand, did not initially place much emphasis on preparing ministers but expected all graduates to teach at least two year.[69] Even Tuskegee, however, opened a Bible school in 1893.

The curriculum of the schools evolved as the preparation of entering students improved. Initially none of the schools had collegiate departments, rather they had students from the grammar school level to the first levels of high school. The earliest course offerings reflect the elementary level of their students. By 1886, however, these schools had instituted the educational format that they would use through the remainder of the century. The Nashville Institute, Fisk, and Atlanta University offered a liberal arts education which at the collegiate level embraced the classical approach. Nashville Institute, by then Roger Williams University, was less rigid in its course structure than Fisk and Atlanta University. It allowed students interested in mathematics and the sciences to concentrate on advanced courses in these disciplines in the second year, bypassing most of the language courses. Nevertheless, most students were required to take several courses in Greek and Latin before graduation, just as students in the other institutions. An examination of the 1885-86 catalogues for Roger Williams, Fisk, and Atlanta University, shows the importance these schools placed on Greek and Latin studies for their college students. At Roger Williams students were required to have eight of their first twelve courses in Greek and Latin; six of the ten courses required during the first three years at A.U. centered on Greek and Latin Literature, grammar, history, and culture; and the course offerings at Fisk required nine classes of Greek and Latin combined and two courses each of French and German to go with the eleven non-language courses a student took in the first three years of his college study. It was the opinion of the administrators of these schools that a command of the classical languages and literature helped one understand one's own language and disciplined one's mind. Furthermore, the study of Greek was also helpful in the study of the New Testament. Though some minor changes occurred in the curriculum of these schools by 1902, their educational philosophy and their academic approach remained constant; the predominance of language studies held steady throughout the period. Tuskegee, however, did not adopt the pattern found in so many schools committed to training ministers, teachers, and others for the work of uplift. Instead of concentrating on the development of classical language skills, Tuskegee concentrated on teaching future teachers the practical skills they needed to teach an illiterate population. The 1885-86 catalogue of Tuskegee lists no college degree courses, but the Normal department had 141 students enrolled. The four-year curriculum in this department included such courses as spelling and diction exercises, basic geography, penmanship, geometric drawings, elementary Botany and Zoology, American Literature, the U.S. Constitution, and methods of teaching. Tuskegee also offered courses at night to accommodate students who worked during the day. If uplift was to be successful, the race needed the 70 students enrolled in the degree programs of Fisk, Atlanta University, and Roger Williams, but it also needed the 141 studying in Tuskegee's Normal department.

That there were differences in the curriculum of the three classical schools and Tuskegee cannot be denied, but by 1885-86 these schools resembled each other in at least two ways. In the senior year, students at all four schools took courses in such disciplines as economics, sociology, and political science. The weight in the senior year, however, fell on the courses in Moral Philosophy and the Evidences of Christianity. These courses were taught by the presidents of the schools as the final preparation of students about to take their place in society.

At Roger Williams University, the presidents, who throughout the period were Baptist ministers, used Francis Wayland's, **The Elements of Moral Science** as the text for the class on Moral Philosophy, as did Booker T. Washington at the Tuskegee Institute. Wayland, who was professor of Moral Philosophy, and president of Brown University when he published the book in 1835, believed that men and women had a moral obligation to be obedient to the creator of the universe. He thought that natural religion revealed duties and obligations to God and that revealed religion intensified those obligations of obedience. That obedience included a number of actions relevant to blacks concerned about uplift. Because he was assured that all men and women had been created with the potential for progressive moral and intellectual improvement, Wayland believed that all people were to demonstrate their obedience to God by developing their abilities to their maximum. Self-improvement was an obligation, and neither the obligation nor the potential was determined by race, for God was the father of all humanity and all were brothers.[70] Wayland concluded that obedience to God also entailed human love for one another because of humanity's common parentage. "He is the father of us all," wrote Wayland, "and he requires that every one of his children conduct himself toward others, who are also his children, as he shall appoint."[71] And obedience to God also meant that people were obligated to improve society by cultivating the moral nature of humanity. Disavowing violence, he argued that right would prevail through human suffering in the cause of moral right.

Wayland's emphasis on human improvement, brotherhood, and the redemptive qualities of human suffering confirmed all that uplift meant to a politically weak, economically powerless, educationally deprived, recently freed black population. While the values of the course reflected the prevailing values of the society, those values also affirmed black possibility. Wayland's ideas, as taught to college seniors, affirmed that humanity, black humanity, could be uplifted, but that it was up to the race to do the job in obedience to God.

Atlanta University and Fisk required students to take the Evidences of Christianity, a course in Christian apologetics. The textbook for the course was Mark Hopkins', **Evidences of Christianity,** written in 1884 when Hopkins was president of Williams College in Massachusetts. Like Wayland, Hopkins was concerned about the reasonableness of Christianity.

115

He believed Christianity confirmed the best of human intellectual achievements. Essential to Hopkins' argument was his position that Christianity sought to elevate humanity. He saw humanity as having the potential to improve, to develop morally and spiritually, and Christianity as the religion that was compatable with that capacity for growth. Christianity, according to Hopkins, was a moral religion that spoke of God as a Father whose concern for His creation was best exhibited by His love, a love that sought to lift humanity. Like the Baptist Francis Wayland, Hopkins also affirmed the brotherhood of humanity; a theme the ministerial elite would repeat in their quest for uplift.

A second feature of the schools was that by 1885 all three had develop porgrams in agricultural and industrial training. As early as 1869, the catalogue for Atlanta University listed an Agricultural Department. Furthermore, the catalogue stated that it was the school's intention that the department would "become a prominent one in the institution" with all students reckoned as belonging to it.[72] In 1880, Atlanta University owned fifty acres of land which was cultivated by students interested in agriculture. The school offered a Bachelor of Science degree for those who did their course work in the field. By 1886, however, the university no longer emphasized the agricultural program; it developed, rather, a mechanical arts program for students enrolled in its high school level programs. At Fisk, Roger Williams, and Tuskegee, Industrial Departments were functioning as part of the college program, all of which were funded by the Slater Foundation. Fisk noted this new direction in its catalogue:

> While distinctively Industrial Education is not made a prominent or characteristic feature in Fisk University, all the methods of instruction and all the arrangements of home life in the boarding department are devised with the view of forming correct ideas and habits which shall help prepare the student for the practical duties and occupations of life.[73]

All students who boarded at Fisk were required to give an hour a day in manual labor. Courses were also offered in a variety of practical programs such as printing, sewing, and cooking. Yet, despite the increased attention given to manual labor at the classically-oriented schools, manual training was not given the emphasis the academic courses received. Only Tuskegee placed the industrial program on a par with its academic work. The philosophy of self-sufficient manual labor was not foreign to Booker T. Washington, but the gift of almost 500 acres of land to the school in the early 1880's and Slater Fund support for the industrial arts program gave life to Washington's dreams. By 1886, Tuskegee's catalogue informed readers that "work is required of all for purposes of discipline and instruction and of teaching the dignity of labor."[74]

Though few ministers saw an industrial education as the ideal, preferring the classical training, the manual training did provide a person with a chance to be an honest, self-respecting, hard-working member of society, which in itself was an upward step. And whether the education taught one to conjugate Latin verbs or lay bricks, as long as it led to the uplifting of the race, it served its purpose.

5. SUMMARY

Education was an early interest of the ministers and it continued to grow in importance for them. Whites, mainly from the North, played an important role in helping blacks secure an education by establishing schools, teaching, and helping blacks help themselves. Blacks were deeply involved as students, teachers, and administrators. And the black ministers were in the forefront. Accepting the idea that ministers should prepare themselves for the responsibilities of their high calling and also believing that they were models for the race, they first sought to educate themselves and their peers in the ministry. By the turn of the century, the leadership of the black denominations was being assumed either by trained men or by men who, despite their own disadvantages, advocated ministerial training. The ministers were also convinced that the masses of freedmen had to be educated if the race was to reach its potential. Education was aligned with the highest concepts of Christianity and was the only way the race could protect itself from the ravages of racism. It is no surprise that black denominational efforts to start schools of higher learning increased in the wake of the dismantling of the political gains of Reconstruction. As the hope of political solutions to racial problems in America became more remote, the ministers were more convinced than ever that education was the only way to insure survival with dignity. To be sure, the ministers sometimes disagreed about the appropriate style of education, but that debate took place within a common affirmation of education. The concern for uplift tempered the debate and allowed advocates of both the classical and the industrial types of education to see value in the positions held by the other side. Education for uplift was important. Indeed, but 1902 education held the greatest potential for fulfilling the hope and belief of the ministers that the race could and would be uplifted.

[1]*Charles O. Boothe, **The Cyclopedia of the Colored Baptists of** Alabama: Their Leaders and Their Work (Birmingham: Alabama Publishing Co., 1895), p. 167.*

[2]*McAlpine's career is described in several works including: Boothe,* **The Cyclopedia of the Colored Baptists of Alabama,** *pp. 166-8; A.W. Peques,* **Our Baptist Ministers and Schools** *(Springfield, Mass.: Willey and Co., 1892; reprint ed., New York: Johnson Reprint Corporation, 1970), pp. 327-332; William J. Simmons,* **Men of Mark: Eminent, Progressive and Rising** *(George M. Rewell and Co., 1887; reprint ed., Chicago: Johnson Publishing Co., Inc., 1970), pp. 353-356.*

[3]*An excellent two-part historical summary of the legal status of black education in each of the then thirty-five states and the District of Columbia through the year 1868 was prepared in 1871 at the request of the first United States Commissioner of Education. The first part describes black education in and around the District of Columbia and the second part provides information regarding restrictions on black education in the various states. The report is a classic in the field of education and served as the basis for several studies of black education in the 1800's and well into this century. It has been republished as the* **History of Schools for the Colored Population** *(reprint ed., New York: Arno Press, 1969). Pages 305-400 were those most useful to the study. Further information on the education and literacy levels of the freedman at the War's end is provided by several studies of blacks in the specific states before and during Reconstruction. Among these are: John W. Blassingame,* **Black New Orleans 1860-1880** *(Chicago: University of Chicago Press, 1973), pp. 107-137; Peter Kolchin,* **First Freedom: The Responses of Alabama's Blacks to Emancipation and Reconstruction** *(Westport, Connecticut: Greenwood Press Publishers, 1972), pp. 79-99; Vernon Lane Wharton,* **The Negro in Mississippi 1865-1890** *(New York: Harper & Row, 1947), pp. 243-265.*

[4]*U.S. Department of Commerce, Bureau of the Census, Bulletin* **29, Negroes in the United States** *(Washington: Government Printing Office, 1915), p. 27.*

[5]*For most of the period between 1865 and 1902, blacks desired and gratefully accepted white teachers, white administrators, and white controlled schools, but in the wake of political setbacks, increased discrimination against blacks, and an increase in the number of trained*

black teachers, some blacks began to question white leadership in educational institutions for blacks. The tensions that came to a head after the period covered by this book began to surface in the last decade of the nineteenth century and carried over into the new century. Some of the tensions are discussed in three essays in Daniel Culp's, *Twentieth Century Negro Literature* under the title "Is it Time for the Negro Colleges in the South to be Put Into the Hands of Negro Teachers." See also James M. McPherson, "White Liberals and Black Power in Negro Education, 1865-1910," *American Historical Review* 8 (June 1970): 1357-86.

^{6}U.S. Department of Interior, Bureau of Education, Bulletin 1916, No. 38, *Negro Education: A Study of the Private and Higher Schools for Colored People in the United States, Volume 1* (Washington: Government Printing Office, 1917), p. 289.

^{7}Dwight Oliver Wendell Holmes, *The Evolution of the Negro College* (New York: Bureau of Publications, Teachers College, Columbia University, 1934; reprint ed., New York: Arno Press, 1969), pp. 31-49. Further insight into the educational work of the Freedman's Bureau, of those involved in it and affected by it, can be gained through letters written to General O.O. Howard by the General Superintendent of Education in 1870. O.O. Howard, *Letters from the South Relating to the Condition of Freedmen* (Washington, D.C.: Howard University Press, 1870). John and LaWanda Cox argue that Gen. Howard's concern for educating the freedman rested on his belief that education alone would give blacks what they needed to preserve their freedom. This conclusion was also reached by many prominent black clergymen. See John and LaWanda Cox, "General O.O. Howard and the 'Misrepresented Bureau,'" *The Journal of Southern History* 19 (November 1953): pp. 453-4.

^{8}See Augustus Field Beard, *A Crusade of Brotherhood: A History of the American Missionary Association* (Boston: American Mission Soceity, 1909; reprint ed., Boston: Pilgrim Press, 1972); Holmes, *The Evolution of the Negro College*, pp. 76-101; Eloise Turner Welch, "The Background and Development of the American Missionary Association's Decision to Educate Freedmen in the South, With Subsequent Repercussions" (Ph.D. dissertation, Bryn Mawr College, 1975).

^{9}Agencies affiliated with other northern denominations, though active, spent less money and had less impact on the black community than either the Baptists or Methodists. Biddle University in North Carolina, however, did graduate four members of the ministerial elite, even though it was supported by the Board of Missions for the Presbyterian Church.

^{10}A letter from the Council of Bishops, reprinted in the Freedmen's Aid Society of the Methodist Episcopal Church, *Fourth Annual Report* (Cincinnati: Western Methodist Book Concern Print, 1871), p. 2, states that mission and education go hand in hand. "The emancipation of four millions of slaves has opened at our door a wide field calling alike for *mission and educational work. . . . Religion and education alone can make freedom a blessing to them."*

[11]Holmes, **The Evolution of the Negro College,** p. 105.

[12]A.W. Peques, **Our Baptist Ministers and Schools,** pp. 618-9.

[13]Among die-hard white supremacists it was not hard to find those who did not believe blacks could be educated at all. Even more moderate whites felt that a classical education was useless for blacks. Some scholars even believed that the incidence of black criminality rose with the increase of education. (See I.W. Newby, **Jim Crow's Defense: Anti-Negro Thought in America, 1900-1930** [Baton Rouge, La.: Louisiana State University Press, 1965], pp. 174-178 and H. Shelton Smith, **In His Image, But . . .: Racism in Southern Religion, 1780-1910** [Durham, NC: Duke University Press, 1972], pp. 255-57, 273-4).

[14]See Atticus G. Haygood, **Our Brother in Black: His Freedom and His Future** (New York: Phillips & Hunt, 1881), pp. 144-57.

[15]Home Mission Board reports included in the Southern Baptist Convention Annuals during the period demonstrate the types of issues raised by the Board. Also Southern Baptist relations to black education are discussed in both Rufus Spain, **At Ease in Zion: A Social History of Southern Baptists, 1865-1902** (Nashville: Vanderbilt University Press, 1961), pp. 84-93 and John Eighmy, (Churches in Cultural Captivity: A History of the Social Attitudes of Southern Baptists (Knoxville: The University of Tennessee Press, 1972), pp. 32-40.

[16]John F. Slater, "Letter of the Founder," in **Reports of John F. Slater Fund, 1882-1891;** Organization of the Trustees of the John F. Slater Fund for the Education of Freedmen, 1882; A.G. Haygood editor (Baltimore: John Murphy & Co., 1882), p.4.

[17]See Holmes, **The Evolution of the Negro College,** pp. 168, 170.

[18]Edward M. Brawley, "The Duty of Colored Baptists in View of the Past, the Present, and the Future," in **The Negro Baptist Pulpit: A Collection of Sermons and Papers by Colored Baptist Ministers** (Philadelphia: American Baptist Publication Society, 1890; reprint ed., Freeport, New York: Books for Libraries Press, 1971), p. 292. In another essay in this same volume, "Baptist and General Education," Brawley reminds his readers of the numerous efforts northern Baptists had made in behalf of black education.

[19]M.C.B. Mason, "Did the American Negro Make in the Nineteenth Century Achievements Along the Lines of Wealth, Morality, Education, Etc., Commensurate with His Opportunities? If so, What Achievements did He Make?," in Daniel Culp, **Twentieth Century Negro Literature** (J.L. Nichols and Co., 1902; reprint ed., Miami: Mnemosyne Publishing

Co., Inc., 1969), p. 35.

[20]George A. Goodwin, "Is it Time for the Negro Colleges in the South to be Put in the Hands of Negro Teachers," in Culp, **Twentieth Century Negro Literature,** pp. 132-9.

[21]Examples of the importance the men who became the ministerial elite place on education are numerous. A few of these are worth noting. William McAplpine's reluctance to enter the ministry without an education was not without precedent. George Washington Dupree, who became an important Baptist leader in Kentucky after the Civil War, had refused to respond to a call to preach for several years in the 1840's becuase he could not read or write at the time. (See Simmons, **Men of Mark,** pp. 599-607 and Peques, **Our Baptist Ministers and Schools,** pp. 175-183). Other men made great sacrifices to attain their educations. Thomas Oscar Fuller, a North Carolina Baptist, was already attending school when he was called to preach. But the call seemed to keep him in school despite his mother's death and the financial hardships he encountered. (See Thomas O. Fuller, **Twenty Years of Public Life, 1890-1910** [Nashville: National Baptist Publishing Board, 1910], Chapters 1 and 2). C.H. Phillips, an outstanding leader in the CME Church, not only completed college after his call to the ministry, but he went on to complete a degree in medicine at Meharry Medical School. He wanted to be able to respond to a variety of needs he saw and felt that if he could not preach, he could always practice medicine. (See C.H. Phillips, **From the Farm to the Bishopric: An Autobiography** [Nashville: Parthenon Press, 1932], Chapter 2-9). Others like William Simmons worked themselves into poor health in their attempts to secure their education. (See Simmons, **Men of Mark,** p. 7).

[22]Booker T. Washington, "The Colored Ministry: Its Defects and Needs," in **The Booker T. Washington Papers,** ed. Louis R. Harlan, Vol. 3, 1889-95 (Urbana, Illinois: University of Illinois Press, 1974), ppl 71-75. Originally delivered as a commencement address at Fisk University in June, 1890, the address received nationwide attention after its publication in the **Christian Union** paper in August, 1890, and later in the Indianapolis **Freeman.** Washington's criticism of the educational level of the ministers in the South caused quite a stir as many ministers took offense at his opinions. The ministers' reactions were alluded to in another article Washington wrote defending his earlier opinion which appeared in November, 1890 in the Indianapolis **Freeman** (See **Papers,** pp. 101-103). As evidence of the validity of his views, Washington attached a letter of support he had received from Bishop Daniel Payne of the AME Church (See **Papers,** pp. 97-99).

[23]"From Daniel Payne," Ibid., p. 98.

[24]Tuskegee Normal and Industrial School, **Catalogue of the Tuskegee Normal and Industrial School, Tuskegee, Alabama 1893-94** (Tuskegee: Normal School Press, 1894), p. 40.

[25]Wesley J. Gaines, *The Gospel Ministry: A Series of Lectures* (Atlanta: W.J. Gaines, 1899), p. 41.

[26]Albert W. Peques, "The Necessity of a Trained Ministry," in *The United Negro: His Problems and His Progress*, ed. J.W.E. Bowen and I. Garland Penn (Atlanta: D.E. Luther Publishing Co., 1902), p. 119.

[27]William E. Partee, "The Negro as a Christian," in Culp, *Twentieth Century Negro Literature*, pp. 309-313.

[28]*The Independent*, 5 March 1891, p. 332.

[29]Edward M. Brawley, "Is the Young Negro an Improvement, Morally, On His Father," Culp, *Twentieth Century Negro Literature*, pp. 255-6. Other ministers who were part of the elite clergy also articulated their views that the minister had to be uplifted so that he could uplift the race. A.W. Peques who stated at the 1902 Conference in Atlanta that "The minister is more than a shepherd. . . . He not only leads to where the food is but he has largely to do with its preparation." (See "The Necessity of a Trained Ministry," in Bowen and Penn, *The United Negro*, p. 119). L.B. Ellerson, a Presbyterian minister, presented the view that blacks had to have trained leadership if their religious life was to reach its potential. (See Ellerson, "The Negro as a Christian," in Culp, *Twentieth Century Negro Literature*, pp. 313-315). John B.L. Williams of the Methodist Episcopal Church was yet another member of the ministerial elite who saw the minister as a leader whose example was the model for uplift. Therefore the minister had to be uplifted if the race was to be uplifted and that uplift began with education. (See Williams "To What Extent is the Negro Pulpit Uplifting the Race," in Culp, *Twentieth Century Negro Literature*, pp. 120-121).

[30]R.P. Wyche, "To What Extent is the Negro Pulpit Uplifting the Race," in Culp, *Twentieth Century Negro Literature*, p. 122.

[31]S.N. Vass, "The Work of the American Baptist Publication Society," in Bowen and Penn, *The United Negro Literature*, p. 122.

[32]Gaines, *The Gospel Ministry*, p. 33.

[33]Nashville Normal and Theological Institute, *Catalogue of the Officers and Students of the Nashville Normal and Theological Insitute, Nashville, Tennessee, for the Academic Year 1880-81* (Nashville: Marshall & Bruce, 1881), p. 21.

[34]See William Hicks, *History of Louisiana Negro Baptists and Negro Baptist Beginnings in America* (Nashville: National Baptist Publishing Board, 1914), pp. 28, 29 and ff.

[35]Thomas O. Fuller, *Twenty Years of Public Life*, pp. 112-3.

[36]A.W. Peques, *Our Baptist Ministers and Schools,* p. 618. On pages 554-622 Peques provides additional information on the Baptist schools including historical sketches of the major institutions supported by black Baptists and the Baptist Home Mission Society. Further information can be gathered on the number of schools suppported by the black denominational boards by comparing the schools listed in Volume 1 of the U.S. Department of Interior Bulletin on **Negro Education** published in 1916 with the dates those institutions were founded in Volume 2 of the same report. This process will not provide the reader with the total number of schools that were started, but it will help the reader determine how many of the major schools that were started survived until 1915 when the study was completed.

[37]Wesley Gaines places the effort to establish a school in Georgia within the broader issues that confronted a growing AME denomination in Chapters 8,9,12,14,16, and 19 of **African Mehtodism in the South or Twenty-Five Years of Freedom** (Atlanta: Franklin Publishing House, 1890).

[38]See B.A. Johnson, "History of Livingstone College" in **Afro-American Encyclopedia; or, The Thoughts, Doings, and Sayings of the Race,** compiled and arranged by James T. Haley (Nashville: Haley and Florida, 1896), pp. 313-321.

[39]Charles H. Phillips, **The History of the Colored Methodist Episcopal Church in America** (Jackson, Tennessee: Publishing House CME Church, 1898; reprint ed., New York: Arno Press, 1972), p. 91.

[40]Haley, **Afro-American Encyclopedia,** pp. 327-332. Also see Isaac Lane, **Autobiography of Bishop Isaac Lane, LL.D.** (Nashville, Tennessee: The Publishing House of the ME Church, South, 1916), Chapters 13,14 and 17.

[41]This number does not include the eighteen men who studied at such schools as Augusta Institute (Atlanta Baptist Seminary), Roger Williams University, Le Moyne Institute, Shaw University, and Benedict College which trained many Baptist leaders but which were considered under the auspices of the Baptist Home Mission Society, even though they received substantial support from black Baptists. Selma University also received support from the Society, but remained under the control of black Baptists in Alabama for the period under consideration. Therefore, persons who attended Selma are included in the number I cited.

[42]See the catalogues of Tuskegee Normal and Industrial School, Tuskegee, Alabama, 1893-94 and 1901-02; catalogue of the Nashville Institute, Nashville, Tennessee, 1873-74, 1880-81, 1885-86, 1894-95, and 1901-02.

[43] Elijah P. Marrs, *Life and History of the Rev. Elijah P. Marrs* (Louisville: The Bradley and Gilbert Company, 1885; reprint ed., Miami: Mnemosyne Publishing Co., Inc., 1969), p. 103.

[44] Gammon School of Theology, *Circular of the Gammon School of Theology. Clark University, Atlanta, Georgia 1885-86* (Atlanta: Clark University Press, 1886), pp. 11-12. Also see Gammon Catalogues for years 1894-95 and 1901-02.

[45] See Morris Brown College, *Catalogue, Morris Brown College, Atlanta, Georgia 1898-99* (Atlanta: Morris Brown, 1899).

[46] Prior to the Civil War northern blacks in their conventions had often expressed their concern for the establishment of a college for blacks which they felt would promote the elevation of the race. The project that developed out of this concern did not succeed, however. See Howard Holman Bell, ed., *Minutes of the Proceedings of the National Negro Convention, 1830-1864* (New York: Arno Press and The New York Times, 1969). Especially relevant are the minutes from the 1831, 1832, and 1853 conventions.

[47] Theophilus G. Steward, "The Bible and Education" in *Pioneer Echoes: Six Special Sermons* (Baltimore: Hoffman and Co., 1889), pp. 30-40.

[48] Edward R. Carter, "Can the Negro Atain What Other Races Have?" in *Bibliographical Sketches of Our Pulpit* (Atlanta: E.R. Carter, 1888), p. 81.

[49] J.S. Flipper, "Is the Young Negro an Improvement, Morally, On His Father," in (Twentieth Century Negro Literature, p. 258. Other men also saw a relationship between education and Christian responsibility and behavior. Among these was E.M. Brawley, a leading Baptist, who believed that the gospel in its fullest power made the greatest impact on educated people. He believed that salvation was totally independent of education, but the fullest joys and power of the Christian religion were unleashed through education. (See Brawley, "Is the Young Negro and Improvement, Morally, On His Father," *Twentieth Century Negro Literature*, pp. 254-57). Citing the positive qualities of black Christian worship and practice, William E. Partee, a highly trained Presbyterian minister from North Carolina, nevertheless was convinced that the highest degree of moral and religious life could not be reached without an education. "Education help us to be better Christians . . . and as we get more knowledge of Bible truths such as education can give us we will be better Christians." (See Partee, "The Negro as a Christian," *Twentieth Century Negro Literature*, pp. 309-313). L.B. Ellerson, a Presbyterian pastor in Florida, firmly believed that the ministry had to take responsibility for the lack of training found in the race, but still affirmed the idea that the quality of black religious life and practive would improve with education. (Ellerson, "The Negro as a Christian," *Twentieth Century Negro Literature*, pp. 313-15).

[50]J.S. Flipper, "Is the Young Negro an Improvement, Morally, on His Father?," **Twentieth Century Negro Literature**, p. 259.

[51]M.C.B. Mason, "Did the American Negro Make in the Nineteenth Century Achievements Along the Lines of Wealth, Morality, Education, Etc., Commensurate with His Opportunities? If so, What Achievements did He Make?," Ibid., p. 37.

[52]Lucius H. Holsey, "The Work of an Enemy," in **Autobiography, Sermons, Addresses and Essays** (Atlanta: Franklin Printing and Publishing Co., 1898), p. 179.

[53]J.W.E. Bowen and I. Garland Penn, **The United Negro**, p. 35. Among others advocating the importance of Christian education as an enhancer of and complement to other educational endeavors were W.D. Chappelle, an AME minister (See Bowen and Penn, **The United Negro**, pp. 77-83), E.W.D. Isaac, a Baptist leader who was also an officer of the 1902 Congress (Bowen and Penn, **The United Negro**, pp. 49-54), and E.M. Brawley (See "Baptists and General Education" and "The Duty of Colored Baptists" in **The Negro Baptist Pulpit: A Collection of Sermons and papers by Colored Baptist Ministers** (Philadelphia: American Baptist Publication Society, 1890; reprint ed., Freeport, New York: Books for Libraries Press, 1971), pp. 237-250 and 287-300.

[54]Theophilus G. Steward, **Fifty Years in the Gospel Ministry** (Philadephia: AME Book Concern, 1921), p. 103.

[55]E.R. Carter, "Can the Negro Attain What Other Races Have?," in **Biographical Sketches of Our Pulpit**, p. 82.

[56]Thomas O. Fuller, **Twenty Years of Public Life, 1890-1910**, pp. 43-45 and Alexander Walters, **My Life and Work** (New York: Fleming H. Revell Co., 1917), pp. 112-131. Fuller reacted to his constitutents' fears that they would be disfranchised by writing an open letter in which he stressed the importance of education as the way to secure black rights in the long run. In his address to the called meeting of the Afro-American Council, Walters argued that education was the most important factor in the development of the race and would be the most important reason why the race would achieve equality.

[57]Bowen and Penn, **The United Negro**, p. 34.

[58]S.G. Atkins, "Should Blacks Be Given an Education Different From That Given to the Whites," in **Twentieth Century Negro Literature**, pp. 80-83.

[59]E.R. Carter, "Can the Negro Attain What Other Races Have?," in **Bibgraphical Sketches of Our Pulpit**, p. 83.

CONCLUSION

The year 1865 witnessed the defeat of the Confederate Army and signaled new hope for black Americans who had endured a long and cruel bondage. But despite the hope freedom held, blacks had to face the fact that although they had lived in America for almost 250 years, those years had not prepared the race to assume the awesome responsibilities of freedom. Chattel slavery had not helped the freedman develop skills and abilities needed to flourish in a free and open society. For nearly 250 years blacks had been subject to rules and regulations established by people who often failed to see or treat them as fully human. It is therefore no surprise that as freedom dawned the newly freed black population was economically powerless, educationally illiterate, and politically impotent. Yet the freedman was expected to compete successfully with others who had nevenr known slavery. And if blacks were to survive and prosper in the changed situation, they had to move beyond the degradation of slavery.

Uplift was not easy. Not only did it mean the preparation of blacks to assume the responsibilities of freedom, but it also meant incorporating blacks into a white-dominated society as free men and women. As W.E.B. Dubois said, the job entailed merging the best of the black past with the best elements of American society and culture. This would have been a formidable task under the best of circumstances, but in light of the slave experience and the reluctance of some whites to view blacks as fully human, the task was even less promising. But the hope of the race rested with the accomplishment of uplift.

The post-Civil War period was crucial for establishing whether or not uplift was achievable. The years from 1865 to the turn of the century were characterized by the ebb and flow of black progress and regress which became a precursor of much of what black existence in America would mean. Though the issue of uplift was not settled in those years, the battle lines were drawn and black potential was demonstrated. By 1902, blacks no longer questioned whether uplift was possible but only wondered when it would become reality.

the other ills that plagued the freedman. Surely others could do as much if given the opportunity.

But the hope of uplift so frequently articulated by the leading ministers was rooted in something far more fundamental than their own notable achievements. The hope of uplift was valid because it rested on Christian principles. The emphasis on the fallenness of humanity, the redemption of humanity purchased through the sacrifice of Christ, and the salvation that was available to all repentant sinners who accepted Christ as their Saviour appealed to black ministerial leaders. But so did the themes of the fatherhood of God and the brotherhood of man so common in more liberal theological circles. The black clerical elite had no problem in affirming both traditions. For them, black equality was insured both by the fact that all humanity had God as father and by the fact that the sacrifice of Christ applied to all people. For the black ministerial elite Christianity was the ground out of which aspirations for uplift grew. It was Christianity that most clearly articulated their rightful demands for equality and which affirmed black potential.

Convinced that Christianity affirmed the goals of uplift, the elite ministers sought practical ways to translate the race's potential and promise of uplift into reality. To some of the ministerial elite, politics appeared to provide the first opportunity to accomplish that goal. Several of the leading clergymen sought to create new possibilites for the race through the structures of partisan politics; they became active as candidates for constitutional conventions and elective office. Others served in a variety of positions within political parties. But because blacks were almost totally connected with the Republican party, the resurgence of the Democratic party spelled an end to meaningful political involvement before the close of the century. The subsequent reversals led the leading ministers to a disillusionment with politics as means by which uplift would be accomplished. Yet even in the midst of this change in attitude, the ministerial elite were willing to accommodate themselves to the values espoused in the temperance movement in the hope that those values would salvage the last vestiges of possiblity for uplift that politics held for the race.

Even before they abandoned politics and accepted temperance as the means of uplifting the race, however, most of the ministers viewed education as having the greatest potential for uplift. Throughout the thirty-seven year period between 1865-1902, the black ministerial elite believed in the uplifting qualities of education. But with the failure of politics to fulfill the promise of uplift, education seemed to be the surest means by which new possibilities for the race would be realized. The growing importance of education in the work of uplift led to a greater interest among the ministers in the development of black-controlled schools which would join with existing white-operated schools that were already training blacks. Although the leading ministers expressed a desire to secure an educated clergy first, they were also concerned about providing a Christian education for the masses. The schools that they

The black church was the only institution blacks controlled in the years between 1865 and 1902, and it played a crucial role in interpreting what uplift meant and how blacks should see themselves in relation to the larger society. And no one in the black church or the black community had a greater influence in determining the church's interpretation of uplift than the black ministerial leadership. Serving as the leaders of the most powerful black institution, the elite black clergy were frequently the coordinators of the attempt to uplift the race.

Uplift, as advocated by the leading ministers, appears simple at first glance, but in fact the concept was, as I have argued throughout, paradoxical. On the one hand, the concept was accommodationist in that it embraced American ideals and culture. The black ministerial elite wanted blacks to become an integral part of American life rather than merely existing on the periphery, as they had done during slavery. Uplift then meant equipping the freedman so that he or she could function as an American. But ironically, much of what America stood for denied black possibility. Even liberal whites rarely thought that blacks would ever be fully integrated into American society. Most were convinced that blacks, though capable of improvement, were essentially inferior to whites and incapable of functioning as equals in America. The black ministerial leadership, however, rejected the claims of black inferiority and argued that blacks were capable of achieving all that whites had achieved and indeed had the potential of making their own unique contributions to the furtherance of American greatness. Therefore, even as the leading black ministers sought to accommodate themselves to American values and move blacks into the mainstream of American culture, they also affirmed black possibility in such a way as to reject what Americans actually practiced in terms of race relations and what had become a very real part of the culture blacks sought to adopt. Blacks would be Americans, but Americans who were equal to all other Americans, and who shared equally in the bright promise of the nation. Accommodation and possibility then were inter-related aspects of what uplift was all about.

The role the black ministerial leaders assumed in the quest for uplift was a result of their leadership in the church, but it also reflected the fact that they were seen as part of the black community. Their experiences, through varied, were similar to the experiences of their constituents. Because of this, they became both examples of what uplift entailed and models that the community could emulate as it attempted to be uplifted. The leading ministers accommodated themselves to American values. They believed in the home, the family, and the school as the bedrock of a Christian nation and emulated the American model of these ideals in their own lives. Yet because they had been uplifted, they stood as examples of what the race could do if it adopted the principles that undergirded civilized nations everywhere. The ministerial elite had risen from slavery, illiteracy, illegitimacy, poverty, and all help found adopted prevailing educational principles and methodologies. Whether the schools emphasized the skills needed for manual labor or concentrated on teaching the classical languages, they reflected the values of the dominant society, but even in the midst of this accommodationism, black possibility was reborn.

The turn toward education meant that uplift would be a long-term process that might take decades, if not generations, to accomplish. But the ministerial leaders had a faith that blacks could endure for the time needed to accomplish uplift. And the institutions that were created on the basis of accommodation ironically led to the creation of a generation of leaders who helped uplift the race to the point where equality, though not yet attained, is at least not merely a dream any longer.

BIBLIOGRAPHY

A. *PRIMARY SOURCES*

    1. Denominational Histories

Gaines, Wesley. **African Methodism in the South or Twenty-five Years of Freedom.** *Atlanta: Franklin Publsihing House, 1890.*

Hicks, William. **History of Louisianna Negro Baptists and Negro Baptist Beginnings in America.** *Nashville: National Baptist Publishing Board, 1914.*

Mixon, Wanfield H. **History of African Methodist Episcopal Church in Alabama with Biographical Sketcehs.** *Nashville: AME church School Union, 1902.*

Payne, Daniel A. **History of African Episcopal Church.** *Nashville: Publishing House of the African Methodist Episcopal Sunday School Union, 1891; reprint ed., New York: Arno Press, 1869.*

Phillips, C.H. **the History of the Colored Methodist Episcopal Church in America.** *Jackson, Tennessee: Publishing House CME Church, 1898; reprint ed., New York: Arno Press, 1972.*

Wayman, Alexander Walker. **The Recollection of AME Ministers, or Forty Years' Experience in the African Methodist Episcopal Church.** *Philadelphia: AME Book Rooms, 1882.*

    2. Autobiographies

Anderson, Robert. **The Life of Robert Anderson.** *Macon, Georgia: J.W. Burke, 1891; reprint ed., Atlanta Foote and Davis Co., 1900.*

Fuller, Thomas Oscar. **Twenty Years of Public Life, 1890-1910.** *Nashville: National Baptist Publishing Board, 1910.*

Heard, William Henry. **From Slavery to the Bishopric in the AME Church: An Autobiography.** *Philadelphia: AME Book Concern, 1924; reprint ed., New York: Arno Press, 1969.*

133

Holsey, L.H. **Autobiography, Sermons, Addresses and Essays.** *Atlanta: Franklin Printing and Publishing Compnay, 1898.*

Holtzclaw, William H. **The Black Man's Burden.** *New York: The Neale Publishing Comapny, 1915.*

Jamison, M.F. **Autobiography and Work of Bishop M.F. Jamison, D.D.** *Nashville: Publishing House of the ME Church, South, 1912.*

Lane, Isaac. **Autobiography of Bishop Isaac Lane, LL.D.** *Nashville: The Publishing House of the ME Church, South, 1916.*

Marrs, Elijah P. **Life and History of the Rev. Elijah P. Marrs.** *Louisville: Bradley and Gilbert Company, 1885.*

Morant, John J. **Mississippi Minister.** *New York: Vantage Press, 1958.*

Newton, Alexander Heritage. **Out of the Briars.** *Philadelphia: AME Book Concern, 1910.*

Phillips, Charles Henry. **From the Farm to the Bishopric: An Autobiography.** *Nashville: Parthenon Press, 1932.*

Proctor, Henry Hugh. **Between Black and White: Autobiographical Sketches.** *Boston: Pilgrim Press, 1925; reprint ed., Freeport, New York: Books for Libraries Press, 1972.*

Steward, Theophilus Gould. **Fifty Years in the Gospel Ministry** *Philadelphia: AME Book Concern, 1921.*

Walters, Alexander. **My Life and Work.** *New York: Fleming H. Revell, 1917.*

3. *Sermon Collections*

Brawley, E.M. **The Negro Baptist Pulpit.** *Philadelphia: American Baptist Publication Society, 1890; reprint ed., Freeport, New York: Books for Libraries Press, 1971.*

Channing, William Ellery. **Discourses, Reviews, and Miscellaneous.** *Boston: Carter and Hendee, 1830.*

Channing, William Ellery. **Unitarian Christianity and Other Essays.** *Edited by Irving H. Bartlett. New York: The Liberal Arts Press, 1957.*

Clinton, G.W. **Christianity Under the Searchlight.** *Nashville, Tennessee: Natioanl Baptist Publishing Board, 1909.*

Floyd, Silas X. *National Perils: An Address Delivered at Atlanta, Georgia, Monday, January 2, 1899.* Augusta, Georgia: the Georgia Baptist Print, 1898.

Haygood, Atticus G. *The New South: Gratitude, Amednment, Hope. A Thanksgiving Sermon for November 25, 1880.* Oxford, Georgia, 1880.

Hood. J.W. *The Negro in the Christian Pulpit, or, The Two Characters and Two Destinies, As Delineated in Twenty-One Practical Sermons.* Raleigh: Edwards, Broughton and Co., 1884.

Parker, Theodore. *Additional and Occassional Sermon in Two Volumes,* Volume 1. Boston: Little, Brwon and Co., 1855.

Payne, Daniel A. *Sermons and Addresses, 1851-1891.* New York: Arno Press, 1972, reprint.

Steward, Theophilus G. *Pioneer Echoes: Six Special Sermons.* Baltimore: Hoffman and Co., 1889.

4. Biographical Sketches

Carter, Edward Randolph. *Biographical Sketches of Our Pulpit.* Atlanta: E.R. Carter, 1888.

_____. *The Black Side.* Atlanta; E.R. Carter, 1894.

Peques, Albert W. *Our Baptist Ministers and Schools.* Springfield, Mass.: Willey and Co., 1892; reprint ed., New York; Johnson Reprint Corporation, 1970.

Simmons, Wiliam J. *Men of Mark: Eminent, Progressive and Rising.* Chicago: Johnson Publishing Co., 1970, reprint.

5. Yearbooks and Encyclopedias

Boothe, Charles O. *The Cyclopedia of the Colored Baptists of Alabama: their Leaders and Their Work.* Birmingham: Alabama Publishing Co., 1895.

Haley, James T., Complier. *Afro-American Encyclopedia.* Nashville: Haley and Florida, 1895.

Wayman, Alexander. *Cyclopedia of African Methodism.* Baltimore: Methodist Episcopal Book Depository, 1882.

6. Contemporary Theological Works

Clarke, William N. *An Outline of Christian Theology.* Cambridge: John
Wilson and Son, 1894.

Munger, Theodore. *The Freedom of Faith.* Boston: Houghton, Mifflin
and Company, 1883.

Wayland, Francis. *The Elements of Moral Science.* Boston: Gould and
Lincoln, 1857.

7. Convention Proceedings

Bell, Howard Holman, ed. *Minutes of the Proceedings of the National
Negro Conventions, 1830-1864.* New York: Arno Press, 1969.

Bowen, J.W.E. and Penn, I. Garland, editors. *The United Negro: His
Problems and His Progress.* Atlanta: D.E. Luther Publishing
Co., 1902.

South Carolina. *Proceedings of the Constitutional Convention, 1868.*
Charleston, S.C.: Denny and Perry, 1868. Reprint ed.,
New York: Arno Press, 1968.

8. Governmment Documents

U.S. Commissioner of Education. *History of Schools for the Colored
Population.* Reprint ed., New York: Arno Press, 1969.

U.S. Congress. House. *Menphis Riots and Massacres.* 39th Congress.
1st Session. 1866. Washington, D.C.: Government Printing
Office, 1866. Reprint ed., New York: Arno Press, 1969.

U.S. Congress. House. *New Orleans Riots.* 39th Congress. 2nd Session.
1867. Washington, D.C.: Government Printing Office, 1867.
Reprint ed., New York: Arno Press, 1969.

U.S. Department of Commerce. Bureau of the Census. Bulletin 129.
Negroes in the United States. Washington, D.C.: Government
Printing Office, 1915.

U.S. Department of Commerce. Bureau of the Census. *Negro
Population, 1790-1915.* Washington, D.C.: Government Printing
Office, 1918.

U.S. Department of Commerce and Labor. Bureau of the Census. Bulletin
8. *Negroes in the United States.* Washington, D.C.: Government
Printing Office, 1904.

U.S. Department of the Interior. Bureau of Education. Bulletin 1916.

No. 38. **Negro Education: A Study of the Private and Higher Schools for Colored People in the United States.** *Volume 1. Washington, D.C.: Government Printing Office, 1917.*

U.S. Department of the Interior. Census Office. **Report on Statistics of Churches in the United States at the Eleventh Census: 1890.** *Washington, D.C.: Government Printing Office, 1894.*

9. *Miscellaneous*

Atlanta University Publications

DuBois, W.E.B., ed. **Some Efforts of American Negroes for Their Own Social Betterment.** *Atlanta: Atlanta University Press, 1898.*

_____. **The Negro church.** *Atlanta: Atlanta University Press, 1903.*

Other Books and Essays

Cantwell, J.S., general ed. **Manuals of Faith and Duty.** *Boston: Universalist Publishing House, 1888. Vol. 1:* **The Fatherhood of God,** *by John Coleman Adams.*

Culp, D.W. **Twentieth Century Negro Literature.** *J.L. Nichols and Co., 1902; reprint ed., Miami: Mnemosyne Publishing Co., Inc., 1969.*

Gaines, Wesley J. **The Gospel Ministry: A Series of Lectures.** *Atlanta: W.J. Gaines, 1899.*

Garnet, Henry Highland. "An Address to the Slaves of the United States of America." In **Chronicles of Black Protest.** *Edited by Bradford Chambers. New York: New American Library, 1968.*

Garnet, Henry Highland. **The Past and Present Condition and the Destiny of the Colored Race.** *Reprint ed., Miami: Mnemosyne Publishing Inc., 1969.*

Gladden, Washington. **Ruling Ideas of the Present Age.** *Boston and New York: Houghton, Mifflin and Company, 1895.*

Harlan, Louis R., ed. **The Booker T. Washington Papers,** *Volume 3, 1889-95. Urbana, Illinois: Unversity of Illinois Press, 1974.*

Haygood, Atticus G. **Our Brother in Black: His Freedom and His Future.** *New York: Phillips and Hunt and Nashville: Southern Methodist Publishing House, 1881.*

Howard, O.O. **Letters from the South Relating to the Condition of Freedmen.** *Washington, D.C.: Howard University Press, 1870.*

Jordan, L.G. **Up the Ladder in Foreign Missions.** *Nashville: National Baptist Publishing Board, 1903; reprint ed., New York: Arno Press, 1980.*

Penn, I. Garland. **The Afro-american Press and Its Editors.** *Springfield, Mass.: Willey and Co., 1891; reprint ed., New York: Arno Press, 1980.*

Redkey, Edwin R., ed. **Respect Black: The Writings and Speeches of Henry McNeal Turner.** *New York: Arno Press, 1971.*

Sewall, Samuel. **The Selling of Joseph.** *Boston: Bartholemew Green and John Allen, 1700: reprint edition, New York: Arno Press, 1969.*

Slater, John F. "Letter of the Founder." **Reports of John F. Slater Fund, 1882-1891.** *Editor A.G. Haygood. Baltimore: John Murphy and Co., 1882.*

Woolman, John. **The Work of John Woolman.** *Reprint edition, New York: Arno Press, 1969.*

B.   SECONDARY SOURCES

1. General Histories of the Period

Blassingame, John W. **Black New Orleans 1860-1880.** *Chicago: University of Chicago Press, 1973.*

Cartwright, Joseph H. **The Triumph of Jim Crow: Tennessee Race Relations in the 1880's.** *Knoxville: University of Tennessee Press, 1976.*

Cruden, Robert. **The Negro in Reconstruction.** *Englewood Cliffs, N.J.: Prentice-Hall, 1969.*

Drimmer, Melvin. **Black History: A Reappraisal.** *Garden City, New York: Doubleday and Company, 1967.*

Holt, Thomas. **Black Over White: Negro Political Leadership in the South During Reconstruction.** *Urbana, Illinois: University of Illinois Press, 1977.*

Kolchin, Peter. **First Freedom: The Responses of Alabama's Blacks to Emancipation and Reconstruction.** *Westport, Conn.: Greenwood Press, Publishers, 1972.*

Litwack, Leon F., and Stampp, Kenneth M., ed. **Reconstruction: An Anthology of Revisionist Writings.** Baton Rouge, Louisiana State University Press, 1969.

Logan, Frenise A. **A Negro in North Carolina, 1876-1894.** Chapel Hill: The University of North Carolina Press, 1964.

McPherson, James M. **The Struggle for Equality: Abolitionists and the Negro in the Civil War and Reconstruction.** Princeton University Press, 1964.

Taylor, Alrutheus Ambush. **The Negro in South Carolina During the Reconstruction.** Washington, D.C.: The Association for the Study of Negro Life and History, 1924.

Wharton, Vernon Lane. **The Negro in Mississippi, 1865-1890.** New York: Harper Torchbooks, 1965.

Woodward, C. Vann. **The Strange Career of Jim Crow.** New York: Oxford University Press, 1866.

2. Religious Histories

Ahlstrom, Sidney E. **A Religious History of the American People.** New Haven: Yale University Press, 1972.

The American Church History Series. New York: Charles Scribner's Sons, 1911. Vol. 11: **History of the Methodist Church, South** by Gross Alexander.

Chiles, Robert E. **Theological Transition in American Methodism: 1790-1935.** New York: Abingdon Press, 1965.

Eighmy, John Lee. **Churches in Cultural Captivity: A History of the Social Attitudes of Southern Baptists.** Knoxville: The University of Tennessee Press, 1972.

Farish, Hunter Dickinson. **The Circuit Rider Dismounts: A Social History Southern Methodism 1865-1900.** Richmond: The Dietz Press, 1938.

Fordham, Monroe. **Major Themes in Northern Black Religious Thought, 1800-1860.** Hicksville, New York: Exposition Press, 1975.

Frazier, E. Franklin. **The Negro Church in America.** New York: Schocken Books, 1964.

Handy, Robert T. **A Christian America: Protestant Hopes and Historical Realities.** New York: Oxford University Press, 1971.

Smith, H. Shelton. *In His Image, But. . . .: Racism in Southern Religion, 1780-1910.* Durham: Duke University Press, 1972.

Smith, H. Shelton, Handy Robert T., and Loetscher, Lefferts A. *American Christianity: An Historical Interpretation with Representative Documents.* Volume II 1820-1960. New York: Charles Scribner's Sons, 1963.

Smith, James Ward, and Jamison, A. Leland. *Religion in American Life. Volume 1: The Shaping of American Religion.* Princeton: Princeton University Press, 1961.

Spain, Rufus B. *At Ease in Zion: A Social History of Southern Baptists, 1865-1900.* Nashville: Vanderbilt University Press, 1961.

Woodson, Carter G. *The History of the Negro Church.* Washington, D.C.: The Associated Publishers, 1921.

3. Other Historical and Theological Interpretations

Beard, Augustus Field. *A Crusade of Brotherhood: A History of the American Missionary Association.* Boston: American Mission Society, 1909. Reprint ed., Boston: Pilgrim Press, 1972.

Clarke, Erskine. *Wrestlin' Jacob: A Portrait of Religion in the Old South.* Atlanta: John Knox Press, 1979.

Cone, Cecil. *The Identity Crisis in Black Theology.* Nashville: The African Methodist Episcopal Church, 1975.

Cone, James. *Black Thology and Black Power.* New York: The Seabury Press, 1969.

Franklin, John Hope. *From Slavery to Freedom: A History of Negro Americans.* 3rd edition. New York: Afred A. Knopf, 1967.

Mitchell, Henry. *Black Belief: Folk Beliefs of Blacks in America and West Africa.* New York: Harper and Row, Publishers, 1975.

Raboteau, Albert J. *Slave Religion: "The Invisible Institution" in the Antebellum South.* New York: Oxford University Press, 1978.

Sobel, Mechal. *Trabelin' On: Slavery Journey to an Afro-Baptist Faith.* Westport, Connecticut: Greenwood Press, 1979.

Weber, Timothy P. *Living in the Shadow of the Second Coming: American Premillenialism 1875-1925.* New York: Oxford Press, 1979.

Williams, Daniel Day. *The Andover Liberals: A Study in American Theology.* New York: King's Crown Press, 1941.

Wilmore Gayraud. **Black Religion and Black Radicalism.** Garden City,
New York: Doubleday and Company, Inc., 1972.

    4. Studies of Ministerial Leadership

Hall, David. **The Faithful Shepherd: A History of the New England
Ministry in the Seventeeth Century.** Chapel Hill: The University
of North Carolina Press, 1972.

Hamilton, Charles V. **The Black Preacher in America.** New York: William
Morrow and Company, Inc. 1972.

Holifield, E. Brooks. **The Gentlemen Theologians: American Theology
in Southern Culture (1795-1860).** Durham, North Carolina:
Duke University Press, 1978.

Hutchinson, William R. **The Transcendentalist Ministers: Church Reform
in the New England Renaissance.** New Haven: Yale University
Press, 1959.

Scott, Donald M. **From Office to Profession: The New England Ministry
1750-1850.** University of Pennsylvannia Press, 1978.

Youngs, William T. **God's Messengers: Religious Leadership in Colonial
New England, 1700-1740.** Baltimore: The John Hopkins
University Press, 1976.

    5. Reference Books

An American Dictionary of the American Language, 1850 ed. S. v. "Uplift."

A Dictionary of American English on Historical Principles, 1944 ed. S.v.
"Uplift."

A Dictionary of Americanisms on Historical Principles, 1951 ed. S.v.
"Uplift."

A Dictionary of the English Language, 1819 ed. S.v. "Uplift."

The Century Dictionary, 1911 ed. S.v. "Uplift."

The Oxford English Dictionary, 1933 ed. S.v. "Uplift."

    6. Slave Narratives

Rawick, George P. **The American Slave: A Composite Autobiography.
Volume 1: From Sundown to Sunup: The Making of the Black
Community.** Westport, Conn.: Greenwood Publishing Co., 1972.

_____. *The American Slave: A Composite Autobiography: Volume 19: God Struck Me Dead.* Westport, Conn.: Greenwood Publishing Co., 1972.

7. *Miscellaneous*

Brignano, Russell C. *Black Americans in Autobiography: An Annotated Bibliography of Autobiographies and Autobiobraphical Books Written Since the Civil War.* Durham: Duke University Press, 1974.

Freedmen's Aid Society of the Methodist Episcopal Church. *Fourth Annual Report.* Cincinnati: Western Methodist Book Concern Print, 1871.

Gusfield, Joseph R. *Symbolic Crusade: Status Politics and the American Temperance Movement.* Urbana, Illinois: University of Illinois Press, 1963.

Holmes, Dwight Oliver Wendell. *The Evolution of the Negro College.* New York: Bureau of Publications, Teachers College, Columbia University, 1934. Reprint ed., New York: Arno Press, 1969.

Newby, I.W. *Jim Crow's Defense: Anti-Negro Thought in America, 1900-1930,* Baton Rouge, Louisiana: Louisiana State University Press, 1965.

Ofari, Earl. *"Let Your Motto Be Resistance": The Life and Thought of Henry Highland Garnet.* Boston: Beacon Press, 1972.

Puckett, Newbell Niles. *Folk Beliefs of the Southern Negro.* Chapel Hill: The University of North Carolina Press, 1926.

Wagner, Clarence M. *Profiles of Black Georgia Baptists.* Gainesville: Clarence M. Wagner, 1980.

Welch, Eloise Turner. "The Background and Development of the American Missionary Association's Decision to Educate Freedmen in the South, With Subsequent Repercussions." Ph. D. dissertation, Bryn Mawr College, 1975.

C. *ARTICLES*

Barney, William L. "Johnson and Reconstruction: Swinging Around the Circle Again." *Reviews in American History* 8 (September 1980): 366-71.

Belz, Herman, "The New Orthodoxy in Reconstruction Historiography." *Reviews in American History* 1 (March 1973): 106-113.

Colored Methodist Episcopal Church. **The Independent** 5 March, 1891, pp. 331-2.

Cooper, Frederick. "Elevating the Race: The Social Thought of Black Leaders, 1827-1850." **The American Quarterly** 24 (1972): 604-625.

Cox, John and LaWanda. "General O. O. Howard and the 'Misrepresented Bureau'." **The Journal of Southern History** 19 (November 1953): 453-4.

Cox, LaWanda and John. "Negro Suffrage and Republican Politics: The Problem of Motivation in Reconstruction Historiography." **The Journal of Southern History** 33 (August 1967): 303-330.

Cox, LaWanda. "Reconstruction Foredoomed? The Policy of Southern Consent." **Reviews in American History** 1 (December 1973): 541-7.

Kolchin, Peter. "Race, Class, and Poverty in the Post-Civil War South." **Reviews in American History** 7 (December 1979): 515-26.

Les Benedict, Michael. "Preserving the Constitution: The Conservative Basis of Radical Reconstruction." **Journal of American History** 61 (June 1974): 65-90.

Linden, Glenn M. "A Note on Negro Suffrage and Republican Politics." **Journal of Southern History** 36 (May 1970): 411-20.

McPherson, James M. "White Liberals and Black Power in Negro Education, 1865-1910." **American Historical Review** 8 (June 1970): 1357-86.

Moore, James Tice. "Redeemers Reconsidered: Change and Continuity in the Democratic South, 1870-1900." **The Journal of Southern History** 44 (August 1978): 357-78.

Nieman, Donald G. "Andrew Johnson, the Freedman's Bureau, and the Problems of Equal rights, 1865-1866." **The Journal of Southern History** 44 (August 1978): 399-420.

Wheeler. Edward L. "Beyond One Man: A General Survey of Black Baptist History." **Review and Expositor** (Volume LXX, No. 3, Summer 1973): 314-19.

D. CATALOGUES

Atlanta University. **Catalogue of the Normal and Preparatory Departments of Atlanta University, Incorporated 1867. Atlanta, Georgia, 1869-70.** *Atlanta: Economical Book and Job Printing House, 1870.*

_____. **Catalogue of the Officers and Students of Atlanta University, Atlanta, Georgia with a Statement of the Courses of Study, Expenses, Etc. 1879-80.** *Atlanta: Atlanta Constitution Power Book and Job Press, 1880.*

_____. **Catalogue of the Officers and Students of Atlanta University, Atlanta, Georgia with a Statement on the Courses of Study, Expenses, Etc. 1885-86.** *Atlanta: Constitution Job Office Print, 1886.*

_____. **Catalogue of the Officers and Students of Atlanta University, Atlanta, Georgia with a Statement of the Courses of Study, Expenses, Etc. 1894-95.** *Atlanta: The Foote and Davis Co., 1895.*

_____. **Catalogue of the Officers and Students of Atlanta University, Atlanta, Georgia with a Statement of the Courses of Study, Expenses, Etc. 1901-02.** *Atlanta: Atlanta Univeristy Press, 1902.*

Fisk University. **First Annual Catlogue of the Fisk University and Normal School 1867-8, Nashville, Tennessee.** *Nashville: Press and Times Book and Job Printing Establishment, 1868.*

_____. **Catalogue of the Officers and Students of Fisk University, Nashville, Tennesee, for the College Year 1879-80.** *Nashville, Tenn.: Marshall and Bruce, Stationers and Printers, 1880.*

_____. **Catalogue of Officers and Students of Fisk University Nashville, Tennessee, for the College Year 1885-86.** *Nashville, Tenn.: Wheeler, Osborn & Duckworth MF'G. Co., 1886.*

_____. **Catalogue of the Officers and Students of Fisk University, Nashville, Tennessee, for 1894-95.** *Nashville, Tenn.: Marshall and Bruce Co., Stationers and Printers, 1895.*

_____. **Catalogue of the Officers and Students of Fisk University, Nashville, Tennessee 1901-02.** *Nashville, Tenn.: Brandon Printing Company, 1902.*

Gammon School of Theology. **Circular of the Gammon School of Theology. Clark University, Atlanta, Georgia 1885-86.** *Atlanta: Clark University, 1886.*

_____. **Circular of the Gammon School of Theology. Clark University, Atlanta, Georgia 1894-95.** *Atlanta: Clark University, 1902.*

_____. **Circular of the Gammon School of Theology. Clark University, Atlanta, Georgia 1901-02.** *Atlanta: Clark University, 1902.*

Morris Brown College. **Catalogue, Morris Brown College, Atlanta, Georgia 1898-99.** *Atlanta: Morris Brown College, 1899.*

The Nashville Institute. **A Catalogue of the Officers and Students of the Nashville Institute, 1873-74.** *Nashville, Tenn.: Wheeler, Marshall and Bruce, Printers and Stationers, 1874.*

The Nashville Normal and Theological Institute. **Catalogue of the Officers and Students of the Nashville Normal and Theological Institute, Nashville, Tennessee, for the Academic Year 1880-81.** *Nashville: Marshall & Bruce, 1881.*

Roger Williams University. **Twenty-Second Annual Catalogue of the Officers and Students of the Roger Williams University, Nashville, Tennessee, 1885-86.** *Nashville: Office of the Roger Williams Record, 1886.*

_____. **Thirty-First Annual Catalogue of the Officers and Students of Roger Williams Univeristy, Nashville, Tennessee, 1894-95.** *Nashville: Office of the Rogerana, 1895.*

_____. **Thirty-Eighth Annual Catalogue of the Officers and Students of Roger Williams University, Tennessee, 1901-02.** *Nashville: Nationaal Baptist Publishing Board, 1902.*

Tuskegee State Normal School. **Catalogue of the Tuskegee State Normal School at Tuskegee, Alabama for the Academic Year 1881-82. Hampton, Va.: Normal School Steam Press, 1882.**

_____. **Catalogue of the Tuskegee State Normal School at Tuskegee, Alabama for the Academic Year, 1885-86.** *Tuskegee, Alabama: Normal School Press, 1886.*

Tuskegee Normal and Industrial School. **Catalogue of the Tuskegee Normal and Industrial School, Tuskegee, Alabama 1893-94.** *Tuskegee, Alabama: Normal and Industrial School Press, 1894.*

Tuskegee Normal and Industrial Institute. **Catalogue Tuskegee Normal and Industrial Institute, Tuskegee, Alabama 1901-02.** *Tuskegee, Alabama: Tuskegee Institute Steam Print, 1902.*

APPENDIX

PERSONAL BACKGROUND (Name/Date & Place of Birth)	FAMILY & PARENTAGE	STATUS at BIRTH SLAVE	STATUS at BIRTH FREE	EDUCATION	SECULAR JOBS or POSITION	DENOMINATIONAL AFFILIATION	POLITICAL AFFILIATIONS	COMMUNITY AFFILIATIONS
ANDERSON, J.H. June 30, 1848 Frederick, Maryland				Livingstone College, D.D. Limited formal education		African Methodist Episcopal Zion		
ATKINS, S.G. June 11, 1863 Chatham County, North Carolina		X		St. Augustine Academic; Livingston College	School Master	African Methodist Episcopal Zion Secretary of Education for A.M.E. Zion Church		Organizer and President, North Carolina Teacher's Association; President Slater Industrial School
BOOTHE, CHARLES O. June 13, 1845 Mobile County, Alabama		X		Literate; Limited formal education		Baptist; Baptized 1866; Ordained 1868; Pastor, Meridian, Mississippi and Dexter Avenue in Montgomery		
BOUEY, HARRISON N. August 4, 1849 Columbia County, Georgia				Graduated from Baptist Theological Seminary Augusta, Georgia, 1873	Painter Apprentice	Baptist Baptized 1870 Pastor; initiated S.C. Mission to Africa 1879-82; S.S. Missionary Cor. Sec. Ala. St. Miss. Bd.	Republican; Sheriff in South Carolina; Probate Judge in South Carolina	Financial Agent for Selma University

APPENDIX

PERSONAL BACKGROUND (Name/Date & Place of Birth)	FAMILY & PARENTAGE	STATUS AT BIRTH		EDUCATION	SECULAR JOB OR POSITION	DENOMINATIONAL AFFILIATION	POLITICAL AFFILIATIONS	COMMUNITY AFFILIATIONS
		SLAVE	FREE					
BOWEN, JOHN W.E. Ca. 1855 New Orleans, La.	Mother Slave; Father free. Father purchased him and mother Ca. 1858.	X		A.B., New Orleans Un., B.D., Boston College 1885; Ph.D., Boston College, 1887.	Educator	Methodist Episcopal Church; Licensed 1872; Field Secretary, M.E. Church Missionary Society, Pastor.		Teacher, Central Tennessee College; Professor, Howard University; Professor and President, Gammon Theological Seminary; American Historical Association Member.
BRAWLEY, EDWARD M. March 18, 1851 Charleston, S.C.	Free Parents; Married 1877, First wife died the same year. Second marriage, 1879, 4 children.		X	B.A., Bucknell University; A.M., Bucknell University; D.D., State University, Louisville, Kentucky	Shoemaker, Educator Editor	Baptist; converted 1865; Licensed 1872 or 1873; Ordained 1875; Missionary in S.C. for American Baptist Publication Society; Pastor; Editorial Secretary; National Baptist Publishing House		President, Alabama Baptist Normal and Theological School

APPENDIX

PERSONAL BACKGROUND (Name/Date & Place of Birth)	FAMILY & PARENTAGE	STATUS AT BIRTH SLAVE	FREE	EDUCATION	SECULAR JOB OR POSITION	DENOMINATIONAL AFFILIATION	POLITICAL AFFILIATIONS	COMMUNITY AFFILIATIONS
CARTER, JAMES M. July 4, 1855 or 1858 DeSoto Parish, Louisiana	Married 1875 Nine children.	X		No earned degrees; attended several schools		Baptist; converted 1878; Ordained 1883 Pastor, Secretary, N.W. Louisiana Baptist Convention; Elected Corresponding Secretary, Louisiana Baptist State Convention 1887.		
CHAPPELLE, W.D. November 16, 1857 Fairfield County, S.C.		X		B.A., Allen University	Businessman; Teacher	A.M.E.; converted 1881; Ordained Deacon, 1883; Elder, 1885; Pastor, Presiding Elder; Corresponding Secretary and Editor African Methodist Episcopal Church.		President, Allen University, 1897-99; Real and personal property in access of $10,000 in 1900.

APPENDIX

PERSONAL BACKGROUND (Name/Date & Place of Birth)	FAMILY & PARENTAGE	STATUS AT BIRTH SLAVE	FREE	EDUCATION	SECULAR JOB OR POSITION	DENOMINATIONAL AFFILIATION	POLITICAL AFFILIATIONS	COMMUNITY AFFILIATIONS
BROWN, STERLING N. Nov. 21, 1857 Roane County, Tennessee				B.A., Fisk, 1885; Oberlin Theological Seminary; A.M., Fisk University, 1891	Educator	Congregationalist; Pastor		Member, Washington School Board; Professor, Howard University
CAIN, RICHARD H. 1825-1887 Virginia			X	B.A.; Wilberforce University	Politician	African Methodist Episcopal Church; Converted 1841; Ordained in M.E. Church 1844; Ordained Deacon in A.M.E. Church in 1859; Elected Bishop, 1880.	Republican; Member S.C. Constitutional Convention; S.C. State Senate; Representative to Congress from S.C., 1879.	President, Paul Quinn College, Texas; Property Owner, S.C. Property valued at $3,400 in 1876.
CARTER, EDWARD R. 1856 Clarke County, Georgia		X		Theological Department, Atlanta Baptist Sem. 1884	Apprentice Shoemaker	Baptist; converted 1875; Pastor; Vice-President, Georgia State Baptist Sunday School Convention	Temperance Movement Activist	Grand Worthy Templar for Georgia; Member, Centennial Committee of the Colored Baptists of Georgia.

APPENDIX

PERSONAL BACKGROUND (Name/Date & Place of Birth)	FAMILY & PARENTAGE	STATUS AT BIRTH SLAVE	STATUS AT BIRTH FREE	EDUCATION	SECULAR JOB OR POSITION	DENOMINATIONAL AFFILIATION	POLITICAL AFFILIATIONS	COMMUNITY AFFILIATIONS
CLANTON, SOLOMON T. March 27, 1857 Glencoe, St. Mary's Parish, Louisiana	Married 1883; Nine children	X		B.A., New Orleans University, 1878; B.D., Union Theological Seminary, Chicago, 1883.	Teacher	Baptist; Ordained 1881; Pastor Sunday School Missionary; Recording Secretary, Baptist Foreign Missionary Convention; Corresponding Secretary, American National Baptist Convention; Financial Secretary, Minister's Mutual Aid Society of La.		
CLARK, GEORGE V. January 1, 1851 Oxford, Georgia	Mother was a major influence.	X		Studied at Howard 1872 & 1881.	Teacher	Congregationalist; converted 1868; Pastor	Active in Temperence Movement.	First black teacher employed in DeKalb County, Ga.
CLINTON, GEORGE W. March 28, 1859 Cedar Creek Township, Lancaster County, S.C.	Father died during George's youth; Mother was a major influence. Grandparents influenced him. Married; one child.			B.A. Brainard Institute	Educator; Editor	A.M.E. Zion; converted 1869; began preaching, 1879, Ordained Bishop; 1897; Pastor, Editor, *Star of Zion*.		

APPENDIX

PERSONAL BACKGROUND (Name/Date & Place of Birth)	FAMILY & PARENTAGE	STATUS AT BIRTH SLAVE	FREE	EDUCATION	SECULAR JOB OR POSITION	DENOMINATIONAL AFFILIATION	POLITICAL AFFILIATIONS	COMMUNITY AFFILIATIONS
COFFEE, T.W. July 4, 1853 Lauderdale County, Alabama	Taken from Mother at age 8; Married 1881	X		Teacher Certificate, LeMoyne Institute; D.D. Payne University, 1900.	Editor; Writer	A.M.E.; converted as Baptist 1868 or 1869; Licensed A.M.E. Exhorter, 1871; Ordained 1881; Pastor, Church Publications editor.		Editor, *Birmingham Era* and *The Vindicator*, Eufala, Alabama.
DAVIS, I.D. 1858 Laurens, S.C.		X		B.A., Biddle University, 1881. B.D., Biddle Seminary, 1884.	Teacher	Presbyterian; Licensed 1883; Ordained, 1884; Moderator Catauba Presbytery; Stated Clerk, Fairfield Presbytery; Pastor.		Principal, Lauren County, S.C.
DUPREE, GEORGE W. July 24, 1826 or 1827 Gellatin County, Kentucky	Mother died in his youth; taken from his father. Married 1848; Purchased his freedom after 1855.	X		No formal education. Self taught.		Baptist; converted, 1842; began preaching 1845; Ordained, 1851, Pastor, Organized first Minister's and Deacon's Meeting; Moderator First District Association; Moderator, General Association of Kentucky.		Grand Master and Senior Warden, Masons

APPENDIX

PERSONAL BACKGROUND (Name/Date & Place of Birth)	FAMILY & PARENTAGE	STATUS AT BIRTH SLAVE	FREE	EDUCATION	SECULAR JOB OR POSITION	DENOMINATIONAL AFFILIATION	POLITICAL AFFILIATIONS	COMMUNITY AFFILIATIONS
DURHAM, James J. April 13, 1849 Spartanburg County, South Carolina	Son of wealthy white planter and female slave.		X	A.B., Fisk University, 1881, M.D., Meharry, 1882.	Apprentice Blacksmith; Medical Doctor.	Baptist; converted 1867; Licensed, 1867; Ordained, 1868; Pastor; Missionary, American Baptist Publication Society; Secretary and Financial Agent, Baptist Educational, Missionary and Sunday School Convention.		Established health Clinic in Nashville; owned property valued at about $3,000 in 1886.
FLIPPER, SIMEON J. February 22, 1859 Atlanta, Georgia	Father was an Atlanta business-man in 1870's.			Completed Junior year at Atlanta University.	Teacher	A.M.E.; converted 1877; Licensed, 1880; Ordained Deacon, 1882; Ordained Elder, 1884; Pastor; Secretary, A.M.E. General Conference of Georgia.		Trustee, Morris Brown College; Secretary, Trustee and Executive Boards, Morris Brown College; Deputy Grand Master, Union Grand Lodge; Trustee, Masonic Orphan's Home.

APPENDIX

PERSONAL BACKGROUND (Name/Date & Place of Birth)	FAMILY & PARENTAGE	STATUS AT BIRTH SLAVE	STATUS AT BIRTH FREE	EDUCATION	SECULAR JOB OR POSITION	DENOMINATIONAL AFFILIATION	POLITICAL AFFILIATIONS	COMMUNITY AFFILIATIONS
FRIERSON, A.U. Prior to Civil War South Carolina	Parents were salves.	X		B.A., Biddle University, 1885; B.D., Biddle Seminary, 1888.	Teacher	Presbyterian; Missionary, Freedmans' Bureau Presbyterian Church.		Professor, Greek language and literature, Biddle University.
FULLER, THOMAS O. October 25, 1867 Franklinton, N.C.	Parents had been slaves; both were uneducated but were Christians. Father was carpenter and wheelwright.		X Born after Emancipation	B.A., Shaw University, 1890; A.M., Shaw, 1893, Ph.D., Alabama A & M University, 1906.	Teacher; Educator	Baptist; Licensed, 1886; Ordained, 1890; Vice Moderator, local Association; Pastor; Recording Secretary, North Carolina State Sunday School Convention.	Republican; N.C. State Senator, 1898.	Assistant Teacher with American Baptist Home Mission Society; School Principal; President, Howe Institute, Memphis.
GADDIE, DANIEL A. May 21, 1836-1911 Kentucky				D.D., State University of Kentucky, 1887.	Smithing	Baptist; Moderator, General Association of Kentucky Baptists; Treasurer, American National Baptist Convention; Moderator, Central District Association.	Active in the Temperance Movement.	Trustee, State University, Louisville, Kentucky.

APPENDIX

PERSONAL BACKGROUND (Name/Date & Place of Birth)	FAMILY & PARENTAGE	STATUS AT BIRTH SLAVE	FREE	EDUCATION	SECULAR JOB OR POSITION	DENOMINATIONAL AFFILIATION	POLITICAL AFFILIATIONS	COMMUNITY AFFILIATIONS
GAINES, WESLEY. J. October 4, 1840 Wilkes County, Georgia	Parents were slaves; 13 brothers and sisters were slaves. Family not separated during slavery. Parents were Christian; Father was member M.E. Church, South; Mother was Baptist; Married 1863; one child.	X		No earned degree; D.D., Wilberforce University.		A.M.E.; converted M.E. Church, South, 1849, Licensed to exhort, 1864; Licensed to preach, 1865; joined A.M.E. Church, 1866; Ordained Deacon, 1866; Ordained Elder, 1867; Pastor; Presiding Elder Atlanta District; Elected Bishop, 1888.		General Superintendent and Treasurer, Morris Brown College.
GAYLES, G.W. June 29, 1844 Wilkinson County, Mississippi	Parents were slaves.	X		Little formal education; literate; self-taught.	Politician; Editor	Baptist, coverted, 1866; Ordained, 1867; Missionary for Bolivar and Sunflower counties, 1872; Pastor; Corresponding Secretary, Baptist State Missionary Convention of Mississippi; 1874; President, Baptist State Missionary Convention, 1880.	Republican; Member, Board of Police, 1869; Justice of the Peace, 1870; Member, State Legislature; State Senator, 1877; Member State Executive Committee.	Escaped slavery and joined Union Army, 1863; Editor, *Baptist Signal*.

APPENDIX

PERSONAL BACKGROUND (Name/Date & Place of Birth)	FAMILY & PARENTAGE	STATUS AT BIRTH SLAVE	FREE	EDUCATION	SECULAR JOB OR POSITION	DENOMINATIONAL AFFILIATION	POLITICAL AFFILIATIONS	COMMUNITY AFFILIATIONS
GILBERT, M.W. July 25, 1862 Mechanicsville, South Carolina	Parents were slaves; Father was Methodist Minister prior to Civil War; later became Baptist. Married, 1883, 7 children.	X		A.B., Madison University, 1887; A.M., Colgate, 1890; D.D., Colgate University, 1898.	Teacher; Educator	Baptist; converted, 1878; Licensed, 1880; Ordained, 1882; Pastor, Educational Missionary American Baptist Home Mission Society.		President, Florida Baptist Academy; Professor, Colored State College, Orangeburg, S.C.
GOODWIN, GEORGE A. February 20, 1861 Augusta, Georgia	Father died when he was young. Reared by Mother and an uncle. Married 1895.			Graduated, Atlanta Baptist College.	Teacher	Baptist; Ordained 1889; Pastor.		Member, Florida State Teacher's Association; Secretary, Georgia State Teacher's Association.
HARRISON, ZECHARIAH March 1, 1866 Murray, Kentucky			X Born after Emancipation.	No degree; some theological study.		Baptist; Ordained, 1877; Pastor, General Superintendent, Sunday School State of Kentucky, 1889.		Member, Literary Society.

APPENDIX

PERSONAL BACKGROUND (Name/Date & Place of Birth)	FAMILY & PARENTAGE	STATUS AT BIRTH SLAVE	STATUS AT BIRTH FREE	EDUCATION	SECULAR JOB OR POSITION	DENOMINATIONAL AFFILIATION	POLITICAL AFFILIATIONS	COMMUNITY AFFILIATIONS
HEARD, WILLIAM H. June 25, 1850 Elbert Couty, Georgia	Parents were slaves on different plantations. Father spent 3 nights per week with Mother.	X		No degrees; Studied at several schools.	Teacher; Politician; Railway Postal Clerk, 1880; Minister Resident and Consul General Liberia, 1895.	A.M.E.; converted, 1879; Licensed, 1880; Ordained Deacon, 1881; Ordained Elder, 1883; Pastor, Bishop, 1908.	Republican; elected to S.C. Legislature from Abeville County, S.C., 1876.	
HOLMES, WILLIAM E. January 22, 1856 Augusta, Georgia	Both parents were slaves on different plantations. Mother was literate and taught William to read.	X		A.B. Atlanta Baptist Seminary, 1881, M.A., University of Chicago, 1884.	Teacher	Baptist; converted, 1874; Baptized, 1875; Licensed, 1878; Ordained, 1881; Corresponding Secretary, Missionary Baptist Convention of Georgia, 1883.		Trustee, Spelman Seminary; Secretary, Faculty, Atlanta Baptist Seminary; owned property valued at approx. $5,000 in 1888.
HOLSEY, LUCIUS H. July 3, 1842 Hancock County, Georgia	Son of white slave owner and black female slave. Married 1862 to ex-slave of an M.E. Church, South Bishop. 14 children.	X		No formal education; literate; self-taught.	Farmer	C.M.E.; converted, M.E. Church, South, 1858; Licensed 1868 ; Ordained Deacon, 1869; Elder, 1869; Bishop, 1873; Secretary, C.M.E. College of Bishops, General Corresponding Secretary, C.M.E. Church.		

APPENDIX

PERSONAL BACKGROUND (Name/Date & Place of Birth)	FAMILY & PARENTAGE	STATUS AT BIRTH SLAVE	FREE	EDUCATION	SECULAR JOB OR POSITION	DENOMINATIONAL AFFILIATION	POLITICAL AFFILIATIONS	COMMUNITY AFFILIATIONS
HOOD, JAMES W. May 30, 1831 Kennett Township, Chester County, Pennsylvania	Both parents were free. Father was a preacher. Parents home served as a station on the Underground R.R.		X	No degrees; limited education.		A.M.E. Zion; Licensed 1856; Ordained Deacon, 1860; Elder, 1862; Bishop, 1872; Pastor.	Member, N.C. "Colored Convention", 1865; Constitutional Convention, 1867; strong temperance advocate.	Agent State Board of Education; Assistant Superintendent of Public Instruction; Assistant Superintendent under Freedman's Bureau; Grand Master, North Carolina Masons, most eminent Grand Patron, Order of the Eastern Star.
JAMISON, MONROE F. November 27, 1848 Georgia	Parents were slaves.	X		Literate; no formal education.		C.M.E.; converted 1867 (joined M.E. church, south); Licensed as exhorter, 1870; Ordained Deacon, 1874; Pastor; Secretary, Church Extension Department C.M.E. Church 1890 (elected Bishop, 1910).		

APPENDIX

PERSONAL BACKGROUND (Name/Date & Place of Birth)	FAMILY & PARENTAGE	STATUS AT BIRTH SLAVE	FREE	EDUCATION	SECULAR JOB OR POSITION	DENOMINATIONAL AFFILIATION	POLITICAL AFFILIATIONS	COMMUNITY AFFILIATION
JOHNSON, W.D. June 4, 1862 Hephzibah, Georgia	Christian parents.			No degrees; Studied at several schools, including Atlanta Baptist Seminary.		Baptist; converted, 1871; Pastor, Member, Executive Board, State Baptist Sunday School Convention.		Chairman, Board of Directors for Walker Baptist Institute; Director, Colored State Fair.
JONES, JOSHUA H. June 15, 1856 Pine Plains, S.C.				A.B., Claflin University, 1885, B.D., Howard University, 1887; D.D., Wilberforce University.	Educator	A.M.E.; converted, 1866; Licensed, 1874; Pastor.		Trustee, Wilberforce University; President, Wilberforce, 1900.
KENNEDY, PAUL H. September 1, 1848 Elizabeth, Kentucky		X		No degree; Studied at Nashville Institute.	Author; Publisher	Baptist, converted, 1873; Pastor, Missionary, Association and State Convention Missionary.		Author and Publisher, *Baptist Directory and Year Book of Kentucky.*
LANE, ISAAC March 3, 1834 Madison County, Tennessee	Lane had little knowledge of parents. Married 1854, 11 children.	X		No formal training; self-taught.	Farmer	C.M.E.; converted, 1854, M.E. Church, South; Licensed exhorter, 1856; preach, 1865; Ordained Deacon, 1866, Elder, 1867; Bishop, 1873.		

APPENDIX

PERSONAL BACKGROUND (Name/Date & Place of Birth)	FAMILY & PARENTAGE	STATUS AT BIRTH SLAVE	FREE	EDUCATION	SECULAR JOB OR POSITION	DENOMINATIONAL AFFILIATION	POLITICAL AFFILIATIONS	COMMUNITY AFFILIATIONS
LIPSCOMBE, E.H. September 29, 1858 Durham, North Carolina	Married 1882; 4 children.			A.B., Shaw University, 1879; M.A.; Shaw, 1882.	Teacher; Editor	Baptist; converted, 1877; Ordained, 1883; Editor, North Carolina Baptist State Convention Paper; Clerk, Baptist State Convention.	Republican; strong temperance advocate.	Professor, Shaw University; President, Western Union Institute, 1886.
LOVE, E.K. July 27, 1850 Marion, Alabama		X		Graduated, Augusta Institute, 1877.	Editor; Teacher	Baptist; converted, Licensed to preach, 1868; Ordained, 1875; Pastor, Missionary, Baptist Home Mission Society; Treasurer, Sunday School Baptist State Convention, 1888.		Associate Editor, State Newspaper.

APPENDIX

PERSONAL BACKGROUND (Name/Date & Place of Birth)	FAMILY & PARENTAGE	STATUS AT BIRTH FREE	SLAVE	EDUCATION	SECULAR JOB OR POSITION	DENOMINATIONAL AFFILIATION	POLITICAL AFFILIATIONS	COMMUNITY AFFILIATIONS
MARRS, ELIJAH P. January, 1840 Shelby County, Kentucky	Both parents had been slaves, Father purchased his own freedom.		X	No earned degree; literate	Farmer; Teacher	Baptist; converted 1851; Licensed, 1873; Pastor, Member and Secretary, Executive Board; Central District Association; Treasurer, General Association of Kentucky.	Republican; delegate, 1869 Political Convention; President County Republican Club; stront temperance advocate.	Sgt., Union Army; Secretary, Loyal League (organized to protect blacks from Ku Klux Klan).
MASON, M.C.B. March 27, 1859 Houma, Louisiana	Parents were slaves.		X	A.B., New Orleans University; B.D., Gammon Theological Seminary; Ph.D., Syracuse University.	Denominational Executive	M.E. Church; Field Agent, M.E. Church Freedman's Aid Society; Assistant Corresponding Secretary Freedman's Aid Society, 1893; Corresponding Secretary F.A.S., 1896; Senior Corresponding Secretary, 1900.		

APPENDIX

PERSONAL BACKGROUND (Name/Date & Place of Birth)	FAMILY & PARENTAGE	STATUS AT BIRTH SLAVE	STATUS AT BIRTH FREE	EDUCATION	SECULAR JOB OR POSITION	DENOMINATION AFFILIATION	POLITICAL AFFILIATIONS	COMMUNITY AFFILIATION
McALPINE, WILLIAM H. June, 1847 Buckingham County, Virginia	Mother was slave; no mention of father; separated from family at age 8 years old.	X		No degree; attended Talladega College.	Teacher	Baptist; converted, 1864; Licensed, 1869; Ordained, 1871; Pastor, President; Baptist Foreign Mission Convention 1880-82.		President, Selma Institute; Editor, *Baptist Pioneer.* 1978-82. Trustee, Lincoln Normal University.
McEWEN, A.N. April 29, 1849 La Fayette County, Mississippi	Both parents were slaves. Married 1870.	X			Editor	Baptist; converted, 1870 Ordained, 1876; Pastor; Chairman, Baptist State Mission Board. Alabama	Republican; Member, Alabama Republican State Executive Board.	Trustee, Selma University; Editor, *Montgomery Herald;* Editor, *Baptist Leader.* 1887.
MIXON, W.H. April 25, 1859 Dallas County, Alabama	Parents were slaves; lived on separate plantations. Married 1898; 2 children.	X		No degree; limited study at Selma University.	Editor	A.M.E.; converted 1876; Ordained Deacon, 1879; Elder, 1880; Pastor.	Republican; Member, National Republican Convention, 1896.	President, Executive Board, Payne University, Selma, Alabama; Editor, *Dallas Post;* Secretary and Treasurer, Payne University.

APPENDIX

PERSONAL BACKGROUND (Name/Date & Place of Birth)	FAMILY & PARENTAGE	STATUS AT BIRTH SLAVE	STATUS AT BIRTH FREE	EDUCATION	SECULAR JOB OR POSITION	DENOMINATIONAL AFFILIATION	POLITICAL AFFILIATIONS	COMMUNITY AFFILIATIONS
MORANT, JOHN J. Alabama	Parents had been slaves.		X Born after Emancipation.	B.A., Wilberforce, 1896; B.D., Wilberforce, 1899.		A.M.E.; converted age 8; Licensed, prior to 1889.		
NEWTON, A.H. November 5, 1837 Craven County, North Carolina	Father was a slave; Mother was free. Married 1859; 3 children; wife died 1868. Remarried 1877.		X	No earned degrees but attended several schools and was literate.	Soldier	A.M.E.; became active in 1866; Ordained Deacon, 1874; Pastor.	Republican; active in temperance movement.	Owned home and additional property.
OWEN, A.F. January 1, 1854 Wilcox County, Alabama	Married 1882.			Attended Leland University for 4 years; studied classical and theological courses.	Editor; Teacher	Baptist; converted, 1872; Licensed, 1873; Ordained, 1877; Pastor, Secretary, Louisiana Baptist State Convention; Editor *Baptist Pioneer*; Superintendent of Missions in Alabama.		School Principal; Trustee, Selma University.

APPENDIX

PERSONAL BACKGROUND (Name/Date & Place of Birth)	FAMILY & PARENTAGE	STATUS AT BIRTH SLAVE	STATUS AT BIRTH FREE	EDUCATION	SECULAR JOB OR POSITION	DENOMINATIONAL AFFILIATION	POLITICAL AFFILIATIONS	COMMUNITY AFFILIATIONS
PARTEE, W.E. 1860 Concord, North Carolina	Married, 1886			A.B., Biddle University; B.D., Biddle University	Educator	Presbyterian; Licensed, 1883; Ordained, 1884; Pastor.		School Teacher; Principal.
PEQUES, ALBERT W. November, 1859 Cheraw, South Carolina	Married 1890; One daughter	X		A.B., Bucknell University, 1886; M.A. Bucknell University, 1887; Ph.D., Selma University, 1891.	Educator	Baptist; converted, 1877; Licensed, 1881; Ordained, 1888; Pastor, active in National Baptist Education Convention; helped create National Baptist Convention, U.S.A.		School Principal; Professor at Shaw University.
PETERSON, B.H. Shortly before Civil War Florida	Both parents were slaves	X		A.B., Lincoln University; B.D., Lincoln University; Summer School; Hampton Institute and University of Chicago.	Educator	Baptist; Pastor		School Principal; Professor, Selma University; Professor Tuskegee Institute

APPENDIX

PERSONAL BACKGROUND (Name/Date & Place of Birth)	FAMILY & PARENTAGE	STATUS OF BIRTH		EDUCATION	SECULAR JOB OR POSITION	DENOMINATIONAL AFFILIATION	POLITICAL AFFILIATIONS	COMMUNITY AFFILIATIONS
		SLAVE	FREE					
PETTIFORD, WILLIAM R. January 20, 1847 or (1848) Granville County, North Carolina	Parents were free; owned a farm until 1857. 1st marriage, 1869; wife died 1870. 2nd marriage, 1873; wife died 1874. 3rd marriage, 1880; 3 children.		X	No degrees; studied 7 years at State Normal; studied at Selma University.	Teacher; Businessman	Baptist; converted 1868; Licensd, 1879; Ordained, 1880; Pastor, President, Birmingham Ministerial Union. President; Baptist State Convention.		Trustee, Selma University; President, Negro American Publishing Company; President, Alabama Penny Savings Bank.
PHILLIPS, C.H. January 17, 1858 Milledgeville, Georgia	Both parents were slaves. Parents were Christian. Father was M.E. Church South Minister licensed in 1856. Three brothers were ministers. Married 1880.	X		A.B.; Central Tennessee College; M.D., Meharry; M.A., Central Tennesee College; D.D., Philander Smith and Wiley College.	Doctor; Teacher	C.M.E.; converted, 1874; Licensed, 1878; elected Bishop, 1902; Pastor; Editor, *Christian Index.*	Active in temperance movement; advocated prohibition.	Outspoken opponent of Kentucky separate Coach Law, 1892.
POLLARD, ROBERT T. October 4, 1860 Gainesville, Alabama	Both parents were slaves. Father was a minister.	X		Completed normal course and two years of college at Selma University.	Teacher	Baptist, converted, 1872; Ordained, 1885; Pastor; Moderator of Association; Recording Secretary, State Convention; Member, Executive Committee, State Convention.		

APPENDIX

PERSONAL BACKGROUND (Name/Date & Place of Birth)	FAMILY & PARENTAGE	STATUS AT BIRTH SLAVE	FREE	EDUCATION	SECULAR JOB OR POSITION	DENOMINATIONAL AFFILIATION	POLITICAL AFFILIATIONS	COMMUNITY AFFILIATIONS
PRICE, J.C. February 10, 1854-1893 Elizabeth City, North Carolina	Father was a slave; mother was free.		X	A.B., Lincoln University, Pennsylvania; B.D., Lincoln University, 1881.	Educator	A.M.E. Zion; converted 1873; Licensed, Ca., 1875; Ordained Elder, 1882; Pastor; Delegate Ecumenical Council, 1881.	Active in temperance movement.	President, Livingston College; President, National Afro-American League.
PROCTER, HENRY H. December 8, 1868 Near Fayetteville, Tennessee		Born after Civil War.	X	A.B. Fisk University, 1891; B.D., Yale University, 1894.	Teacher	Congregationalist, converted between 1884-1891 at Fisk at Moody-Sankey Revival.		
PURCE, CHARLES L. 1856 Charleston, S.C.	Father was free; mother was a slave.			Attended Benedict College; graduated Richmond Institute.		Baptist, converted 1875; Licensed 1878; Ordained, 1883; Pastor.		Professor of Latin and Greek, Selma University; President, Selma University, 1886.
REVELS, Hiram R. September 1, 1822 Fayetteville, North Carolina		X		A.B., Kno	Politician	M.E.; spent time with A.M.E. and Presbyterian but ended career as he started with M.E. Church, Pastor.	Republican; Mississippi State Legislator; U.S. Senator from Mississippi; Alderman, Natchez, Mississippi; Secretary of State, Mississippi.	Freedman's Bureau Agent; President, Alcorn University.

APPENDIX

PERSONAL BACKGROUND (Name/Date & Place of Birth)	FAMILY & PARENTAGE	STATUS AT BIRTH SLAVE	FREE	EDUCATION	SECULAR JOB OR POSITION	DENOMINATIONAL AFFILIATION	POLITICAL AFFILIATION	COMMUNITY AFFILIATIONS
SIMMONS, FRANCIS April 15, 1856 Monroe County, Georgia	Married, 1883			No degree; 2 years study at Atlanta University; some study at Augusta Institute.	Educator Politician	Baptist; converted, 1871; Ordained minister, 1877; Pastor; Missionary for Georgia.		
SIMMONS, WILLIAM J. June 29, 1849-1890 Charleston, South Carolina	Both parents were slaves; his mother escaped from slavery along with William and two sisters. Married 1874; 7 children.	X		A.B., Howard University.		Baptist; converted, 1867; Licensed and Ordained, 1879; Pastor, President, American National Baptist Convention, 1886.	Republican; County Campaign Chairman, Republican Party in Florida.	President, State University, Louisville; Editor, *American Baptist.*
SISSION, SAMUEL S. June 11, 1862 or 1863 White Plains, Calhoun County, Alabama.	Both parents were slaves; family stayed together during slavery. Married, 1888.	X		No degree; literate with some formal education.		Baptist; converted, 1871; Licensed 1882; Ordained Ga., 1884; Pastor.		
STARKS, JOHN JACOB 1871 or '72 Greenwood County, South Carolina.	Parents were together with family; father was farmer. Married, 1897.		X Born after Emancipation.	A.B., Morehouse College, 1898 (Atlanta Baptist Seminary).	Educator	Baptist, converted, called, Licensed, 1891; Ordained before 1898; Pastor.		School Teacher; School Principal.

APPENDIX

PERSONAL BACKGROUND (Name/Date & Place Of Birth)	FAMILY & PARENTAGE	STATUS AT BIRTH SLAVE	STATUS AT BIRTH FREE	EDUCATION	SECULAR JOB OR POSITION	DENOMINATIONAL AFFILIATION	POLITICAL AFFILIATIONS	COMMUNITY AFFILIATIONS
STEWARD, THEOPHILUS G. Ca. 1842 New Jersey	Married, 1866.		X		Teacher	A.M.E.; joined the Annual Conference, 1864; Ordained, Elder, 1865; Pastor, Secretary, Annual Conferences.	Republican; active in politics.	
STOKES, A.J. July 25, 1858 Orangeburg County, South Carolina				A.B., Benedict College, 1884.	Editor	Baptist; converted, 1870 in Methodist Church; baptized as Baptist, 1871; Ordained, 1874; Pastor, Missionary.		School Commissioner; Editor.
TAYLOR, BARTLETT February 14, 1815 Louisville, Kentucky	Mother was slave; Father was plantation owner. Purchased freedom; married, 1840; 3 daughters. 1st wife died. Remarried, 1848. 1 son.	X		No degrees; self taught; literate.	Butcher	A.M.E.; called Ca. 1862; appointed A.M.E. itinerant for Kentucky, 1866; Pastor, Delegate, General Conference, A.M.E. Church.		Trustee, Wilberforce University; Treasurer, Wilberforce University. Property owner.

APPENDIX

PERSONAL BACKGROUND (Name/Date & Place of Birth)	FAMILY & PARENTAGE	STATUS AT BIRTH SLAVE	FREE	EDUCATION	SECULAR JOB OR POSITION	DENOMINATIONAL AFFILIATION	POLITICAL AFFILIATIONS	COMMUNITY AFFILIATIONS
TAYLOR, PRESTON November 7, 1849 Shreveport, Louisiana	Enlisted in Union Army, 1864.	X			Editor; Businessman	Disciple of Christ; began as Pastor Ca. 1867; General Evangelist for Disciples of Christ.	Staunch opponent of Kentucky and Tennessee Jim Crow Laws.	Editor, *Our Colored Brethren*; State Grand Chaplain for Masons; State Grand Master of Odd Fellows. Owned large funeral business; 16 employees.
TURNER, HENRY M. February 1, 1833 Newberry Court-House, South Carolina	Mother was free born; father was of German extraction. Married 1857; 14 children.	X		No degrees; self taught.	Apprentice Blacksmith; worked in Law Office.	A.M.E.; converted, 1848, M.E. Church, South, Licensed, 1858, A.M.E. Church; Ordained, Deacon 1860; Elder, 1862; Bishop 1880; Pastor, Army Chaplain; Presiding Elder, A.M.E. Church in Georgia; Manager, A.M.E. Publication Dept. 1876.	Republican; Member, Georgia Constitutional Convention, 1867; elected to Georgia State Legislature in 1868, 1870; appointed Post-master, Macon, Georgia, 1869; Coast Inspector; U.S. Customs; U.S. Government Detective.	

APPENDIX

PERSONAL BACKGROUND (Name/Date & Place of Birth)	FAMILY & PARENTAGE	STATUS AT BIRTH SLAVE	FREE	EDUCATION	SECULAR JOB OR POSITION	DENOMINATIONAL AFFILIATION	POLITICAL AFFILIATIONS	COMMUNITY AFFILIATIONS
TYLER, MANSFIELD November, 1826 Near Augusta, Georgia		X		No formal education; literate; strong advocate of education.		Baptist; converted, 1855; called to preach, 1855; Ordained, 1868; Pastor, Moderator, Alabama District Association; President, Baptist State Convention, 1876-1886.		Chairman, Board of Trustees, Selma University.
VANDERVALL, R.B. 1832 Nesley's Bend (North of Nashville), Tennessee	Parents were slaves on different plantations; father permitted to visit once a year. Purchased his freedom and hired wife's time to keep his family together.	X		No formal education; literate; strong advocte of education; 3 surviving children completed college.		Baptist; converted, 1847; began preaching 1848; President, Tennessee State Sabbath School Convention President, State Baptist Convention.		Trustee, Roger Williams University.
VANN, MICHAEL April 5, 1860 Madison County (Near Jakson), Tennessee	Oldest of 12 children. 1st married 1882; wife died, 1883. 2nd marriage, May, 1890.			A.B., Roger Williams University, 1881.	Teacher; Missionary.	Baptist; converted, 1879; Ordained, 1888; Pastor; Corresponding Secretary Baptist State Convention of Tennessee; President, American National Baptist Convention, 1892-95.		President, Alumni Association; Roger Williams University; Trustee, Memphis Baptist Institute.

APPENDIX

PERSONAL BACKGROUND (Name/Date & Place of Birth)	FAMILY & PARENTAGE	STATUS AT BIRTH SLAVE	STATUS AT BIRTH FREE	EDUCATION	SECULAR JOB OR POSITION	DENOMINATIONAL AFFILIATION	POLITICAL AFFILIATIONS	COMMUNITY AFFILIATIONS
VAUGHN, C.C. December 27, 1846 Dinwiddle County, Virginia	Parents slaves; white owner freed him and his family in Ohio in 1852. Married, 1879.	X		A.B., Berea College.	Teacher	Baptist; converted, 1869; Licensed, 1876; Ordained, 1878: Pastor.	Republican; elected chairman State Convention of Colored Men of Kentucky, 1884.	Joined Army in 1864; Sarteant in Union Army during Civil War; Treasurer, Grand United Order of Odd Fellows; State Grand Chief, Independent Order, Good Sumaritans; High Worthy National Grand Chief, Good Sumaritans.
WALKER, C.T. January 11, 1858 Richmond County, Georgia				No degrees; studied at Augusta Institute.		Baptist, converted, 1873; Licensed 1876; Ordained, 1877; Pastor; Moderator, Western Union Association; Secretary, Walker Baptist Association; Treasurer, American National Baptist Association; Treasurer, American National Baptist Convention.		Manager, *Weekly Sentinel*.
WALKER, GEORGE W. October 25, 1820 or (1819) — Dec. 1892 Pulaski, Tennessee	Married ca. 1850; 3 children (Teacher), Doctor, Printer)			No degrees; self-taught; literate.		Baptist; converted, 1846; baptized, 1847; Pastor; member Baptist Foreign Mission Convention; Treasurer; Louisiana Baptist State Convention.		Trustee, Leland University; Founder and Treasurer, Old Folks Home at New Orleans.

APPENDIX

PERSONAL BACKGROUND (Name/Date & Place of Birth)	FAMILY & PARENTAGE	STATUS AT BIRTH SLAVE	STATUS AT BIRTH FREE	EDUCATION	SECULAR JOB OR POSITION	DENOMINATIONAL AFFILIATION	POLITICAL AFFILIATIONS	COMMUNITY AFFILIATIONS
WALTERS, ALEXANDER August 1, 1858 Bardstown, Kentucky	Both parents were slaves. Paternal grandfather was a white slave owner. Married 1877; 5 children.	X		No degrees; studied at several institutions.	Teacher	A.M.E. Zion; converted, 1870; Licensed, 1877; Ordained Deacon, 1879; Elder, 1881; Bishop, 1892; Pastor; Secretary, A.M.E. Zion General Conference.		Mason; member of Odd Fellows; member United Brethren of Friendship Fraternal Society; President, Afro-American Council, 1898.
WHITE, WILLIAM J. December 25, 1831 Ruckersville, Georgia				No degrees; limited formal education; literate.	Teacher; Editor; Apprentice Carpenter; Apprentice Cabinet Maker.	Baptist, converted, 1855; Licensed, exhorter, 1858; Licensed preacher; Ordained, 1866; Pastor, Treasurer, Missionary Baptist Convention 1870-86; Executive Board, Missionary Baptist Convention, 1870-92; Corresponding Secretary, State Convention.		Editor, *The Georgia Baptist;* Vice President, Spelman Seminary Trustees; Secretary, Board of Trustees, Atlanta Baptist Seminary.
WHITTAKER, J.W. December 23, 1860 Atlanta, Georgia				A.B., Atlanta University, 1884; B.D., Hartford Seminary, 1887.		Congregationalist; Ordained, 1886; Pastor.		Chaplain, Tuskegee Institute; Financial Secretary, Tuskegee Institute.

APPENDIX

PERSONAL BACKGROUND (Name/Date & Place of Birth)	FAMILY & PARENTAGE	STATUS AT BIRTH SLAVE	FREE	EDUCATION	SECULAR JOB OR POSITION	DENOMINATIONAL AFFILIATION	POLITICAL AFFILIATIONS	COMMUNITY AFFILIATIONS
WHITTED, J.A. March 10, 1860 Hilsboro, North Carolina				A.B., Lincoln University, Pennsylvania, 1885.		Baptist; converted, 1877; Ordained, 1886; Pastor.		Principal, Warrenton, North Carolina (school owned by Shiloh Baptist Association).
WILKINS, C.S. March 15, 1859 Jefferson County, Georgia				Graduate, Atlanta Baptist Seminary, 1884.		Baptist; Licensed to preach, 1878; Pastor; Secretary, Executive Committee; Sunday School Baptist State Convention; Clerk, Southwestern Union Baptist Association.		Had financial affiliation with the *Weekly Sentinel* paper published in Georgia.
WILLIAMS, JOHN B.L. November 22, 1853 Baltimore, Maryland			X	Studied in Catholic and Public high school; graduated, Gammon Theological Seminary, 1885.		M.E. Church; converted, 1870; Licensed, preach, 1875; Ordained, Elder, before 1880; Pastor; Presiding Elder, Atlanta District, 1880-84; Secretary, Annual Conference, 15 years.		
WYCHE, R.P. Before 1860 Granville County, North Carolina	Father was a Carpenter.			A.B.; Biddle University, 1877; A.M., Biddle University; D.D., Biddle University.		Presbyterian; Licensed and Ordained between 1877 and 1881; Pastor, Moderator, Catawba Synod, North Carolina.		Principal, LaGrange and Newnan, Georgia, Teacher, LaGrange Seminary.